LUTHER LIBRARY
MIDLAND COLLEGE
FREMONT NE 68025

MIDLAND LUTH

3 7206 00048 7314

Mental Retardation

Definition, Classification, and Systems of Supports

10th Edition

American Association on Mental Retardation

616.8588
M528R
2002

Copyright © 2002 by the American Association on Mental Retardation

Published by
American Association on Mental Retardation
444 North Capitol Street, NW
Suite 846
Washington, DC 20001-1512

Printed in the United States of America

Library of Congress Cataloging-in-Publication Data

Mental retardation : definition, classification, and systems of supports. — 10th ed.
  p. cm.
  Includes bibliographical references and indexes.
  ISBN 0-940898-81-0
    1. Mental retardation — Classification.   I. American Association on
  Mental Retardation.

RC570 . C515 2002
616.85'88'0012--dc21   2002066469

241126

THE AAMR AD HOC COMMITTEE
ON TERMINOLOGY AND CLASSIFICATION

Ruth Luckasson, JD, Chair
Regents Professor and Professor of
   Special Education
Coordinator of Mental Retardation
   and Severe Disabilities: Studies in
   Educational Equity for Diverse
   Exceptional Learners
College of Education
University of New Mexico
Albuquerque, NM

Sharon Borthwick-Duffy, PhD
Professor of Education
Graduate School of Education
University of California at Riverside
Riverside, CA

Wil H.E. Buntinx, Drs
Health Care Psychologist
Director Research and Development
St. Anna Foundation
Governor Kremers Center / Department
   of Health Organization, Policy, and
   Economics
University of Maastricht
Maastricht (Netherlands)

David L. Coulter, MD
Department of Neurology
Harvard Medical School
Institute on Community Inclusion
Children's Hospital
Boston, MA

Ellis M. (Pat) Craig, PhD
Psychologist
Texas Department of Mental Health
   and Mental Retardation
Austin, TX

Alya Reeve, MD
Assistant Professor
Department of Psychiatry
Research Assistant Professor
Department of Neurology
University of New Mexico Health
   Sciences Center
Albuquerque, NM

Robert L. Schalock, PhD
Professor Emeritus and Former Chair
Department of Psychology
Hastings College
Principal
Bob Schalock and Associates
Chewelah, WA

Martha E. Snell, PhD
Coordinator of Special Education
Department of Curriculum,
   Instruction, and Special Education
Curry School of Education
University of Virginia
Charlottesville, VA

continued

THE AAMR AD HOC COMMITTEE ON TERMINOLOGY AND CLASSIFICATION

continued

Deborah M. Spitalnik, PhD
Professor of Pediatrics
Executive Director
The Elizabeth M. Boggs Center on
  Developmental Disabilities
University of Medicine and Dentistry
  of New Jersey
Robert Wood Johnson Medical
  School
New Brunswick, NJ

Scott Spreat, EdD
Executive Director
Woodland Center for Challenging
  Behaviors
Woods Services Incorporated
Langhorne, PA

Marc J. Tassé, PhD
Clinical Assistant Professor of
  Psychiatry
Communication Education Director
Center for Development and Learning
University of North Carolina at
  Chapel Hill
Chapel Hill, NC

©American Association on Mental Retardation

TABLE OF CONTENTS

TABLES

FIGURES

APPENDIX

PREFACE

Since its founding in 1876, the American Association on Mental Retardation (AAMR) has led the field of mental retardation in understanding, defining, and classifying the condition of mental retardation. The Association has attempted to fulfill its responsibility by formulating and disseminating manuals and related information on terminology and classification through the years.

The AAMR's first edition on definition was published in 1921 in conjunction with the National Committee for Mental Hygiene. A second edition of that manual was published in 1933, and a third in 1941. The Committee on Nomenclature of the AAMR (then the American Association on Mental Deficiency) published the fourth edition in 1957, which was an etiological classification system.

The fifth edition, a comprehensive manual on terminology and classification, was published in 1959 (Heber) and reprinted with minor corrections in 1961 (Heber). Two dramatic changes in the 1959 manual were raising the IQ ceiling to one standard deviation below the mean (i.e., an IQ of approximately 85 or below) and the formal introduction of an adaptive behavior criterion to the definition of mental retardation.

The sixth edition (Grossman, 1973) lowered the IQ ceiling to two standard deviations below the mean (i.e., an IQ of about 70 or below). Several other important changes were introduced in the 1973 manual, including: (a) inserting the word *significantly* before the term *subaverage general intellectual functioning*; (b) raising the limit of the developmental period from age 16 to 18; and (c) omitting the borderline level of retardation (i.e., IQ about 70 to 85).

The seventh edition (Grossman, 1977) included relatively minor corrections and changes.

The eighth edition (Grossman, 1983) further clarified that the upper IQ range for the diagnosis of mental retardation was a guideline and with clinical judgment could extend to approximately 75.

The ninth edition (Luckasson et al., 1992) of the manual retained some aspects of the 1983 definition and classification system (e.g., the IQ guidelines of approximately 70 to 75 or below), but departed from the previous definitions and classifications systems in four important ways: (a) it expressed the changing understanding that mental retardation is a state of functioning; (b) it reformulated what ought to be classified (intensities of supports) as well as how to describe the systems of supports that people with mental retardation require; (c) it represented a paradigm shift, from a view of mental retardation as an absolute trait expressed solely by an individual to an expression of the interaction between the person with limited intellectual functioning and the environment; and (d) it extended the concept of adaptive behavior another step, from a global description to specification of particular adaptive skills.

The 2002 10th edition, *Mental Retardation: Definition, Classification, and Systems of Supports,* reflects 10 years of experience with — and critiques of — the 1992 System. During that time, the AAMR Terminology and Classification Committee has held public forums, integrated the literature on mental retardation since 1992, and sought input from Association members and others. This work has greatly benefited from the generous comments and challenges of many. The result is found in the ensuing 12 chapters that build on the 1992 System. Key aspects of the 2002 System include:

• The 2002 System retains: (a) the term *mental retardation*; (b) the essential features of the 1992 System including its functional orientation and supports emphasis; (c) the three diagnostic criteria related to intellectual functioning, adaptive behavior, and age of onset; and (d) maintains a strong commitment that classification based on intensities of needed supports should be the primary focus of a classification system and the preferred direction for the field.

• The 2002 System incorporates: (a) a standard deviation criterion to the intellectual and adaptive behavior components; (b) a fifth dimension of Participation, Interactions, and Social Roles; (c) factor analytic and conceptual work on adaptive behavior that suggests that conceptual, social, and practical skills can adequately represent this multidimensional component of the definition; (d) recent work on supports assessment and supports intensity determination; (e) an expansion of the previous three-step process into a Framework for Assessment; (f) an expanded discussion regarding diagnostic and classification considerations and recommendations regarding other populations including "the forgotten generation"; (g) an expanded discussion of clinical judgment in reference to the circumstances in which it is required, its definition, and a number of clinical judgment guidelines; and (h) a discussion of the relationship between the 2002 System and other classification systems, such as *DSM–IV, ICD–10,* and *ICF.*

The manual retains the term *mental retardation.* Many individuals with this disability urge elimination of the term because it is stigmatizing and is frequently mistakenly used as a global summary about complex human beings. After considerable deliberation by a number of groups, there is no consensus of an acceptable alternative term that means the same thing. Thus, at this time, we were unable to eliminate the term, despite its acknowledged shortcomings. The purpose of the 2002 manual was to define and create a contemporary system of diagnosis, classification, and systems of supports for the disability currently known as mental retardation. To accomplish that, we had to use the commonly understood term for the disability.

With the 1992 System, the concept of mental retardation was expanded signif-

©American Association on Mental Retardation

icantly with the emphasis on a functional orientation, an ecological perspective, and the use of the supports paradigm for both classification and service provision purposes. Based on the critiques of the 1992 System, the AAMR Terminology and Classification Committee, which authored the 2002 manual, recognized that although we were attempting to respond to the paradigm shift in mental retardation, we needed to attend to ensuring adequate and appropriate services to users of the system. Our primary challenge in 1992 was to reflect the paradigm shift; the challenge of the 2002 System has been to integrate the vast amount of commentary and research that has occurred since the 1992 System's publication and to operationalize more clearly the multidimensional construct of mental retardation and best-practice guidelines regarding diagnosis, classification, and planning supports for individuals with mental retardation.

The field of mental retardation is currently in a state of flux regarding not just a fuller understanding of the condition of mental retardation, but also the language and process used in naming, defining, and classifying. For example, we are in the midst of discussions about the nature of intelligence; the relationship between intelligence and adaptive behavior; the implementation of the supports paradigm; the best way to conceptualize disabling conditions the impact of consumer and reform movements; and the effects of terminology upon individual lives.

This state of flux is both frustrating and challenging. It is frustrating because it prohibits one from relying on past language, definitions, and models of mental retardation that can be a source of stability and permanence to some. However, the state is also challenging, as it provides the opportunity to incorporate the current and evolving understanding of the condition of mental retardation and the factors that influence the lives of people in their societies. Whether perceived from a positivistic or social perspective, the condition of mental retardation is being thought of differently today throughout the world. The 2002 AAMR *Definition, Classification, and Systems of Supports* captures that changed vision and builds on our more than 125 years of collegial work, attempting to understand and support individuals with mental retardation.

MENTAL RETARDATION:

Mental retardation is a disability characterized by significant limitations both in intellectual functioning and in adaptive behavior as expressed in conceptual, social, and practical adaptive skills. This disability originates before age 18.

The following five assumptions are essential to the application of this definition:

1. Limitations in present functioning must be considered within the context of community environments typical of the individual's age peers and culture.

2. Valid assessment considers cultural and linguistic diversity as well as differences in communication, sensory, motor, and behavioral factors.

3. Within an individual, limitations often coexist with strengths.

4. An important purpose of describing limitations is to develop a profile of needed supports.

5. With appropriate personalized supports over a sustained period, the life functioning of the person with mental retardation generally will improve.

PART 1

OVERVIEW AND DEVELOPMENT

© American Association on Mental Retardation

CHAPTER 1
DEFINITION, THEORETICAL MODEL, FRAMEWORK FOR ASSESSMENT, AND OPERATIONAL DEFINITIONS

OVERVIEW

In this 2002 manual, *Mental Retardation: Definition, Classification, and Systems of Supports* (10th ed.), the American Association on Mental Retardation (AAMR), through its Ad Hoc Committee on Terminology and Classification (T&C Committee), continues its history of contributing practical and up-to-date information on the definition and classification of the state of functioning currently known as mental retardation. With this work, the AAMR attempts to state, describe, organize, and extend the thinking in the field of mental retardation that has occurred over the past 10 years since the publication of the AAMR's 1992 manual, *Mental Retardation: Definition, Classification, and Systems of Supports* (9th ed.; Luckasson et al.). The present manual contains and describes the logical continuation in conceptualizing mental retardation as functional and contextual.

Often discussions of this disability become confusing because aspects of what is loosely referred to as "the definition" are not separated for consideration. Therefore, we begin this analysis of the current status of mental retardation by providing a framework for thinking about the three separate aspects of naming, defining, and classifying. Each of the aspects is distinct but related to the others.

NAMING, DEFINING, AND CLASSIFYING

NAMING

In naming, a specific term is attached to something or someone. It is a powerful process that carries many messages about perceived value and human relationships. Currently people with mental retardation and others in the field are struggling to identify a new name for this disability. So far, no new consensus term has emerged. The history of the condition we now know as mental retardation is replete with name changes, including feebleminded, mentally defective, mentally deficient, and others. These new names arose as new theoretical frameworks appeared and older names came to signal stigma and distorted power relationships. It is likely that the name mental retardation will change in the near future.

Luckasson and Reeve (2001) suggested a list of guiding questions to ask when names or terms are considered:

- Does this term name this and nothing else?
- Does this term provide consistent nomenclature?
- Does this term facilitate communication?
- Does this term incorporate current knowledge and is it likely to incorporate future knowledge?
- Does this term meet the purposes for which it is being proposed?
- Does this term contribute positively to the portrayal of people with the disability? (pp. 48–49)

DEFINING

In defining, the name or term is explained as precisely as possible. The definition should establish the boundaries of the term and separate who or what is included within the term from who or what is outside the term. The importance of a definition is that it establishes meaning, and should help meet the basic human drive for understanding. But this meaning function of a definition also explains some of the tensions over proposed definitions: reasonable people can disagree over what the meaning of mental retardation is. The meaning proposed in the 1992 manual was that the condition is functional and interactionist rather than statistical. That functional and interactionist meaning continues and is further extended in this 2002 manual. (See the definition, p. 1.)

Luckasson and Reeve (2001) suggested a list of guiding questions to ask when definitions are considered:

- Does this definition indicate the boundaries of the term, that is, who or what is inside the boundaries and who or what is outside the boundaries?
- Does this definition indicate the class of things to which it belongs?
- Does this definition differentiate the term from other members of the class?
- Does this definition use words that are no more complicated than the term itself?
- Does the definition define what something is, not what it is not?
- Does this definition allow some generalizations about characteristics of the individual or group named by the term?
- Is this definition consistent with a desired theoretical framework?
- Does this definition contribute positively to the portrayal of people included in the term? (p. 49)

CLASSIFYING

In classifying, what has been included in the term by its definition is divided into subgroups according to stated principles. Many different types of classification sys-

©American Association on Mental Retardation

tems, based on many different criteria, are used in many different fields. For example, medical disease classification systems might be based on etiology or prognosis or even DNA analysis. Plant classification systems might be based on heredity patterns or even leaf shape. Historically mental retardation classification systems were based on designating the person into an IQ band as in the classification system of mild, moderate, severe, and profound. In the 1992 manual, AAMR proposed a new classification system based on the intensities of needed supports. This 2002 manual maintains this strong commitment for a supports-based classification system and also explains the use of multiple classification systems. (For a full discussion of the classification system, see chaps. 7 & 9.)

Luckasson and Reeve (2001) suggested a list of guiding questions to ask when classification systems are considered:

- Does this classification system allow coding into groups, based on some consistent and meaningful criteria?
- Does this classification system facilitate record keeping?
- Does this classification system provide consistent nomenclature?
- Does this classification system facilitate communication?
- Does this classification system allow some generalizations about the individual or group?
- Does this classification system create a principled organizing system for incorporating new knowledge?
- Does this classification system promote planning and allocation of resources?
- Does this classification system contribute to meaningful predictions for individuals or groups?
- Is this classification system consistent with a desired theoretical framework?
- Does this classification system contribute positively to the portrayal of individuals or groups? (p. 51)

Defining and classifying are the focus of this manual. Naming, although an important aspect of thinking about the disability, is beyond the scope of this manual. Other groups, such as The Consortium on Language, Image, and Public Information and individual organizations, are exploring possible alternatives to the name "mental retardation." If changes occur, they are likely to occur in different settings according to different purposes and timetables. For example, the scientific name of the condition might remain the same; the common usage name might change over extended time; the term used in organizational titles might change, depending on the schedules and roles of the organizations; legislative language might remain constant; and so on. Some coordination of possible name changes is likely, but uniformity, if it occurs, is in the future.

2002 DEFINITION OF MENTAL RETARDATION

The 2002 AAMR definition of mental retardation is as follows:

> Mental retardation is a disability characterized by significant limitations both in intellectual functioning and in adaptive behavior as expressed in conceptual, social, and practical adaptive skills. This disability originates before age 18.

This definition, like AAMR definitions of mental retardation of the recent past, includes the three broad elements of significant limitations in intellectual functioning, concurrent with and related to significant limitations in adaptive behavior, and manifested during the developmental period.

As in 1992, important assumptions are included as part of the application of the definition of mental retardation. In 2002 we specify the following five assumptions:

Assumption 1: "Limitations in present functioning must be considered within the context of community environments typical of the individual's age peers and culture." This means that the standards against which the individual's functioning must be measured are typical community-based environments, not environments that are isolated or segregated by ability. Typical community environments include homes, neighborhoods, schools, businesses, and other environments in which people of similar age ordinarily live, play, work, and interact. The concept of age peers should also include people of the same cultural or linguistic background.

Assumption 2: "Valid assessment considers cultural and linguistic diversity as well as differences in communication, sensory, motor, and behavioral factors." This means that in order for assessment to be meaningful, it must take into account the individual's diversity and unique response factors. The individual's culture or ethnicity, including language spoken at home, nonverbal communication, and customs that might influence assessment results, must be considered in making a valid assessment.

Assumption 3: "Within an individual, limitations often coexist with strengths." This means that people with mental retardation are complex human beings who likely have certain gifts as well as limitations. Like all people, they often do some things better than other things. Individuals may have capabilities and strengths that are independent of their mental retardation. These may include strengths in social or physical capabilities, strengths in some adaptive skill areas, or strengths in one aspect of an adaptive skill in which they otherwise show an overall limitation.

Assumption 4: "An important purpose of describing limitations is to develop a profile of needed supports." This means that merely analyzing someone's limitations is not enough, and that specifying limitations should be a team's first step in developing a description of the supports the individual needs in order to improve

8   ©American Association on Mental Retardation

functioning. Labeling someone with the name mental retardation should lead to a benefit such as a profile of needed supports.

Assumption 5: "With appropriate personalized supports over a sustained period, the life functioning of the person with mental retardation will generally improve." This means that if appropriate personalized supports are provided to an individual with mental retardation, improved functioning should result. A lack of improvement in functioning can serve as a basis for reevaluating the profile of needed supports. In rare circumstances, however, even appropriate supports may merely maintain functioning or stop or limit regression. The important point is that the old stereotype that people with mental retardation never improve is incorrect. Improvement in functioning should be expected from appropriate supports, except in rare cases.

THEORETICAL MODEL

The theoretical model shown in Figure 1.1 is used throughout this manual to denote the relationship among individual functioning, supports, and the five dimensions encompassing a multidimensional approach to mental retardation. These five dimensions are very similar to the four dimensions found in the 1992 System. The 1992 System had included four dimensions (Intellectual Functioning and Adaptive Skills, Psychological and Emotional Considerations, Health and Physical Considerations, and Environmental Considerations). In contrast, the 2002 System has five dimensions (Intellectual Abilities; Adaptive Behavior; Participation, Interactions, and Social Roles; Health; and Context). The fifth was added to be consistent with the *International Classification of Functioning, Disability, and Health (ICF)* (World Health Organization [WHO], 2001) model of disability. By way of comparison:

The 1992 System:
    Dimension I: Intellectual Functioning and Adaptive Skills
    Dimension II: Psychological and Emotional Considerations
    Dimension III: Health and Physical Considerations
    Dimension IV: Environmental Considerations

The 2002 System:
    Dimension I: Intellectual Abilities
    Dimension II: Adaptive Behavior (conceptual, social, practical skills)
    Dimension III: Participation, Interactions, and Social Roles
    Dimension IV: Health (physical health, mental health, etiology)
    Dimension V: Context (environments, culture)

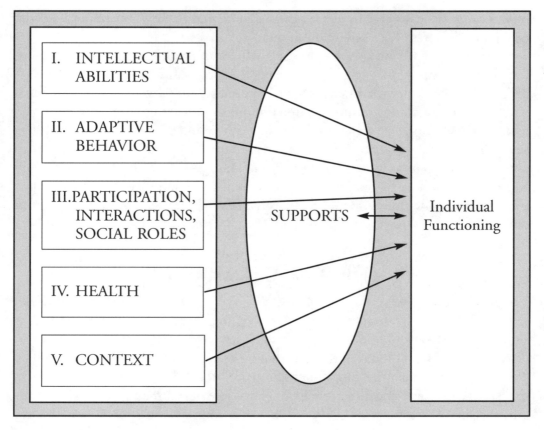

Figure 1.1. Theoretical model of mental retardation.

The 2002 System's theoretical model (see Figure 1.1) continues the ecological focus on the key elements in understanding the condition of mental retardation and the individual's functioning: the person, environments, and supports. However, the model has been changed from the 1992 model (Luckasson et al., p. 10) to reflect the current understanding of the multidimensionality of mental retardation and the mediational role that supports play in individual functioning. As shown in Figure 1.1, each of the multidimensional influences on the individual's functioning is mediated through the supports available to the person. Also note in Figure 1.1 that the need for supports can reciprocally influence functioning.

FRAMEWORK FOR DIAGNOSIS, CLASSIFICATION, AND PLANNING OF SUPPORTS

The 2002 System includes a framework for assessment that involves three functions: diagnosis, classification, and planning supports. As shown in Table 1.1 ("Frame-

©American Association on Mental Retardation

work for Assessment"), each function has a number of primary purposes and appropriate measures and tools. For example, for diagnosis, primary purposes might be to establish eligibility for services, benefits, and legal protections. The three required measures and tools are IQ tests, adaptive behavior scales, and documented age of onset. For classification, primary purposes might be to group for service reimbursement or funding, research, services, and communication about selected characteristics. Appropriate measures and tools might include support intensity scales, IQ ranges or levels, special education categories, environmental assessments, etiology-risk factor systems, levels of adaptive behavior, mental health measures, funding levels, or benefits categories. For planning supports, the primary purpose is to enhance personal outcomes related to independence, relationships, contributions, school and community participation, and personal well-being. Appropriate measures might include person-centered planning tools, self-appraisals, support intensity scales, and elements from individualized plans such as individualized education programs (IEPs).

The Framework for Assessment depicted in Table 1.1 also includes important considerations for assessment, such as a match between measures and purpose; the psychometric characteristics of measures selected; the qualifications of the examiner; sensitivity to the selection of informants, relevant context and environments, the individual's clinical and social history; team input; the individual's behavior in the assessment situation; and the individual's personal goals.

In summary, assessment should follow the following framework:

- There are three major functions of assessment: diagnosis, classification, and planning of supports for the person.

- Each function has a number of possible purposes ranging from establishing service eligibility and research, to organizing information, to the development of a plan for the provision of supports for the individual.

- Selection of the most appropriate measures or tools will depend on the function (diagnosis, classification, planning supports) and specific purpose to be fulfilled. Selection of measures or systems and interpretation of results should address the considerations found in Table 1.1.

OPERATIONAL DEFINITIONS

Throughout the manual, readers will find reference to the terms *mental retardation, intelligence, adaptive behavior, supports, disability,* and *context.* Table 1.2 presents operational definitions for these terms. These operational definitions are used consistently throughout the manual to ensure a clear understanding of key issues involved in diagnosis, classification, and planning supports. These operational definitions are critically important in the assessment of intelligence and adaptive behavior and

TABLE 1.1
Framework for Assessment of Mental Retardation

Function	Purposes	Measures and Tools	Considerations for Assessment
Diagnosis	Establishing eligibility: • Services • Benefits • Legal protections	[a]IQ tests [a]Adaptive behavior scales [a]Documented age of onset	Match between measures and purpose Psychometric characteristics of measures selected Appropriateness for person (age group, cultural group, primary language, means of communication, gender, sensori-motor limitations) Qualifications of examiner Examiner characteristics and potential for bias Consistency with professional standards and practices Selection of informants
Classification	Grouping for: • Service reimbursement or funding • Research • Services • Communication about selected characteristics	Support intensity scales IQ ranges or levels Special-education categories Environmental assessments Etiology-risk factor systems Levels of adaptive behavior Mental health measures Funding levels Benefits categories	Relevant context and environments Social roles, participation, interactions Opportunities/experiences Clinical and social history Physical and mental factors Behavior in assessment situation Personal goals Team input
Planning Supports	Enhancing personal outcomes: • Independence • Relationships • Contributions • School and community participation • Personal well-being	Person-centered planning tools Self-appraisal Assessment of objective life conditions measures Support intensity scales Required individual plan elements (IFSP, IEP, ITP, IPP, IHP)	

Note. IFSP = individualized family service plan; IEP = individualized education program; ITP = individualized transition plan; IPP = individualized program plan; and IHP = individualized habilitation plan.

[a] Required assessments to establish diagnosis of mental retardation.

©American Association on Mental Retardation

the subsequent diagnosis of mental retardation. Hence, readers should pay special attention to the following three operational definitions:

In reference to the *assessment of intelligence.* The criterion for diagnosis is approximately two standard deviations below the mean, considering the standard error of measurement for the specific assessment instruments used and the instruments' strengths and limitations.

In reference to the *assessment of adaptive behavior:* For diagnosis, significant limitations in adaptive behavior should be established through the use of standardized measures normed on the general population, including people with disabilities and people without disabilities. On these standardized measures, significant limitations in adaptive behavior are operationally defined as performance that is at least two standard deviations below the mean of either (a) one of the following three types of adaptive behavior: conceptual, social, and practical, or (b) an overall score on a standardized measure of conceptual, social, and practical skills.

In reference to *context:* The assessment of context, although not typically accomplished with standardized measures, is a necessary component of clinical judgment and integral to understanding the individual's functioning.

TABLE 1.2
Operational Definitions

MENTAL RETARDATION

Mental retardation is a disability characterized by significant limitations both in intellectual functioning and in adaptive behavior as expressed in conceptual, social, and practical adaptive skills. This disability originates before age 18.

The following five assumptions are essential to the application of this definition:

1. Limitations in present functioning must be considered within the context of community environments typical of the individual's age peers and culture.

2. Valid assessment considers cultural and linguistic diversity as well as differences in communication, sensory, motor, and behavioral factors.

3. Within an individual, limitations often coexist with strengths.

4. An important purpose of describing limitations is to develop a profile of needed supports.

5. With appropriate personalized supports over a sustained period, the life functioning of the person with mental retardation generally will improve.

(table continues)

©American Association on Mental Retardation

TABLE 1.2 *(continued)*

INTELLIGENCE

Intelligence is a general mental capability. It includes reasoning, planning, solving problems, thinking abstractly, comprehending complex ideas, learning quickly, and learning from experience.

Limitations in intelligence should be considered in light of four other dimensions: Adaptive Behavior; Participation, Interactions, and Social Roles; Health; and Context.

The measurement of intelligence may have different relevance, depending on whether it is being considered for purposes of diagnosis or classification.

Although far from perfect, intellectual functioning is still best represented by IQ scores when obtained from appropriate assessment instruments. The criterion for diagnosis is approximately two standard deviations below the mean, considering the standard error of measurement for the specific assessment instruments used and the instruments' strengths and limitations.

ADAPTIVE BEHAVIOR

Adaptive behavior is the collection of conceptual, social, and practical skills that have been learned by people in order to function in their everyday lives.

Limitations in adaptive behavior affect both daily life and the ability to respond to life changes and environmental demands.

Limitations in adaptive behavior should be considered in light of four other dimensions: Intellectual Abilities; Participation, Interactions, and Social Roles; Health; and Context.

The presence or absence of adaptive behavior can have different relevance, depending on whether it is being considered for purposes of diagnosis, classification, or planning supports.

For the diagnosis of mental retardation, significant limitations in adaptive behavior should be established through the use of standardized measures normed on the general population including people with disabilities and people without disabilities. On these standardized measures, significant limitations in adaptive behavior are operationally defined as performance that is at least two standard deviations below the mean of either (a) one of the following three types of adaptive behavior: conceptual, social, or practical, or (b) an overall score on a standardized measure of conceptual, social, and practical skills.

(table continues)

© American Association on Mental Retardation

TABLE 1.2 *(continued)*

SUPPORTS

Supports are resources and strategies that aim to promote the development, education, interests, and personal well-being of a person and that enhance individual functioning. Services are one type of support provided by professionals and agencies.

Individual functioning results from the interaction of supports with dimensions of Intellectual Abilities; Adaptive Behavior; Participation, Interactions, and Social Roles; Health; and Context.

The assessment of support needs can have different relevance, depending on whether it is done for purposes of classification or planning supports.

DISABILITY

Disability is the expression of limitations in individual functioning within a social context and represents a substantial disadvantage to the individual.

CONTEXT

Context describes the interrelated conditions within which people live their everyday lives. Context as used here represents an ecological perspective that involves at least three different levels: (a) the immediate social setting, including the person, family, and/or advocates (microsystem); (b) the neighborhood, community, or organizations providing education or habilitation services or supports (mesosystem); and (c) the overarching patterns of culture, society, larger populations, country, or sociopolitical influences (macrosystem or megasystem).

Context should be considered in light of four other dimensions: Intellectual Abilities; Adaptive Behavior; Participation, Interactions, and Social Roles; and Health.

Context can have different relevance depending on whether it is being considered for purposes of diagnosis, classification, or planning supports.

The assessment of context, although not typically accomplished with standardized measures, is a necessary component of clinical judgment and integral to understanding the individual's functioning.

SUMMARY

The 2002 System builds on and extends the 1992 System, incorporating recent developments in mental retardation. Comparing the 1992 and 2002 Systems, we note the following key aspects:

The 2002 System retains (a) the term *mental retardation*; (b) the essential features of the 1992 System, including its functional orientation and supports emphasis; (c) the three diagnostic criteria related to intellectual functioning, adaptive behavior, and age of onset; it also maintains a strong commitment that intensities of needed supports should be the primary focus of a classification system and the preferred direction for the field.

The 2002 System incorporates (a) a standard deviation criterion to the intellectual and adaptive behavior components; (b) a fifth dimension that involves participation, interactions, and social roles; (c) factor analytic and conceptual work on adaptive behavior — suggesting that conceptual, social, and practical skills can adequately represent this multidimensional component of the definition; (d) recent work on supports assessment and supports intensity determination; (e) an expansion of the previous three-step process into the Framework for Assessment (Table 1.1); (f) an expanded discussion regarding diagnostic and classification considerations and recommendations regarding other populations including "the forgotten generation"; (g) an expanded discussion of clinical judgment in reference to the circumstances in which it is required, its definition, and a number of clinical guidelines; and (h) discussion of the relationships between the 2002 System and other classification systems, such as the *Diagnostic and Statistical Manual (DSM–IV–TR)* (American Psychiatric Association, 2000), *International Classification of Diseases (ICD–10)* (WHO, 1993), and *International Classification of Functioning, Disability, and Health (ICF)* (WHO, 2001).

EMERGING CONSENSUS IN THE FIELD

Based on the T&C Committee's analysis of recent work in the field, there seems to be consensus on the following aspects of the definition and classification of the condition of mental retardation:

- Mental retardation is an intellectual disability mirrored by significant limitations in everyday functioning that are present early in life and before age 18.

- A disability is conceptualized as a significant problem in functioning and is characterized in the *ICF* (WHO, 2001) model by marked and severe problems in the capacity to perform ("impairment"), the ability to perform ("activity limitations"), and the opportunity to function ("participation restrictions").

16   ©American Association on Mental Retardation

- Adaptive behavior encompasses the application of conceptual, social, and practical skills to daily life. Its assessment should relate to an individual's typical performance during daily routines and changing circumstances, not to maximum performance.

- Although far from perfect, intellectual functioning is still best represented by IQ scores when obtained from appropriate assessment instruments. The criterion for diagnosis is approximately two standard deviations below the mean of a corresponding group of people considering the standard error of measurement for the specific assessment instruments used and the instruments' strengths and weaknesses.

- Classification systems may be used for a variety of purposes and based on a number of different factors to meet the varied needs of individuals and their families, researchers, clinicians, and practitioners. Aspects of an individual's mental retardation might be classified, for example, on the basis of intensities of needed supports, etiology, levels of measured intelligence, or levels of assessed adaptive behavior.

- The functions or reasons for applying a definition of mental retardation to a person are multiple and may include diagnosis, classification, and planning of supports. Within each function are multiple purposes. For example, the diagnosis function may be applied to determine eligibility for services, research, or legal purposes. Likewise, there are different purposes for classification: to organize information, to plan research, to evaluate, to plan intervention, for eligibility determination, and so forth. Supports planning for a given person should relate to that individual's strengths and needs in each of five dimensions (Intellectual Abilities; Adaptive Behavior; Participation, Interactions, and Social Roles; Health; and Context) and be focused on desired person-referenced outcomes.

- Clinical judgment may play a role in diagnosis, classification, and planning supports.

CHAPTER 2
EVOLUTION OF THE DEFINITION OF MENTAL RETARDATION

A state of mental defect from birth, or from an early age, due to incomplete cerebral development, in consequence of which the person affected is unable to perform his duties as a member of society in the position of life to which he is born. (Tredgold, 1908)

Mental retardation is a disability characterized by significant limitations both in intellectual functioning and in adaptive behavior as expressed in conceptual, social, and practical adaptive skills. This disability originates before age 18. (AAMR, 2002)

OVERVIEW

Many would agree with Benton (1964), who argued that the seeming simplicity and clarity of the concept of mental retardation are deceptive. This chapter will set forth a brief summary of past definitions of mental retardation, trace their changing themes, and review recent criticisms of the 1992 American Association on Mental Retardation (AAMR) definition (Luckasson et al.). By studying the parameters of recent definitions of mental retardation and the related discussions from the field, it should be possible to contribute improvements in both form and function to emerging definitions.

RECURRING THEMES IN DEFINITIONS

The past definitions of mental retardation possess not only recurring themes but also disputable concepts; they have sparked ongoing dialogue and debate by professionals, parents, and, more recently, self-advocates. Table 2.1 sets forth the definitions of mental retardation dating from Tredgold (1908, 1937) and Doll (1941, 1947) to the current 10th definition of the AAMR (Luckasson et al., 2002). The field's explanation of the term *mental retardation* has changed in many ways over this period of 65 years. For example, in the early part of the 20th century, Tredgold and Doll placed an emphasis on *incurability*, a stance that was consistent with the beliefs about the certainty of intelligence testing and the widespread practices of eugenics (Stevens, 1964; Trent, 1994). Individuals with mental retardation were viewed as being predetermined by their limitations and consistently prevented from participating in everyday, typical environments because of their low IQs. By contrast, the first four criteria in Doll's (1941) definition reflect more durable themes that remain in current definitions: (a) social incompetence related to intellectual limitations and (b) developmental limitations occurring before adulthood (Smith, 1997).

TABLE 2.1
Definitions of Mental Retardation

Year and Author	Definition
Tredgold, 1908	A state of mental defect from birth, or from an early age, due to incomplete cerebral development, in consequence of which the person affected is unable to perform his duties as a member of society in the position of life to which he is born. (p. 2) *Emphasis on incurability; refers to an ultimate or permanent status of mental retardation*
Tredgold, 1937	Mental deficiency is a state of incomplete mental development of such a kind and degree that the individual is incapable of adapting himself to the normal environment of his fellows in such a way to maintain existence independently of supervision, control, or external support. (p. 4) *Emphasis on incurability; refers to an ultimate or permanent status of mental retardation*
Doll, 1941	A state of social incompetence obtained at maturity, or likely to obtain at maturity, resulting from developmental arrest of constitutional origin (heredity or acquired); the condition is essentially incurable through treatment and irremediable through training. (p. 215) We observe that six criteria by statement or implication have been generally considered essential to an adequate definition and concept [of mental retardation]. These are (1) social incompetence, (2) due to mental sub normality, (3) which has been developmentally arrested, (4) which obtains at maturity, (5) is of constitutional origin, and (6) is essentially incurable. (p. 215) The concept of the essential incurability of feeble-mindedness is part of the diagnostic picture. If the prognosis suggests a possibility of amelioration of symptoms amounting to prospects of ultimate normality, then a diagnosis of mental retardation is not warranted. (Doll, 1947, as cited in Benton, 1964, p. 22) *Emphasis on incurability; refers to an ultimate or permanent status of mental retardation. The first four of six criteria continue to be themes in current definitions*

(table continues)

©American Association on Mental Retardation

TABLE 2.1 *(continued)*

Year and Author	Definition	IQ Cutoff	Diagnosis	Developmental Period	Adaptive Behavior	Levels of Severity by IQ
5th AAMR Definition: Heber, 1959	Mental retardation refers to subaverage general intellectual functioning which originates during the developmental period and is associated with impairment in one or more of the following: (1) maturation, (2) learning, (3) social adjustment	Less than one standard deviation *(SD)* below the population mean of the age group involved on measures of general intellectual functioning	Both required standardized IQ measures and measure of impairment in one or more aspects of adaptive behavior (e.g., Vineland Social Maturity Scale)	Birth through approximately 16 years	Refers to the effectiveness with which the individual copes with the natural and social demands of the environment. It has two major facets: (a) the degree to which the individual is able to function and maintains him- or herself independently, and (b) the degree to which he or she meets satisfactorily the culturally imposed demands of personal and social responsibility	Level V = -1 to -2 *SD* Level IV = -2 to -3 *SD* Level III = -3 to -4 *SD* Level II = -4 to -5 *SD* Level I = < -5 *SD*
6th AAMR Definition: Heber, 1961	Mental retardation refers to subaverage general intellectual functioning which originates during the developmental period and is associated with impairment in adaptive behavior	Greater than one *SD* below *M* (theoretically 16% of the population)	Standardized IQ and adaptive behavior tests	Birth through age 16	Effectiveness of the individual to adapt to the natural and social demands of his or her environment as reflected in maturation, learning, and social adjustment	Borderline MR: -1 SD; and mild, moderate, severe, profound
7th AAMR Definition: Grossman, 1973	Mental retardation refers to significantly subaverage general intellectual functioning *existing concurrently with* deficits in adaptive behavior, and manifested during the developmental period	Two or more *SDs* below *M* (theoretically 3% of the population)	Standardized IQ and adaptive behavior tests	Upper age limit of 18 years	Effectiveness of degree with which the individual meets the standards of personal independence and social responsibility expected of his or her age and cultural group. May be reflected in the following areas: (a) early years: sensorimotor skills, communication, self-help, socialization; (b) childhood and early adolescence: application of basic academics in daily life, application of reasoning and judgment; (c) later adolescence and adult life: vocational and social responsibilities and performances	Mild, moderate, severe, and profound. Borderline intelligence defined as falling between retardation and average intelligence ("slow learners")

(table continues)

©American Association on Mental Retardation

Table 2.1 *(continued)*

Year and Author	Definition	IQ Cutoff	Diagnosis	Developmental Period	Adaptive Behavior	Levels of Severity by IQ
8th AAMR Definition: Grossman, 1983	Mental retardation refers to significantly subaverage general intellectual functioning resulting in or associated *with concurrent* impairments in adaptive behavior and manifested during the developmental period	IQ of 70 or below on standardized measures of intelligence; upper limit is intended as a guideline and could be extended to 75 or more	Standardized IQ and adaptive behavior tests	Period of time between conception and the 18th birthday	Significant limitations in an individual's effectiveness in meeting the standards of maturation, learning, personal independence, or social responsibility that are expected for his or her age level and cultural group	Mild, moderate, severe, and profound
9th AAMR Definition: Luckasson et al., 1992	Mental retardation refers to substantial limitations in present functioning. It is characterized by significantly subaverage intellectual functioning, *existing concurrently* with related limitations in two or more of the following applicable adaptive skills areas: communication, self-care, home living, social skills, community use, self-direction, health and safety, functional academics, leisure, and work. Mental retardation manifests before age 18	IQ standard score of approximately 70 to 75 or below based on assessment that includes one or more individually administered general intelligence tests	Standardized IQ tests and tests of adaptive behavior skills; coupled with team member observations and clinical judgment; use of valid assessment measures and process	Period of time between conception and the 18th birthday	Adaptive skills refer to an array of competencies that reflect both the ability to fit into a given niche as well as the ability to change one's behavior to suit the demands of a situation. Ten adaptive skill areas were specified with the requirement that an individual evidence sufficiently comprehensive limitations, interpreted as being limitation in 2 or more skills areas applicable to his or her age. The 10 areas: communication, self-care, home living, social skills, community use, self-direction, health and safety, functional academics, leisure, and work	Omitted, as classified by IQ scores. Intensities of supports needed by an individual in adaptive skills areas were added. Intensities change across time and by adaptive skills area for given individuals, thus not a substitute for the IQ levels classification

(table continues)

©American Association on Mental Retardation

TABLE 2.1 *(continued)*

Year and Author	Definition	IQ Cutoff	Diagnosis	Developmental Period	Adaptive Behavior	Levels of Severity by IQ
10th AAMR Definition: Luckasson et al., 2002	Mental retardation is a disability characterized by significant limitations both in intellectual functioning and in adaptive behavior as expressed in conceptual, social, and practical adaptive skills. This disability originates before age 18. Five assumptions: (a) Limitations in present functioning must be considered within the context of community environments typical of the individual's age peers and culture. (b) Valid assessment considers cultural and linguistic diversity as well as differences in communication, sensory, motor, and behavioral factors. (c) Within an individual, limitations often coexist with strengths. (d) An important purpose of describing limitations is to develop a profile of supports. (e) With appropriate personalized supports over a sustained period, the life functioning of the person with mental retardation generally will improve	Performance that is at least two *SDs* below the *M* of an appropriate assessment instrument, considering the standard error of measurement for the specific assessment instruments used and the instruments' strengths and limitations	Standardized IQ tests and tests of adaptive behavior skills; coupled with team member observations and clinical judgment; use of valid assessment measures and process	Period of time between conception and the 18th birthday	Adaptive behavior is the collection of conceptual, social, and practical skills that have been learned by people in order to function in their everyday lives. Limitations in adaptive behavior affect both daily life and the ability to respond to life changes and environmental demands, and should be considered in light of four other dimensions: Intellectual Abilities; Participation, Interactions, and Social Roles; Health; and Context. Significant limitations in adaptive behavior can be established only through the use of standardized measures normed on the general population including people with disabilities and people without disabilities, and are defined as performance that is at least two *SDs* below the *M* of (a) one of the following three types of adaptive behavior: conceptual, social, or practical, or (b) an overall score on a standardized measure of conceptual, social, and practical skills	Depending on the purposes of applying the definition (diagnosis, classification, or planning supports), an individual who is found eligible for mental retardation services may be classified in various ways: by support intensity, IQ range, adaptive behavior limitations, etiology, mental health categories, etc.

Note. Adapted from *Mental Retardation* (5th ed., pp. 72–73), by M. Beirne-Smith, R. F. Ittenback, & J. R. Patton, 1998, Upper Saddle River, NJ: Merrill/Prentice Hall. "What Is Meant by Mental Retardation?" by S. Greenspan, 1999, *International Review of Psychiatry, 11,* 6–18. "Mental Retardation as an Educational Construct: Time for a New Shared View?" by J. D. Smith, 1997, *Education and Training in Mental Retardation and Developmental Disabilities, 20,* 179–183.

Incurability was replaced by an emphasis on present functioning. Heber (1961) described mental retardation "as a symptom rather than a fundamental condition" that is defined by "behavioral, rather than organic manifestations" (p. 3). In 1992 (Luckasson et al.) this emphasis continued: "Mental retardation is a definition of present functioning rather than a permanent state of being, and functioning typically varies during the course of one's life" (p. 19). Thus adaptive behavior and intelligence reflect the two recurring themes in the definition of mental retardation.

ADAPTIVE BEHAVIOR

From its first inclusion (Heber, 1959) as part of the American Association on Mental Deficiency (AAMD, which became the AAMR) definition, the concept of adaptive behavior and its measurement have been seen by most as being important but elusive. The addition of adaptive behavior limitations as a criterion for diagnosing mental retardation was intended to better reflect the social characteristics of the disability, to reduce the reliance upon IQ scores, and to decrease the number of "false positives," or individuals falsely identified as having mental retardation. Despite the development of some 200 scales of adaptive behavior in the last 40 years, consensus on the construct is still lacking (Thompson, McGrew, & Bruininks, 1999). In fact, although adaptive behavior is included currently in all of the major diagnostic systems,

> there is no universal agreement on the factor structure of adaptive behavior, the best method to assess it, the role that adaptive behavior or skill deficits should play in the definition and diagnosis of mental retardation, and the relationship between the concepts of intelligence and adaptive behavior. (Schalock, 1999a, p. 2)

Heber (1959) and his colleagues first introduced the loosely defined term *adaptive behavior* as a characteristic associated with general subaverage intellectual functioning in individuals with mental retardation. Adaptive behavior deficiencies would be understood as difficulties adjusting to ordinary demands made on their life routines. Impaired adaptive behavior might present as problems in maturation, learning, or social adjustment. It is also important that the Heber definition did not view adaptive behavior deficiencies as being fixed, but subject to the social and environmental demands that exist for a given person at various points in his or her life.

Between 1959 and now, there have been many debates over the accuracy of measuring adaptive behavior (and adaptive skills) (e.g., Spreat, 1999) and whether adaptive behavior assessment should be a requirement for diagnosing mental retardation (e.g., Greenspan, 1999b). Regardless, the importance of adaptive behavior increased with the 1973 AAMD definition (Grossman), when measured deficits in adaptive behavior concurrent with subaverage intellectual behavior were made a condition for the diagnosis. From 1973 onward, the criteria for diagnosing mental retardation included simultaneous and significant measured limitations in both

©American Association on Mental Retardation

adaptive behavior (adaptive *skills* in 1992) and intelligence. Yet Greenspan (1997) asserted that IQ still remains "the dominant construct in the definitional equation" (p. 184). To illustrate this point, he challenged that adaptive behavior scores could be used to argue that someone with an IQ score under 70 is not mentally retarded but could not be used to argue for a mental retardation diagnosis when the IQ score is over 70 (p. 184).

In 1992 the concept of global adaptive behavior was replaced by 10 broad adaptive skill areas and the requirement that 2 or more of the 10 skills be documented as deficient. Debate was stimulated by the absence of measures that assessed adaptive behavior skills (rather than the broader concept) and by questions raised over the accuracy of the 10 areas (Greenspan, 1999a). The 1992 definition placed an added emphasis on assessing a person's current functioning given the impact of changing environmental demands and supports. The definition's assumptions stated that improvements in environmental conditions or the presence of needed supports could positively impact an individual's ability to meet the routine demands of life, thereby improving his or her performance on adaptive skill measures; as a result, the life functioning of the person might improve and, in rare cases, the diagnosis of mental retardation might no longer apply.

INTELLIGENCE

Intelligence, as measured by IQ, has predominated as the primary criterion for diagnosing mental retardation. Although some professionals in the field have recommended the return to a definition based only on IQ, others fervently urge that reliance on IQ be reduced and that measures of intelligence reflect the concept more broadly than simply IQ (Greenspan, 1999b; Zigler & Trickett, 1978).

Levels of Severity

Even before the concept of intelligence could be measured, mental retardation had been viewed as a disorder marked by deficits in intellectual ability. In addition, even in the 19th century, criteria were applied to classify individuals with mental retardation by their level of "severity." Two terms were coined in 1877 to describe different levels of intellectual functioning based on decreasing language and speech abilities: *imbecility* and *idiocy* (Field & Sanchez, 1999). Because many professionals (Gould, 1981, p. 159) believed, and still do, that human intelligence was a "single, measurable entity," the arrival of the first successful intelligence test early in the 1900s allowed these terms to be quantified. Mental-age scores replaced the earlier practice of measuring cranial shapes and sizes to predict ability. Classification into "levels of functioning" was dependent on mental age, not adaptive behavior performance — a concept not yet conceived. Since the Binet-Simon intelligence test first appeared at the beginning of the 20th century, classification systems based on numerical scores have been used to place people with mental retardation into subcategories. In 1910 the Committee on Classification of Feeblemindedness of AAMR's precursor organization created three subcategories of individuals with mental retardation; after an individual was categorized as "feebleminded" (a mental age of 12 or less), he or she was then classified into groups by decreasing mental age: "morons," "imbeciles," and "idiots" (Field & Sanchez, 1999). When it was realized that mental age does not grow in a linear fashion, IQ scores replaced mental-age scores as the metric for classifying people by intelligence.

In the early 1950s, the *Diagnostic and Statistical Manual: Mental Disorders (DSM–1)* (as referenced in Trent, 1994), published by the American Psychiatric Association, devised different categories of mental retardation founded on IQ level. These levels, with some differences, were reflected in later AAMR definitions from 1959 until 1983 (see Table 2.1).

The 1992 definition dropped levels of mental retardation based on IQ scores for several reasons: (a) Mental retardation relies on both limitations in IQ and adaptive skills, whereas an individual's "level of severity" was based only on IQ; (b) the accuracy of IQ scores at the extremes of measurement is regarded as less reliable than of those closer to the mean; (c) "mild mental retardation," a condition that represents considerable disadvantage, was a misnomer (Tymchuk, Lakin, & Luckasson, 2001); and (d) too much trust was being put in a person's subclassification, and it often influenced the perception of potential special education placement and types of services as well as adult opportunities for services. When the ninth (1992) edition of the AAMR manual dropped the use of levels of severity as a classification system, IQ scores were used only for making a diagnosis and not for classification. Following a diagnosis of mental retardation, an individual's adaptive skill assessments were examined by an interdisciplinary team and coupled with clinical judgments and findings from observations, interviews, and reports of those who knew the individual well. This process enabled the team to (a) identify strengths and needs for supports across four life dimensions (i.e., Intellectual Functioning and Adaptive Skills; Psychological and Emotional Considerations; Health and Physical Considerations; and Environmental Considerations), and (b) create a profile of the person's needed supports.

Assessment of IQ and "Cutoff" Limits

Starting in 1973, the criterion for having significant limitations in intellectual functioning was increased from one to two standard deviations below the mean. This single change drastically reduced the number of people theoretically eligible to be classified as having mental retardation. Heber's 1961 definition overidentified people as having mental retardation, theoretically labeling 16% of the population, whereas Grossman's 1973 definition, which lowered the IQ cutoff from one to two or more standard deviations below the mean, theoretically labeled only 3% of the population. At the same time, the 1973 definition was made more conservative by

©American Association on Mental Retardation

strengthening the requirement that intellectual and adaptive behavior limitations occur concurrently.

The 1983 AAMR manual (Grossman) specified that the IQ ranges for mild through profound mental retardation include the test's error of measurement (e.g., plus or minus 3 or more IQ points, depending on the measure and the individual's age) rather than citing single IQ score cutoffs. Thus for mild mental retardation, the IQ range was specified as 50–55 to 70–75 and for moderate mental retardation, it was 35–40 to 50–55. MacMillan, Gresham, and Siperstein (1993, 1995) complained that because all psychologists should know the standard error of the mean, there is no need to include standard error in the indicated score ranges. Others argued for using standard deviation cutoffs instead of IQ score cutoffs, so IQ score ranges reflected the standard deviation of the test used.

CRITIQUE OF THE 1992 AAMR DEFINITION

There were several major changes in the 1992 AAMR definition (Luckasson et al.) compared to 1983 (Grossman):

- The global concept of adaptive behavior was replaced by adaptive behavior skills and defined as an array of competencies that reflect both how an individual fits into and functions in a given niche or societal context as well as how that person changes his or her behavior to suit the demands of a situation (p. 39).

- Assessment of global impairments in adaptive behavior was replaced by assessment of strengths and limitations in 10 broad adaptive behavior skill areas, with a requirement for diagnosis of significant limitations in at least 2 developmentally appropriate areas (p. 38).

- The notion of maladaptive behavior was eliminated (p. 43).

- The practice of classifying individuals with mental retardation into IQ-based subgroups (mild, moderate, severe, and profound) was dropped. Instead, professionals were encouraged to accompany diagnoses with descriptions of needed supports (p. 34).

- Application of the definition was contingent on four assumptions: (a) valid assessment, (b) assessment of adaptive skills in a context typical of age peers, (c) limitations coexisting with strengths, and (d) appropriate supports over a sustained period generally yield improvements in life functioning (pp. 6–7).

- Following the diagnosis of those with mental retardation, the design of a supports profile was to include an examination of strengths and needs in three additional human dimensions, beyond the dimension of intellectual functioning and adaptive skills: psychological and emotional; the physical, etiological, and

©American Association on Mental Retardation

health; and environment (pp. 23–26).

- An increased specificity was given to the use of clinical judgment during diagnosis and the profiling of needed supports as it was based on informed observations in a variety of everyday ecologies by those who knew the individual well. Clinical judgment and multiple assessments were viewed as being preferred over the sole reliance on standardized measures, on a single measure of intelligence or adaptive behavior, or on a single evaluator (p. 45).

There have been debates as to whether the 1992 definition changed the IQ cutoff from past definitions (MacMillan et al., 1993, 1995; Reiss, 1994; Schalock et al., 1994). By defining *significantly subaverage intellectual functioning* as "approximately 70 to 75 or below," the authors of the manual intended to provide increased clarity, but *not* to change the cutoff (Reiss, 1994). Similar to the 1983 (Grossman) definition, Luckasson et al. (1992) included significant limitations in intelligence as a requirement for diagnosis, with the benchmark being an IQ standard score of 70 to 75 or below (p. 5). Grossman (1983) had defined *significantly subaverage intelligence* as an IQ of 70 or below on standardized measures of intelligence, but elaborated that "this upper limit is intended as a guideline; it could be extended upward through IQ 75 or more, depending on the reliability of the intelligence test used" (p. 11).

POSITIVE APPRAISAL

There was both positive and negative reaction to the 1992 definition. Some changes viewed as favorable by the AAMR Terminology and Classification (T&C) Committee or by those in the field (e.g., elimination of classification into levels by IQ, increased emphasis on clinical judgment) were cited as unfavorable by others.

One feature praised by some, including many families, was the shift away from a focus on impairment to a heightened consciousness of needed supports (Hodapp, 1995; Polloway, 1997). This shift was linked to the elimination of classification into levels of mental retardation by IQ scores and an emphasis placed on needed supports. However, there was less praise for the elimination of IQ levels as a way to reduce (a) the error of IQ-based classification, (b) practices that segregate by levels, and (c) the stigma of level implications.

A second identified advantage of the 1992 definition was the supports model, conceptualized as part of the system for classifying individuals with mental retardation and meant to replace the deficit model and to provide guidance for the provision of services or supports (Polloway, 1997, p. 176). Some felt that the definition did not go far enough, however, because support was not included in the definition itself (Greenspan, 1997).

Third, the change from a global conceptualization of adaptive behavior into

©American Association on Mental Retardation

adaptive skill areas was favorably regarded by members of the Division on Mental Retardation and Developmental Disabilities in the Council for Exceptional Children (Smith, 1994). The listing of subskills was seen as a way to guide evaluators to assess subskills for other important adaptive skill areas beyond academics. The *DSM–IV* (1994) also included the assessment of adaptive skills as one of the three defining criteria for diagnosis.

Fourth, some praised the specified role of clinical judgment in determining strengths and weaknesses in adaptive behavior and in the diagnosis of mental retardation (Greenspan, 1999a).

Fifth, probably for the first time people with mental retardation were included in forums on the 1992 definition and "indicated in one forum after another that they desire inclusion, access, and independence" (Reiss, 1994, p. 6). Consumer organizations praised the definition as one whose framework for community-based supports promised to stimulate better services. But in this decade consumers have gone further and expressed strong dissatisfaction with continued use of the term *mental retardation* (Snell & Voorhees, in press).

Finally, some saw the elimination of IQ-based levels of severity and the so-called "increase" in the IQ cutoff as reducing the importance of IQ in the definition, which corresponds to its less important role in successful community integration (Greenspan, 1999b).

NEGATIVE APPRAISAL

As Seen in Failure of Adoption

Adoption of a new idea is a complex matter. When analyzing the mental retardation field's acceptance of the 1992 AAMR definition, it is useful to explore the rate-of-adoption concept developed by Rogers (1995) in his classic work *Diffusion of Innovations* (p. 204). *Rate of adoption* refers to the relative speed with which innovations are adopted by members of a system. Many factors affect the rate of adoption, including aspects of the innovation itself and also general factors unrelated to the innovation but nonetheless important to diffusion. According to Rogers, rate of adoption can be explained by five attributes of the innovation itself: (a) whether the innovation is seen as an advantage over the previous idea; (b) whether it is consistent with the values, past experiences, and needs of potential adopters; (c) whether it is perceived as overly complex; (d) whether it is possible to try out parts of the innovation on a smaller basis; and (e) whether the results of the innovation can be observed. The pace at which an innovative idea is adopted is further affected by several variables not specifically related to the innovation itself: (a) whether an individual alone can adopt or whether an entire institution must adopt; (b) the appropriateness of the communication channels used to disseminate information about the innovation; (c) the norms and interconnectedness of the system; and (d) the extent of efforts to promote the innovation.

It seems appropriate to view the adoption of a new definition of mental retardation within Rogers's framework. A recent survey of directors of special education in 50 states indicated that 44 states continue to use the Grossman (1983) definition; only 4 reported using the 1992 AAMR definition (although none used the levels of supports model). Three states based their diagnoses of mental retardation in school-age children on neither model (Denning, Chamberlain, & Polloway, 2000). A survey of published research of investigators working with individuals who have mental retardation indicated that less than 1% applied the 1992 AAMR system for classification (Polloway, Smith, Chamberlain, Denning, & Smith, 1999).

A number of reasons can be cited for the limited adoption of the 1992 definition. First, the change in the mental retardation definition from the 1983 to the 1992 edition required new assessment devices to measure adaptive skills, yet there were no standardized or accepted ways to assess strengths or limitations in the skill areas, short of using a combination of existing devices, informal observation, and clinical judgment. Second, the elimination of IQ-based levels of functioning meant a change in commonly used terminology that had no clear substitute; levels of support were not meant to be substituted (Luckasson, Schalock, Snell, & Spitalnik, 1996), although some misinterpreted support intensity levels as a replacement for levels of impairment (MacMillan, Siperstein, & Leffert, in press). Although some praised the shift to a supports profile, perhaps the legally required individualized education programs for school-age students (and individualized habilation plans for adults) seemed sufficient.

As Seen in Professional Literature

During the period between 1992 and now, the 1992 definition has received some criticism in the professional literature. These key arguments are summarized next.

Elimination of severity levels. Probably most criticized was the removal of the mild, moderate, severe, and profound levels of severity of mental retardation (MacMillan et al., 1993; MacMillan et al., in press). Many regard levels of severity as the fundamental way for educators, psychologists, adult-service providers, and researchers to classify individuals with mental retardation.

Assumed substitution of levels of support for severity levels. Critics decried the substitution of levels of support for levels of severity, though such substitution was never intended (Luckasson et al., 1996). The levels of support were faulted for being deficient in the psychometric qualities needed for measurement and were judged as being subjective, unreliable, and lacking in precision (MacMillan et al., 1993). Some cited the cumbersome nature of support intensity levels as a replacement terminology (Smith, 1994). Concerns were raised as to how existing teacher

©American Association on Mental Retardation

certification requirements that corresponded to levels of severity would be affected (Smith). Luckasson et al. (1996) responded that support levels were never conceptualized to be "statistically measured commodities" but "personalized, individualized, and tailored to the needs of the child and/or the family" (pp. 248–249). The most recent definition of mental retardation published by the American Psychiatric Association in *DSM–IV* (1994) adapted the 1992 AAMR definition but did not drop the levels of severity, which was interpreted by some as criticism of the 1992 AAMR definition (Jacobson & Mulick, 1996).

IQ criterion of 70 to 75. MacMillan et al. (1993) predicted that a significant increase would occur in the number of individuals identified as having mental retardation with the purported change in the IQ cutoff.

Imprecision in use of adaptive behavior skills and their measurement. The 10 adaptive skills set forth in the 1992 definition were not determined empirically, as, for example, through factor analyses of existing adaptive behavior tests to validate the 10 domains as internally consistent and independent skill areas (MacMillan et al., 1993). Some critics have called these skill areas "artificial constructs" (Greenspan, 1997) that do not correspond to any existing tests (Smith, 1994), although recently several tests have reconfigured their test items and scoring into the 10 skill areas. Finally, the criterion of demonstrating significant weaknesses in 2 or more of the 10 skill areas was criticized as failing to uniformly address different age groups: younger, school-age, and adult individuals (MacMillan et al., in press).

Individuals with "mild mental retardation." By cropping levels of severity, MacMillan and his colleagues (MacMillan, Gresham, Bocian, & Lambros, 1998; MacMillan et al., 1993) claimed that the 1992 definition eliminated the mild mental retardation category and questioned whether that definition appropriately served this large group, which represents approximately 75% to 89% of the population with mental retardation (Field & Sanchez, 1999). MacMillan et al. (in press), referring to their earlier work (MacMillan, Gresham, Siperstein, & Bocian, 1996), stated that "Most of the children who fit within the MMR [mild mental retardation] range are being classified by schools as having LD [learning disabilities] rather than mental retardation" due to the stigma of the label that applies to an overly heterogeneous group. A study of 150 grade-school students in five southern California school districts by MacMillan, Gresham et al. (1996) showed that schools were hesitant to diagnose students with low IQs and learning problems as having mental retardation and more often classified them as having learning disabilities.

Estimates from U.S. Department of Education annual counts lent further evidence to this trend as they indicated that the percentage of school-age students classified as having mental retardation has decreased enormously — 40% between the

©American Association on Mental Retardation

1976–1977 school year and 1994–1995 (Beirne-Smith, Ittenback, & Patton, 1998). At the same time, the percentage of students with learning disabilities during this period greatly increased, some estimating an increase as high as 207% (MacMillan, Gresham et al., 1996).

The 1992 definition, MacMillan and colleagues maintained, enlarged the group of people identified as having mental retardation based on IQ scores, while it abandoned the term *mild mental retardation.* MacMillan et al. (in press) also strongly advised that those classified as having mild mental retardation experience different problems in daily functioning from those with moderate to profound mental retardation and should be viewed as having a distinct form of mental retardation with separate classification criteria.

Overrepresentation of minorities. Documentation is abundant regarding the disproportionate number of minority children classified as having mild mental retardation during the school years (MacMillan et al., in press). Many reasons have been cited for this phenomenon, including variation by race in rates of (a) intervention to help avoid referral for special education (minorities often lower) and (b) special-education referral (minorities often higher), and different IQ distributions by race on tests for intelligence (minorities are lower) (Kaufman & Doppelt, 1976). Any change in the IQ cutoff in the definition could further affect the disproportionate representation, assuming use of IQ scores alone for diagnosis. Using the findings of Kaufman and Doppelt, MacMillan et al. (1993) suggested that with an IQ cutoff of 75, 18.4% of African American children and 2.62% of White children would be considered as having mental retardation.

The wide range of heterogeneity in the population. The range of individuals identified with mental retardation differs noticeably by etiology, degree of ability and disability, and behavioral characteristics. Classification by etiology and by levels of mental retardation have allowed professionals to differentiate within this broad group. Individuals with mild mental retardation predominate the population, constituting 75% to 89% of the whole group, whereas those with labels of moderate to profound mental retardation make up only 11% to 25% of the group. A specific identifiable cause for mental retardation can be found for only about 25% to 40% of those with mild mental retardation (McLaren & Bryson, 1987). (For most of those with learning disabilities, etiology also has been considered difficult to determine.) By contrast, specific causes can be identified for 60% to 75% of those with labels of moderate to profound mental retardation.

MacMillan et al. (1993) suggested that with an increase in the upper IQ limits, the "mild" group, which often has no identifiable cause for mental retardation (which they referred to as having "cultural-familial" causes), will double, and the group with lower IQ scores usually detected at an early age (which they referred to

©American Association on Mental Retardation

as having "organic" causes) will become even smaller proportionately. Arguing that these two widely recognized groups have different developmental trajectories and very different ways of learning and adapting in the context of schools and society, MacMillan et al. (1993) questioned whether AAMR could represent their interests when the means for differentiating between the groups has been eliminated.

IMPLICATIONS OF CRITIQUES OF THE 1992 SYSTEM FOR THE 10TH EDITION

A number of implications result from these critical reviews of the 1992 AAMR definition, classification, and systems of supports ("the 1992 System"). Not all are compatible, and many are complex and will be difficult to address with any single revision. Some implications point to the need for new conceptualizations of intelligence and adaptive behavior, which would influence how human ability and capacity are measured.

CRITERIA RELATING TO CAPACITY

"If MR is real, then it must be grounded in the demonstrated incompetencies, needs, and vulnerabilities that cause individuals to be seen as needing supports and protections" (Greenspan, in press). Greenspan, like others, has suggested that the artificial categories of adaptive behavior and IQ that we have invented be replaced with a tripartite model of intelligence. He further noted that IQ (a) is overused, (b) is inadequately contextualized, and (c) reflects a narrow view that is limited to academic intelligence (Greenspan, 1999b).

Adaptive behavior should not be viewed as separate from and subservient to an IQ deficit. Instead of measuring IQ as the indicator of intelligence, Greenspan and others have suggested that a broader, multifaceted construct of the concept be assessed — tripartite intelligence. What is assessed should tap more than the academic realm of intelligence and reflect the practical and social abilities that correspond to successful community integration, making adaptive behavior assessment unnecessary.

Greenspan generally referred to a tripartite model of intelligence as a more logical way to view intelligence and to subsume adaptive behavior within intelligence. This model of competence would reflect the assessment of social, practical, and conceptual intelligence rather than adaptive behavior or skills. Its items would reflect realistic situations met within community environments that require complex decision making, involving contexts and tasks that are critical for survival and success socially, conceptually, and practically. For example, the risks faced in the social domain by someone with low intelligence are being victimized and exploited by others, whereas risks in the practical domain of intelligence are physical (e.g., getting lost, being endangered by exposure, being hit by a vehicle). Assessment would involve a variety of methods, such as observation by knowledgeable informants using rating instruments to judge the responses of individuals to verbal and video-taped incidents tapping credulity and gullibility (Greenspan, Loughlin, & Black, 2001).

Greenspan (1999b) argued that mental retardation is more of a lifelong condition with broad-based deficiencies in various domains of intelligence and one that is highly fluctuating and related mainly to conceptual intelligence. Using measures that tap social and practical intelligence, beyond school-related academics, and lowering the qualifying cutoff would help reduce those in the "mild group," who often disappear when they exit school.

Less critical than Greenspan of IQ measures, MacMillan and his colleagues (in press) expressed concern about the group of individuals they refer to as having "mild mental retardation." They agreed with Greenspan that that the IQ cutoff is arbitrary, but noted that the cutoff score has enormous consequences for those with low IQs.

Like Greenspan, MacMillan et al. (1993) criticized the concept of adaptive behavior and most tests that purport to assess it, but they repeatedly condemned the "2 out of 10 adaptive skill deficit criterion" in the 1992 definition due to an inadequate empirical basis for the 10 skills and the absence of reliable tests for measurement. Although assessment of adaptive behavior is viewed as necessary by MacMillan et al. (in press) as "a bulwark against false positives that would occur if IQ was used as the sole determinant of mental retardation," they claimed that it still fails to embody those dimensions of behavior that are relevant to children's ability to meet the social role expectations of the setting in which they are expected to function.

Both MacMillan and his colleagues and Greenspan agreed that the adaptive behavior criterion in assessment to identify people with mental retardation needs to be reconceptualized to reflect actual problems of adaptation in daily functioning faced by those with mild mental retardation. Rather than basic practical skills of self-care and home-living, the areas of challenge for assessment are those that require planning, decision making, and social judgment. Social competence would emphasize how people behave in the real world (Greenspan, 1999b, p. 15), and thus would measure typical performance, not maximal performance or capacity that is reflected in IQ assessment (Thompson et al., 1999). These critics, therefore, suggested the development of new assessment procedures (for adaptive behavior alone or for adaptive behavior plus intelligence) based on different conceptualizations of human ability and capacity.

©American Association on Mental Retardation

QUANTIFICATION OF SUPPORT

Greenspan (1997) argued that support is of such importance that it should be part of the definition. More recently, Greenspan (in press) proposed the use of a model of competence or needs. This model would (a) involve assessment across a range of life dimensions, (b) leading to a score reflecting the relevance of critical outcomes, (c) that could be used to diagnose those who have disabilities and differentiate them from those who do not have disabilities in relation to a line set by the "keepers of society's purse strings," and (d) would place individuals who qualify on a continuum from very needy to not at all needy. Greenspan's scheme seems like a more refined version of the 1992 supports model and supports profile. Linked either to adaptive skill assessment or to the assessment of social and practical intelligence, this model of competence or needs would require new assessment instruments and a means for classifying different degrees of need or intensities of support.

The current World Health Organization's (WHO) view of disability (WHO, 2001) sets forth multiple determinants of individual functioning for a person with mental retardation (see chap. 7, this volume). Consistent with the 1992 definition and Greenspan' s (in press) view of support, determinants of functioning relate directly to one's support needs. Commonly cited determinants of functioning include (a) adaptive behavior (conceptual, social, and practical skills), (b) intellectual abilities, (c) participation, interactions, and social roles, (d) context (environment, culture, and opportunities), and (e) health (mental and physical) and etiology. When supports are provided that relate to an individual's current needs in one or more of these areas, individual functioning is likely to improve.

MILD MENTAL RETARDATION, LEVELS OF SEVERITY, AND LABELS

The IQ cutoff should be conservative, with some people suggesting that it be lowered significantly, or kept at 70, but accompanied by ways to distinguish between those with limited mental retardation and those with more extensive cognitive disabilities. Citing two or more standard deviations below the norm as the cutoff for a measure of intelligence would prevent more error than citing specific IQ scores. Most agree on the arbitrary nature of numerical boundaries. Greenspan (in press) notes:

> The MR construct is useful in that it allows mostly deserving individuals to get services and supports they often desperately need. It is fiction in that there is no justification for the idea that there is a magical line (let alone one determinable by a test score) dividing those who have or do not have this condition.

Some critics have suggested that the severity subcategories be restored, but disagreed on the basis for those subcategories. Whereas MacMillan and his colleagues want the traditional IQ-based subcategories, Greenspan (in press) argued for subcategories based on the "pervasiveness of needed supports and protections, not on IQ levels."

Critics called for new names for the disability label and the subcategories. For example, Greenspan (1997) suggested (a) that the mild group be renamed to reflect the significance of the disability, (b) the "profound" subcategory be dropped, but (c) the moderate and severe subcategory names be retained. He further emphasized that no subcategory labels be based on IQ. Instead, Greenspan (1999b, in press) proposed that the terms for subcategories be based on more natural functional criteria, such as evidence of an inability to benefit from skilled reading instruction.

If mental retardation is to include heterogeneous groups, MacMillan, Siperstein et al. (1996, in press) recommended that a new, nonstigmatizing term for those in the mild group be adopted, such as *cognitive impairment* or *general learning disability.* These same critics also have proposed narrowing the group of individuals with mental retardation to exclude those with mild mental retardation and adding organicity as part of the prototype of mental retardation (Greenspan, in press; MacMillan, Siperstein, & Gresham, 1996). Under pressure from some members and self-advocates, the AAMR for several years has been debating the recommendation of a name change. The Board of Directors has recently voted to change the name of the organization, to explore an appropriate substitute for the term *mental retardation,* and to present this option to the voting membership in the near future.

SUMMARY

The 10 years since the publication of the ninth edition of AAMR's manual on classification and terminology in mental retardation have brought forth both heated debate and favorable commentary. These comments, coupled with a decade of research, progress, and thinking in the field of mental retardation, have had healthy effects on this 10th edition. There will never be a flawless definition of mental retardation, nor will there be universal agreement on any given definition. Definitions of this construct, however sophisticated, cannot be free from some arbitrariness; but every definition of mental retardation has significant impact on the lives of many individuals. Thus it is critical that those who revise definitions of constructs like mental retardation seriously contemplate the comments of users and consumers as well as strive for improvement in accuracy and correspondence with current understanding of human functioning. The AAMR T&C Committee believes we have followed this recommended course.

There seems to be consensus on the following defining characteristics:

- Mental retardation is a disability characterized by significant limitations in everyday functioning that are present early in life and before age 18.

©American Association on Mental Retardation

- Adaptive behavior is the collection of conceptual, social, and practical skills that have been learned by people in order to function in their everyday lives. Its assessment should relate to an individual's performance during daily routines and changing circumstances, not to maximal performance.

- Although far from perfect, intellectual ability is still best represented by IQ scores when obtained from appropriate assessment instruments administered and interpreted accurately. The criterion for diagnosis is approximately two standard deviations below the mean, considering the standard error of measurement for the specific assessment instrument used and the instrument's strengths and weaknesses.

- Multiple classification systems may be used to meet the varied needs of individuals and their families, researchers, clinicians, and practitioners. Such classification systems can be based, for example, on the intensities of needed supports, etiology, levels of measured intelligence, or levels of assessed adaptive behavior.

- The functions or reasons for applying a definition of mental retardation to a person are multiple and may include diagnosis, classification, and/or planning supports. Each function may have multiple purposes. For example, the diagnostic function may be applied to determine eligibility for services, benefits, or legal protections. Likewise, there are different grouping purposes for classification, including service reimbursement or funding, research, services, communication, and so forth. Supports planning for a given person should relate to that individual's strengths and needs in all five dimensions of individual functioning: Intellectual Abilities; Adaptive Behavior; Participation, Interactions, and Social Roles; Health; and Context.

CHAPTER 3
MULTIDIMENSIONALITY OF MENTAL RETARDATION

> **Mental retardation is a disability characterized by significant limitations both in intellectual functioning and in adaptive behavior as expressed in conceptual, social, and practical adaptive skills. This disability originates before age 18.**

OVERVIEW

Mental retardation is a disability characterized by significant limitations in both intellectual functioning and adaptive behavior (conceptual, social, and practical). A disability is the expression of limitations in individual functioning within a social context and represents a substantial disadvantage to the individual. As represented in the World Health Organization's (WHO) *International Classification of Functioning, Disability, and Health* (2001), an individual's disability may be characterized by marked and severe problems in the capacity to function ("impairments in body functions and structures"), the ability to function ("activity limitations"), and the opportunity to function ("participation restrictions"). Consistent with this conception and the 1992 (Luckasson et al.) AAMR System's "general structure of the definition of mental retardation" (p. 10), a person's disability is considered within the context of environmental and personal factors and the need for individualized supports.

The approach to mental retardation found in the 2002 AAMR *Mental Retardation: Definition, Classification, and Systems of Supports* reflects this multidimensional approach to mental retardation. This approach results in a broader conceptualization of mental retardation, an appreciation of the multidimensionality of behavior, and an emphasis on the individual's needs for supports. A multidimensional approach requires that a comprehensive description of a person with mental retardation includes:

- the existence of mental retardation (as opposed to other disabling conditions);

- a consideration of the person's participation, interactions, and social roles within current living, school or work, and community environments that facilitate or restrict personal well-being factors;

- a consideration of the person's health status, including physical health, mental health, and relevant etiological factors;

- the optimal environments and systems of supports that facilitate the person's independence, relationships, contributions, school and community participation, and personal well-being;

- a profile of needed supports based on the aforementioned factors.

Because of the critical need to approach mental retardation from a multidimensional perspective, this chapter is a summary of the key concepts and emerging patterns in reference to each of the five dimensions discussed in the manual: Intellectual Abilities (Dimension I); Adaptive Behavior — conceptual, social, practical skills (Dimension II); Participation, Interactions, and Social Roles (Dimension III); Health — physical health, mental health, etiological factors (Dimension IV); and Context — environments and cultures (Dimension V).

DIMENSION I:
INTELLECTUAL ABILITIES

Intelligence is a general mental capability. It includes reasoning, planning, solving problems, thinking abstractly, comprehending complex ideas, learning quickly, and learning from experience (Arvey et al., 1994; Gottfredson, 1997). As reflected in this definition, intelligence is not merely book learning, a narrow academic skill, or test-taking smarts. Rather, it reflects a broader and deeper capacity for comprehending our surroundings — catching on, making sense of things, or figuring out what to do. Thus the concept of intelligence represents an attempt to clarify, organize, and explain the fact that individuals differ in their ability to understand complex ideas, to adapt effectively to their environments, to learn from experience, to engage in various forms of reasoning, to overcome obstacles by thinking and communicating (Neisser, Boodo, Bouchard, & Boykin, 1996).

As discussed in chapter 4, there have been a number of attempts to clarify the nature of intelligence, including whether it is composed of: (a) a primary or single factor (i.e., general intelligence or "*g*"), or multiple dimensions (i.e., fluid and crystallized intelligence) (Horn & Cattell, 1966); (b) planning and simultaneous and successive processing (Das, Naglieri, & Kirby, 1994; Naglieri & Das, 1997); (c) analytical, creative, and practical intelligence (Sternberg, 1988); or (d) conceptual, practical, and social intelligence (Greenspan & Driscoll, 1997). As discussed more fully in chapter 4, presently the empirical data suggest strongly that intellectual

©American Association on Mental Retardation

functioning can be explained best by a general factor of intelligence (Carroll, 1997a, 1997b).

The assessment of intellectual functioning is essential in making a diagnosis of mental retardation, as virtually all definitions of mental retardation make reference to significantly subaverage intellectual functioning as one of the diagnostic criteria. Therefore, in reference to this 2002 manual, readers should note the following implications of intelligence on the multidimensionality of mental retardation:

- Limitations in intelligence should be considered in light of four other dimensions: Adaptive Behavior; Participation, Interactions, and Social Roles; Health; and Context.

- The measurement of intelligence may have different relevance, depending on whether it is being considered for purposes of diagnosis or classification.

- Although far from perfect, intellectual functioning is still best represented by IQ scores when obtained from appropriate assessment instruments.

DIMENSION II:
ADAPTIVE BEHAVIOR (CONCEPTUAL, SOCIAL, AND PRACTICAL SKILLS)

Adaptive behavior is the collection of conceptual, social, and practical skills that have been learned by people in order to function in their everyday lives. The concept of adaptive behavior (as expressed in conceptual, social, and practical adaptive skills) found in this 2002 manual is a continuation of the historical attention given to adaptive behavior in the diagnosis of mental retardation (McGrew, Bruininks, & Johnson, 1996; Thompson et al., 1999; Widaman & McGrew, 1996). The concept of adaptive skills implies an array of competencies and, thus, provides a firmer foundation to two key points made throughout this 2002 manual: (a) Adaptive skill limitations often coexist with strengths in other adaptive skill areas; and (b) a person's strengths and limitations in adaptive skills should be documented within the context of community and cultural environments typical of the person's age peers and tied to the person's individualized needs for supports.

Based on extensive work by Thompson et al (1999), Greenspan and Granfield (1992), Kamphaus (1987a), Widaman and McGrew (1996), and Widaman, Stacy, and Borthwick-Duffy (1993), there is an emerging consensus that the structure of adaptive behavior consists of the following three factor clusters: (a) Cognitive, Communication, and Academic Skills (i.e., conceptual skills); (2) Social Competence Skills (i.e., social skills); and (c) Independent Living Skills (i.e., practical skills). Examples of conceptual, social, and practical adaptive skills are found in Table 3.1.

TABLE 3.1
Examples of Conceptual, Social, and Practical Adaptive Skills

Conceptual
- Language (receptive and expressive)
- Reading and writing
- Money concepts
- Self-direction

Social
- Interpersonal
- Responsibility
- Self-esteem
- Gullibility (likelihood of being tricked or manipulated)
- Naiveté
- Follows rules
- Obeys laws
- Avoids victimization

Practical
- Activities of daily living
  - Eating
  - Transfer/mobility
  - Toileting
  - Dressing
- Instrumental activities of daily living
  - Meal preparation
  - Housekeeping
  - Transportation
  - Taking medication
  - Money management
  - Telephone use
- Occupational skills
- Maintains safe environments

 ©American Association on Mental Retardation

A fourth factor-cluster, Motor or Physical Competence (or development), is found in many factor-analytic studies of adaptive behavior (see Thompson et al., 1999). This factor, which involves gross- and fine-motor skills and ambulating, is included in this 2002 manual in the dimension of Health (chap. 10). Problem behavior, which is sometimes referred to as *maladaptive behavior,* is discussed in chapters 5 and 10.

As discussed in chapter 5, it is widely known that the construct of adaptive behavior has not historically been as securely embedded as intelligence in formal definitions of mental retardation or in diagnostic practice. In spite of the fact that previous definitions have indicated that intelligence and adaptive behavior should have equal weight (see Table 2.1), in practice IQ has typically dominated and thus has been overemphasized both in terms of professional decision making and classification. However, with the recent advances in the development and standardization of adaptive behavior scales, and the increased understanding of the adaptive behavior construct as outlined in chapter 5, we anticipate that both adaptive behavior and intelligence will be assessed and thoroughly considered in the diagnostic process. Thus readers should note the following implications of adaptive behavior on the multidimensionality of mental retardation:

- Limitations in adaptive behavior affect both daily life and the ability to respond to life changes and environmental demands.

- Limitations in adaptive behavior should be considered in light of four other dimensions: Intellectual Abilities; Participation, Interactions, and Social Roles; Health; and Context.

- The presence or absence of adaptive skills can have different relevance, depending on whether they are being considered for purposes of diagnosis, classification, or planning supports.

- For diagnosis, significant limitations in adaptive behavior should be established through the use of standardized measures normed on the general population, which includes people with disabilities and people without disabilities.

DIMENSION III:
PARTICIPATION, INTERACTIONS, AND SOCIAL ROLES

Environments are conceptualized as the specific settings in which a person lives, learns, plays, works, socializes, and interacts. Positive environments foster growth, development, and well-being of the individual. For people with mental retardation, these positive environments constitute settings that are typical of their age peers and that are consistent with the individual's cultural and linguistic diversity. It is within such settings that the individual with mental retardation is most likely to experience participation and interactions and assume one or more valued social roles.

The civil and disability rights movements throughout the world have advocated for greater opportunities for people with mental retardation for increased participation in the mainstream of life and greater levels of inclusion, valued social roles, and normalized social relations and interactions. As discussed in chapter 7, the *International Classification of Functioning, Disability, and Health* (WHO, 2001) model of disability also stresses the key role that participation, interactions, and social roles play in the life of people with disabilities.

PARTICIPATION AND INTERACTIONS

Participation and interactions are best reflected in the direct observation of engagement in everyday activities. The application of direct observation of engagement in activity as a quality indicator derives from work in both the United States (see, e.g., Risley & Cataldo, 1973; M. Jones, Risley, & Favell, 1983) and the United Kingdom (see, e.g., Felce, 2000). It also parallels ecological research using direct observations by Sackett and Landesman-Dwyer (1977). The central focus of the direct observations is the individual's interaction with their material and social worlds. Behavior reflecting adaptive functioning is characterized by the extent to which the individual is actively engaged with (attending to, interacting with, participating in) his or her environment. The importance of this participation and interaction is expressed well by Risley and Cataldo who stated that "the direction and extent of engagement with the physical and social environment appears to be an almost universal indication of the quality of a setting for people" (p. 38).

SOCIAL ROLES

Role status refers to a set of valued activities that are considered normative for a specific age group. Examples include one's living arrangement, employment setting, educational level, community participation, recreation-leisure patterns, and health status. For youth, attending school is a valued, age-specific activity, whereas for high-school graduates and adults, living and working in the community are valued activities.

Participation, interactions, and social roles are influenced greatly by opportunities afforded the individual. Thus in reference to this 2002 manual, readers should note the implications of these factors to the multidimensionality of mental retardation:

- *Participation* refers to an individual's involvement in and execution of tasks in real life situations. It denotes the degree of involvement, including society's response to the individual's level of functioning.

- Lack of participation and interactions can result from hampered availability or accessibility of resources, accommodations, and/or services.

- Lack of participation and interactions frequently limits the fulfillment of valued social roles.

DIMENSION IV:
HEALTH (PHYSICAL HEALTH, MENTAL HEALTH, AND ETIOLOGICAL FACTORS)

PHYSICAL AND MENTAL HEALTH

The WHO (1980, 1993) defined *health* as a state of complete physical, mental, and social well-being. Physical and mental health conditions influence human functioning across the other four dimensions: Intellectual Abilities; Adaptive Behavior; Participation, Interactions, and Social Roles; and Context.

For people with mental retardation, the effects of physical and mental health on functioning range from *greatly facilitating* to *greatly inhibiting*. Some individuals enjoy robust good health with no significant activity limitations that allows them to participate fully in social roles, such as work, recreation, or leisure activities. On the other hand, some individuals have a variety of significant health limitations, such as epilepsy or cerebral palsy, that greatly impair body functioning in areas such as mobility and nutrition and that severely restrict personal activities and social participation. Similarly, some individuals may have activity and other limitations related to a mental illness. Most individuals with mental retardation are somewhere between these extremes. Contextual factors, such as the environments in which individuals live, learn, work, play, socialize, and interact with others, influence the degree to which they are able to function and participate. Environmental factors may create actual or potential dangers or fail to provide appropriate protection and supports. Individuals with mental retardation may have difficulty recognizing physical and mental health problems, negotiating the health or mental health care system, communicating symptoms and feelings, and understanding treatment plans.

ETIOLOGY

The approach to etiology found in this 2002 manual builds on the approach described in the ninth AAMR manual (Luckasson et al., 1992). In the 1992 manual and here *etiology* is conceptualized as a multifactorial construct composed of four categories of risk factors (biomedical, social, behavioral, and educational) that interact across time, including across the life of the individual and across generations from parent to child. As discussed more fully in chapter 8, the multifactorial construct replaces prior historical approaches that divided the etiology of mental retardation into two broad types: mental retardation of biological origin and mental retardation due to psychosocial disadvantage (Grossman, 1983).

The multifactorial approach to etiology discussed in chapter 8 (see Table 8.2) expands the list of causal factors in mental retardation in two directions: types of factors and timing of factors. One direction expands the types of factor categories to four groupings: (a) biomedical (factors that relate to biologic processes, such as genetic disorders or nutrition); (b) social (factors that relate to social and family interaction, such as stimulation and adult responsiveness); (c) behavioral (factors that relate to potentially causal behaviors, such as dangerous [injurious] activities or maternal substance abuse); and (d) educational (factors that relate to the availability of educational supports that promote mental development and the development of adaptive skills).

The second direction describes the timing of the occurrence of causal factors according to whether these factors affect the parents of people with mental retardation, the person with mental retardation, or both. This aspect of causation is termed *intergenerational* to describe the influence of factors present during one generation on the outcomes of the next generation. Current ideas about intergenerational effects stress their origin in preventable and reversible influences of adverse environments and how understanding these effects should lead to enhanced individual and family supports.

The concepts of multidimensionality and intergenerational aspects of mental retardation have important implications for people at three levels of prevention: (a) primary, which involves prevention of the condition that would otherwise result in mental retardation; (b) secondary, which involves actions to prevent an existing condition from resulting in mental retardation; and (c) tertiary, which involves actions to minimize the severity of functional impairments associated with the etiology or to prevent secondary conditions. In addition, readers should note the following implications of physical and mental health on the multidimensionality of mental retardation:

- Physical and mental health conditions can affect the assessment of intelligence and adaptive behavior (e.g., impaired alertness that is caused by sleep disturbances or nutritional deficiencies).

- Medications, such as anticonvulsants and psychotropic drugs, may affect performance (e.g., tiredness and fatigue that influence test performance).

- Assessment of adaptive behavior can also be affected by medications that influence gross- and fine-motor skills or by oral motor conditions that influence communication skills.

©American Association on Mental Retardation

- Assessment of needed supports may also be influenced by the presence of health and mental health conditions. Individuals with mental retardation may need health-related supports to promote functioning and participation, to overcome limitations in mobility (e.g., wheelchair-accessible work settings) or safety (e.g., adaptations to prevent seizure-related injuries).

DIMENSION V:
CONTEXT (ENVIRONMENTS AND CULTURE)

Context describes the interrelated conditions within which people live their everyday lives. Context as used in this 2002 manual represents an ecological perspective (Bronfenbrenner, 1979) that involves at least three different levels: (a) the immediate social setting, including the person, family, and/or advocates (microsystem); (b) the neighborhood, community, or organizations providing education or habilitation services or supports (mesosystem); and (c) the overarching patterns of culture, society, larger populations, country, or sociopolitical influences (macrosystem or megasystem). These various environments are important to people with mental retardation because they frequently determine what the individuals are doing, where they are doing it, when they are doing it, and with whom. Thus environments (as defined by the three systems levels just listed) can provide opportunities and foster well-being.

PROVIDE OPPORTUNITIES

Providing education, living, work, and recreation-leisure services and supports in integrated settings creates situations that allow a person to grow and develop. These opportunities involve *community presence* (the sharing of the ordinary places that define community life), *choice* (the experience of autonomy, decision making, and control), *competence* (the opportunity to learn and perform functional and meaningful activities), *respect* (the reality of having a valued place in one's community), and *community participation* (the experience of being part of a growing network of family and friends) (O'Brien, 1987).

FOSTER WELL-BEING

Recent efforts to identify factors within an individual's environment that foster and enhance one's well-being (e.g., Schalock, 1997) suggest the importance of health and personal safety, material comforts and financial security, community and civic activities, leisure and recreation within a wellness perspective, cognitive stimulation and development, and work that is interesting, rewarding, and worthwhile. In addition, one of the most important aspects of any environment is its quality of stability with associated aspects of predictability and control.

A number of our value orientations and assumptions about behavior are affected by one's environment and culture, including our relation with nature, our sense of time and time orientation, relations we have with others, our sense of self, the use of wealth, one's thinking style, and the provision of either formal or informal supports (Craig & Tassé, 1999). Thus in reference to this 2002 manual, readers should note the following implications of context on the multidimensionality of mental retardation:

- Context should be considered in light of four other dimensions: Intellectual Abilities; Adaptive Behavior; Participation, Interactions, and Social Roles; and Health.

- Context can have different relevance, depending on whether it is being considered for purposes of diagnosis, classification, or planning supports.

- The assessment of context, although not typically accomplished with standardized measures, is a necessary component of clinical judgment and integral to understanding the individual's functioning.

SUMMARY

In summary, mental retardation is not something you have, like blue eyes or a bad heart. Nor is it something you are, like being short or thin. It is not a medical disorder, although it may be coded in a medical classification of diseases; nor is it a mental disorder, although it may be coded in a classification of psychiatric disorders. *Mental retardation* refers to a particular state of functioning that begins in childhood, is multidimensional, and is affected positively by individualized supports (see Figure 1.1). As a model of functioning, it includes the structure and expectations of the systems within which the person functions and interacts: micro-, meso-, and macrosystems. Thus a comprehensive and correct understanding of the condition of mental retardation requires a multidimensional and ecological approach that reflects the interaction of the individual and his or her environment, and the person-referenced outcomes of that interaction related to independence, relationships, contributions, school and community participation, and personal well-being.

©American Association on Mental Retardation

PART 2
DIAGNOSIS

CHAPTER 4
ASSESSMENT OF INTELLIGENCE

Intelligence is a general mental ability. It includes reasoning, planning, solving problems, thinking abstractly, comprehending complex ideas, learning quickly, and learning from experience.

OVERVIEW

The assessment of intellectual functioning is essential to making a diagnosis of mental retardation, as virtually all definitions of mental retardation make reference to significantly subaverage intellectual functioning as one of the diagnostic criteria. The intent of this chapter is to discuss the construct of intelligence, to examine the assessment practices relevant to measuring intellectual functioning, and to review the psychometric properties of existing instruments commonly used to measure this dimension.

The assessment of intellectual functioning is a task that requires specialized professional training. Assessment data should be reported by an examiner(s) experienced with people who have mental retardation and qualified in terms of professional and state regulations as well as meeting a publisher's guidelines for conducting a thorough, valid psychological evaluation of the individual's intelligence functioning. In some instances, this may require an interdisciplinary evaluation. It is important for evaluators to familiarize themselves with the five assumptions essential to the application of the 2002 definition of mental retardation presented in chapter 1 of this manual. Appropriate standardized measures should be determined based upon several individual factors, including the individual's social, linguistic, and cultural background. If necessary, proper adaptations must be made for any motor or sensory limitation.

Although reliance on a general functioning IQ score has been heatedly contested by some researchers (discussed later in this chapter), it remains, nonetheless, the measure of human intelligence that continues to garner the most support within the scientific community (Gottfredson, 1997). If appropriate standardized measures of intelligence are not available (e.g., in some developing countries or when people are observed in cultural settings different from their home countries), the general guideline for consideration of intellectual functioning should be determined by professional clinical judgment and determined to be below the level attained by approximately 97% of individuals (i.e., significantly below average). As further research in this area is reported, a greater degree of precision may emerge that can be applied to this area of concern.

The determination that an individual's intellectual functioning is significantly below the mean fulfills the first requirement for being diagnosed as having mental retardation. Intellectual functioning should be measured using individually administered standardized psychological tests and administered by appropriately trained professionals. The American Educational Research Association (1999), in collaboration with the American Psychological Association and the National Council on Measurement in Education, has published standards to promote the sound and ethical use of tests and provide guidelines to establish proper test development and test use.

NATURE OF INTELLIGENCE

GENERAL INTELLIGENCE "*g*"

Early conceptualization of intelligence was focused on a unifactorial latent trait. Much of the early work in establishing the nature of intelligence was accomplished using data obtained from administering cognitive tasks to groups of individuals and analyzing the resulting data using factor analytic procedures. Spearman (1927) reported that the relationship between the different cognitive scores could be explained by a single factor that he labeled "general intelligence" or "*g*." Thurstone (1938) initially claimed that he failed to find a unique factor explaining the majority of the variance in the intelligence data he analyzed. However, he later acknowledged having erred in making his statistical computations, and when he corrected this error he admitted obtaining a general intelligence "*g*" factor (see Carroll, 1997b).

Carroll (1993) reviewed hundreds of intelligence factor analytic studies published between the 1920s and 1990s. His analysis yielded a three-stratum hierarchical model, where a general intelligence *g* factor sits at the apex of the pyramidal structure. The *g* factor was obtained through second- and third-order factor analyses. In Carroll's model, he reported obtaining as many as 60 discrete narrow abilities (e.g., musical abilities, basic arithmetic) at the first stratum. These narrow cognitive abilities are highly intercorrelated and were further factor analyzed into 10 broader abilities that formed the second stratum of his hierarchical model. Finally, these 10 broad abilities can be further factor analyzed into one single *g* factor (3rd stratum) of intelligence.

©American Association on Mental Retardation

INTELLIGENCE AS A MULTIDIMENSIONAL CONSTRUCT

Some authors have challenged the unifactorial position on intelligence. Some of these multifactorial models were posited by theorists and still await empirical validation (e.g., Gardner's [1993] multiple intelligences), whereas others have garnered some empirical or statistical support (e.g., Das et al.'s [1994] planning, attentional, simultaneous, and successive model [PASS] of cognitive processes). Recent theories of multiple intelligences have ranged from two to eight types of intelligence (see Cattell, 1963; Das et al., 1994; Gardner, 1983; Greenspan, 1981; Sternberg, 1988). A brief review of some of the main theories of multiple intelligences follows.

Cattell (1963) and Horn and Cattell (1966) identified two main factors explaining intellectual abilities that they labeled fluid intelligence (*gf*) and crystallized intelligence (*gc*). In Cattell's model of intelligence, *crystallized intelligence* was defined as more global abilities, such as information and knowledge, that are acquired by the individual through life experiences and education. *Fluid intelligence* was mental power that is essentially innate. Reasoning and memory abilities are examples of *gf*. Cattell defined *gc* as a stable trait, whereas *gf* may in fact decrease with age.

Gardner (1983, 1993) has posited a theoretical model of multiple intelligences. Initially his model consisted of seven different intelligences, each tapping distinctive problem-solving and information-processing capacities with its own distinctive developmental trajectory and dependent on the context. The original seven intelligences in Gardner's model were linguistic, logical-mathematical, spatial, musical, bodily kinesthetic, interpersonal, and intrapersonal. This model continues to evolve and, after further reflection, Gardner (1998) added an eighth independent ability, naturalist intelligence, to his model of multiple intelligences; *naturalist intelligence* is defined as the ability to discriminate among living organisms and other aspects of the environment. Linguistic (i.e., ability to use language), logical-mathematical, and spatial intelligences are the only types of intelligence in Gardner's model that are measured by traditional IQ tests (Davidson & Downing, 2000). Gardner (see Chen & Gardner, 1997) has advocated using nonstandardized methods of assessment of multiple intelligences. Gardner views testing of multiple intelligences as an ongoing process that employs personalized activities in a variety of contexts while using multimedia presentations. His assessment of multiple intelligences cannot be carried out in a single one-session assessment (Gardner, 1993). The most damaging criticism leveled at Gardner's multiple intelligences model continues to be its lack of empirical basis and psychometric validation (Hernstein & Murray, 1994).

Das et al. (1994) proposed conceptualizing intelligence as a four-factor model of cognitive processes. This model comprises planning, attention, and simultaneous and successive processing. Referred to as the PASS model, it originated from the early works of Russian neuropsychologist A. R. Luria. Das et al. defined the *planning process* as self-regulation, ability to analyze and evaluate situations, and ability to use knowledge to solve problems. *Attentional process* is the regulation of one's cognitive activity and focus on specific stimuli while inhibiting responses to other less relevant stimuli. *Simultaneous processing* involves the understanding of groupings of stimuli or identifying the commonalities of a grouping of stimuli. Successive processing involves grouping a number of stimuli into a linear series that makes sense. Unlike simultaneous processing, successive processing stimuli do not necessitate understanding of the gestalt, rather the relationship of the successive processing requires comprehension of the serial order of the stimuli.

Sternberg (1988) proposed a three-factor model of intelligence that he called the triarchic theory of human intelligence. He labeled the first attribute of the triarchic theory *analytical abilities,* which represent the individual's ability to analyze and be critical of one's ideas and those of others. The second component of this triarchical model is *creativity,* the person's ability to generate novel ideas that have a significant contribution. The third component of Sternberg's model is *practical intelligence,* the individual's ability to convert ideas into practical applications and convince others of their usefulness.

Greenspan's model of multiple intelligences has evolved over the years. Some elements of his conceptualization of intelligence have some overlap with Sternberg's triarchic model. Greenspan (1981) initially proposed a model of multiple intelligences that he labeled *personal competence.* Personal competence actually encompassed intellectual abilities (social intelligence and conceptual intelligence) as well as more practical independent living skills. Greenspan and Granfield (1992) presented a comprehensive model of personal or general competence that was explained by two subfactors: *instrumental competence* (e.g., motor functioning, processing speed, conceptual intelligence) and *social competence* (e.g., practical intelligence, social intelligence, temperament). The tripartite model proposed by Greenspan and his colleagues (Greenspan, 1997, in press; Greenspan & Love, 1997; Greenspan, Switzky, & Granfield, 1996) defined *intelligence* as being composed of conceptual intelligence, practical intelligence, and social intelligence. Conceptual intelligence is essentially equivalent to *g.* However, Greenspan (1996, 1997) vehemently opposed the position of using only *g* or a unitary IQ score as representing an individual's intellectual abilities. He defined *practical intelligence* as the performance of everyday skills that are typically measured by adaptive behavior scales and *social intelligence* as an individual's social and interpersonal abilities (e.g., moral judgment, empathy, social skills). *Gullibility* (likelihood of being tricked or manipulated) and *credulity* (readily believing exaggerated or clearly inaccurate claims) have recently been added as critical elements of social intelligence (Greenspan et al., 2001).

©American Association on Mental Retardation

CONCLUSIONS ABOUT THE CONSTRUCT OF INTELLIGENCE

Many of the aforementioned theories of multiple intelligences have not been validated via standardized and quantifiable measures. Gardner's multiple intelligences, with the exception of some useful application in educational settings, continue to remain theoretical. Sternberg failed in his attempts to develop a reliable instrument of measuring his triarchical model of intelligence. The Greenspan and Sternberg models face the common challenge of operationalizing tasks to quantify the constructs of their tripartite models (e.g., social intelligence). Although Greenspan (1997) was optimistic about the possibility of developing a good measure of social intelligence, it continues to prove difficult for psychometricians to conceptualize a reliable and valid assessment instrument (Kihlstrom & Cantor, 2000). Some have attempted to use subtests (e.g., Comprehension and Picture Arrangement) from the Wechsler Intelligence Scale for Children (WISC) as a measure of social intelligence but have failed (see Beebe, Pfiffner, & McBurnett, 2000; Lipsitz, Dworkin, & Erlenmeyer-Kimling, 1993).

Researchers, such as Naglieri and Das (1997), have successfully developed a standardized measure that captures their multiple cognitive processes model. We note, however, that even though the Cognitive Assessment Instrument (Naglieri & Das, 1997) provides individual IQ scores for Planning, Attention, Simultaneous, and Successive, the instrument also yields a Full-Scale IQ that represents the measure of overall cognitive functioning. Similarly, the Wide Range Intelligence Test (Glutting, Adams, & Shelsow, 2000), which evaluates fluid intelligence and crystallized intelligence IQ scores, also provides a Full-Scale IQ that represents the individual's general intellectual functioning.

It is hoped that the science of psychometrics will provide reliable measures of the constructs of multiple intelligences. However, until such a time, these theories of multiple intelligences will continue to remain difficult to evaluate and we will have to rely on the current consensus that intelligence is best conceptualized and captured by a general factor of intelligence.

Currently the empirical data seem to overwhelmingly weigh in favor of conceptualizing intellectual functioning as being explainable by a general factor of intelligence (Carroll, 1997b). This is not to say that intelligence is only one unitary ability; however, a majority of the variance of different intellectual abilities can be explained by a common factor of general intelligence. The meaning of intelligence adopted in this manual was presented as a consensus definition among many researchers in the field of intelligence (see Gottfredson, 1997). *Intelligence* has been defined as a general mental capability that includes the ability to reason, solve problems, think abstractly, plan, and learn from experience, and it reflects a broader capability for comprehending one's surroundings (Gottfredson, 1997; Grossman, 1983).

The determination of subaverage intellectual functioning requires the use of global measures that include different types of items and different factors of intelligence (Reschly, 1987). Hernstein and Murray (1994), in their review of intelligence research, commented that research seemed to support the belief that the existing standardized tests of intelligence adequately measure the general construct of intelligence. However, as others have shown (e.g., Flynn, 1987), it is critically important to use standardized tests with the most updated norms. The instruments most commonly used for the assessment of intellectual functioning are briefly reviewed later in this chapter.

SPECIAL ISSUES RELATED TO THE ASSESSMENT OF INTELLECTUAL FUNCTIONING

CAN WE MEASURE THE INTELLIGENCE OF PEOPLE WITH EXTREME COGNITIVE CHALLENGES?

Many instruments attempt to assess intellectual functioning, and several of the more common ones are described in the following section. Before any such analysis, however, one must address the basic issue of whether any available intelligence test is really appropriate for use with a person who may have mental retardation.

It is generally recognized that a psychometric instrument performs best when used with people who score within two to three standard deviations of the mean. However, the diagnosis of mental retardation, by definition, involves the assessment and evaluation of more extreme performance. Although the manuals for both the WISC–III (Wechsler, 1991) and Wechsler Adult Intelligence Scale (WAIS–III) (Wechsler, 1997) indicate that they can be used to diagnose mental retardation, Kaufman (1994) noted that David Wechsler is reported to have said that he never intended the Wechsler scales to be used with individuals who score far from average (i.e., below or above 2 SDs). In the manual for the Binet scales (Thorndike, Hagen, & Sattler, 1986), there is a similar caution about use of the scale to assess "extreme" populations, noting that extrapolation is needed to create norm group data for people who achieve very high or very low scores. Despite these cautions, Sattler (1988) noted the usefulness of both the Wechsler scales and the Stanford-Binet–IV in making the diagnosis of mental retardation. He did, however, mention that neither instrument was designed for use with people whose test performance yields extremely low or high scores. Although standard practice certainly involves the use of these scales to help in the diagnosis of mental retardation, we must recognize that extreme scores are more subject to measurement error and are perhaps less trustworthy than are scores closer to the mean of the test.

This reliance on the interpretation of extreme scores might be of greater con-

©American Association on Mental Retardation

cern if mental retardation were diagnosed solely on the basis of IQ score. Most mental retardation definitions (including those put forth by AAMR since 1959) require the conjoint assessment of adaptive behavior, and an individual's performance must reflect deficiencies in both areas in order to warrant a diagnosis of mental retardation. By having dual criteria for diagnosing an individual as having mental retardation, there are additional safeguards against false identification. There are those who would argue that the considerable correlation between IQ scores and adaptive behavior among people who have mental retardation, in effect, creates a redundant process to ensure better diagnosis (Spreat, Roszkowski, & Isett, 1983). No such safeguards exist, however, for a false negative, a serious problem that demands the field's attention. *The problems faced by people who have mental retardation but do not receive the diagnosis can be severe. These individuals are vulnerable to the denial of essential supports and exclusion from eligibility for important protections.*

DETERMINING A CUTOFF SCORE

The assessment of intellectual functioning through the primary reliance on intelligence tests is fraught with the potential for misuse if consideration is not given to possible errors in measurement. An obtained IQ standard score must always be considered in terms of the accuracy of its measurement. Because all measurement, and particularly psychological measurement, has some potential for error, obtained scores may actually represent a range of several points. This variation around a hypothetical "true score" may be hypothesized to be due to variations in test performance, examiner's behavior, or other undetermined factors. Variance in scores may or may not represent changes in the individual's actual or true level of functioning. Errors of measurement as well as true changes in performance outcome must be considered in the interpretations of test results. This process is facilitated by considering the concept of standard error of measurement (*SEM*), which has been estimated to be three to five points for well-standardized measures of general intellectual functioning. This means that if an individual is retested with the same instrument, the second obtained score would be within one *SEM* (i.e., ± 3 to 4 IQ points) of the first estimates about two thirds of the time. Thus an IQ standard score is best seen as bounded by a range that would be approximately three to four points above and below the obtained score. This range can be considered as a "zone of uncertainty" (Reschly, 1987). Therefore, an IQ of 70 is most accurately understood not as a precise score, but as a range of confidence with parameters of at least one *SEM* (i.e., scores of about 66 to 74; 66% probability), or parameters of two *SEMs* (i.e., scores of 62 to 78; 95% probability) (Grossman, 1983). This is a critical consideration that must be part of any decision concerning a diagnosis of mental retardation. Both of the primary American mental retardation diagnosis schemes make reference to significantly subaverage intellectual functioning as a defining characteristic of mental retardation. The *Diagnostic and Statistical Manual of Mental Disorders (DSM–IV)* (American Psychiatric Association, 1994) defined *significantly subaverage* as an IQ score of about 70 or below and added a statement concerning measurement error and an example of a Wechsler IQ of 70 considered to represent a range of 65 to 75. The American Association on Mental Retardation (Luckasson et al., 1992) defined it as approximately 70 to 75, taking into account measurement error.

In the 2002 AAMR system, the "intellectual functioning" criterion for diagnosis of mental retardation is approximately two standard deviations below the mean, considering the *SEM* for the specific assessment instruments used and the instruments' strengths and limitations.

It is clear that neither of these organizations intends for a fixed cutoff point for making the diagnosis of mental retardation. Both specify consideration of adaptive behavior skills and the use of clinical judgment. Although a fixed cutoff for diagnosing an individual as having mental retardation was not intended, and cannot be justified psychometrically, use of a fixed cutoff score has become operational in some states (Greenspan, 1999b). The Connecticut Department of Mental Retardation, as one example, operationalizes mental retardation (and access to mental retardation services) *based entirely* on an IQ score below two standard deviations.

This is not as trivial an issue as it might appear on the surface. We note that a fixed IQ score of 70 on a Wechsler scale will identify 2.28% of the population as potentially having mental retardation, whereas a Stanford-Binet–IV score of 70 will identify slightly more than 3% of the population as potentially having mental retardation. In the United States, with a population of approximately 280 million, the difference between these two measures would be slightly more than 2 million individuals. Not only are these two most commonly used tests operating on a slightly different metric, it is common clinical lore that the Stanford-Binet is a more challenging test. The choice of intelligence test will be driven by clinical judgment of which instrument is most appropriate. Clinical judgment should be based on the personal characteristics of the individual to be evaluated. The IQ scores obtained from different intelligence tests themselves are not necessarily equivalent. Given that the diagnostic process involves drawing a line of inclusion/exclusion, there can be little rationale for anything other than a relativistic standard for significantly subaverage intellectual functioning.

The 2002 AAMR System indicates that the *SEM* is considered in determining the existence of significant subaverage intellectual functioning (see above boxed

©American Association on Mental Retardation

statement). In effect, this expands the operational definition of mental retardation to 75, and that score of 75 may still contain measurement error. Any trained examiner is aware that all tests contain measurement error; many present scores as confidence bands rather than finite scores. Incorporating measurement error in the definition of mental retardation serves to remind test administrators (who should understand the concept) and bureaucrats (who might not be familiar with the concept) that an achieved Wechsler IQ score of 65 means that one can be about 95% confident that the true score is somewhere between 59 and 71.

The issue at hand is that any score contains measurement error, which can obscure the individual's actual ability levels. There are mathematical ways with which to estimate an individual's true score, or that score that would reflect an individual's average performance on an infinite number of test administrations. Stanley (1971) reported that an individual's true score on a test can be estimated with the following formula:

True score = mean + reliability X (mean – individual's obtained score)

It is tempting to suggest that examiners use a true score correction when classifying mental retardation; however, there is a significant limitation to Stanley's formula. It will always yield a score that regresses to the mean. Because of this, it will always yield higher estimates of intellectual functioning for people who have mental retardation, and this is not suitable for the diagnosis of mental retardation.

ARE DIFFERENT INTELLIGENCE TESTS EQUIVALENT?

Another important source of possible variation lies in test content differences across different scales and between different age levels on the same scale. For example, scores determined on verbal tests, such as from the Wechsler Verbal scale, frequently differ from those obtained on nonverbal tests (e.g., the Wechsler Performance scale). Variations also may be attributed to differences in the standardization samples, to changes between different editions of the same scale, to shifts to an alternative scale as an individual's chronological age increases, and to variances in the person's abilities or performance. Finally, variances in scores between successive revisions of intelligence measures have also been noted (Evans, 1991).

REVIEW OF COMMONLY AVAILABLE INTELLIGENCE SCALES

The Wechsler scales and the Stanford-Binet are perhaps the two instruments most frequently used to assess intelligence, and they will be briefly discussed below. Also discussed are the Cognitive Assessment Scale and the Kaufman Assessment Battery for Children as well as various adaptations for people with limited verbal ability or profound cognitive impairments. Standard errors of measurement for these scales are found in Appendix 4.1.

WECHSLER INTELLIGENCE SCALE FOR CHILDREN–III

The Wechsler Intelligence Scale for Children–III is the most recent revision of the children's intelligence test that was developed initially by David Wechsler in 1949 (Wechsler, 1991). It is an individually administered instrument, designed for assessing intelligence of individuals whose chronological ages range from 6 years to 16 years, 11 months. The instrument consists of 12 individual subtests and yields three composite scores: Verbal IQ, Performance IQ, and Full-Scale IQ. It also offers four factor-based index scores.

Wechsler (1944) conceptualized intelligence as an aggregate and global entity, and he designed his scale to assess the ability of an individual to act purposefully, think rationally, and deal effectively with his or her environment (p. 3). Consistent with this relatively broad conceptualization of intelligence, the 12 subtests each measure somewhat different facets of intelligence. Although performance on no one subtest reflects all intelligent behavior, it is thought that intelligence is reflected in overall performance.

There are six subtests that purport to measure verbal intelligence (and yield the Verbal IQ score): Information, Similarities, Arithmetic, Vocabulary, Comprehension, and Digit Span. Six subtests measure perceptual-motor abilities and yield the Performance IQ score: Picture Completion, Coding, Picture Arrangement, Block Design, Object Assembly, and Mazes. A 13th subtest, Symbol Search, may be substituted for Coding.

The WISC–III manual (Wechsler, 1991) proposed that this instrument is appropriate for a number of purposes, including educational planning and placement, diagnosis of exceptionality, clinical and neurological assessment, and research.

The WISC–IIII was normed on a standardization sample of 2,200 children from the United States. There were 200 children (100 males, 100 females) from each of 11 age groups, ranging from 6 to 16 years. Race or ethnicity was balanced to reflect racial or ethnic group proportions from the 1980 Census survey. In the WISC–III manual, Wechsler (1991) reported reliability indices for each subtest, the three IQ scores, and the four factor scores. Subtest reliabilities tend to be higher for the verbal subtests (*M* reliability = .82) than for the performance subtests (*M* reliability = .77). Although none of these indices would be sufficient for individual decision making (Anastasi, 1988), all of the reported reliability indices for three IQ scores exceed .90 (Verbal IQ = .95, Performance IQ = .91, Full-Scale IQ = .96). Clearly the reliability of the derived IQ scores is strong enough to permit use in decision making about individuals.

SEM is another index of reliability; in a sense, it is an inverse measure of relia-

©American Association on Mental Retardation

bility. The SEM quantifies the amount of error in a given test score. For interpretative purposes, one can be 95% confident that an individual's true score falls within ± 1.96 SEMs. The SEM for the Full-Scale IQ score is 3.2. This means that we can be 95% confident that an individual whose tested IQ is 65 has a true IQ score somewhere between roughly 59 and 71.

The manual offers evidence of validity for the proposed purposes of the test, including correlations with grades, academic achievement tests, and neurological tests. The correlation of Full-Scale IQ with various measures of academic achievement range from .57 to .74. The correlation between Full-Scale IQ and actual grades is a more modest .47. The manual does report a validation study about the use of the WISC–III in making diagnoses of mental retardation. The study suggests that individuals who were diagnosed as having mental retardation on the basis of WISC–Revised scores and adaptive behavior scores would still be diagnosed as having mental retardation on the basis of WISC–IIII scores. The WISC–III scores average about nine points lower than the WISC–Revised scores. We note that a validity study of this nature is complicated by the fact that measured intelligence is a definitional component of mental retardation.

WECHSLER ADULT INTELLIGENCE SCALE–III

Like the WISC–III, the WAIS–III derives from the work of David Wechsler. It is based on the same concept of global intelligence that pertains to the WISC–III; that is, intelligence is viewed as a multifaceted and multidetermined construct that enables an individual to comprehend and deal effectively with the world. This particular version of the adult Wechsler scale derives from the Wechsler Adult Intelligence Scale–Revised. The Matrix Reasoning subtest was added to improve the ability of the scale to test older adults (up to age 89). Matrix Reasoning replaced Object Assembly as a standard subtest.

The WAIS–III is an individually administered test that was designed to assess intelligence of individuals ranging in age from 16 years to 89 years. Like the WISC–III, the mean IQ score is 100, and the standard deviation is 15. The *SEM* was roughly 2.3 points for the Full-Scale IQ, although this varies as a function of the age group, ranging from 1.98 to 2.58. The six verbal subtests and five perceptual-motor subtests of the WAIS–III yield Verbal IQ scores, Performance IQ scores, and Full-Scale IQ scores.

The WAIS–III was standardized on 2,450 adults from the United States. Thirteen separate standardization groups were created by age classification. Within each group, the number of males and females was roughly equal (except for the 65 to 89 age group, which contained more females), and there was Census-based stratification for race or ethnicity (White, African American, Hispanic), education, and geographic region based on Census reports.

Psychometric properties of the WAIS–III compare favorably with those of the WISC–III. Average split-half reliability coefficient of the Full-Scale IQ was calculated to be .98. Test-retest reliability was .95.

The WAIS–III manual indicates that the scale may be used in diagnosing mental retardation, neuropsychological impairments, and giftedness. As evidence of the scale's usefulness in diagnosing mental retardation, the manual reports that people with mental retardation achieve low scores with minimal variability.

STANFORD-BINET–IV

Some form of the Stanford-Binet intelligence scale has been available since the early 1900s. The Stanford-Binet–IV is the fourth revision of this scale. Like earlier versions of the test, this revision is based on the notion that intelligence is a general factor, comprising a number of subfactors. In the Stanford-Binet–IV, intelligence is composed of verbal reasoning ability, quantitative reasoning ability, abstract/visual reasoning ability, and short-term memory. These are assessed via 15 subtests, 9 of which were derived from the older Stanford-Binet–L-M, and 6 of which were new with this revision.

The Stanford-Binet–IV was designed for use with individuals from the age of 2 years to adulthood. This flexibility is attributable to the use of Standard Age Scores, or derived scores from age-defined subgroups of the norming sample. Although this is a reasonable and appropriate approach, caution must be exercised for use with extreme populations. In the manual, Thorndike et al. (1986) noted that even with samples as large as 500, there were almost no cases that fell beyond three standard deviations from the mean. The implications for assessing people with mental retardation should be fairly clear: These instruments have limited ability to measure IQs below 40.

The test yields a composite IQ score with a mean of 100 and a standard deviation of 16. The *SEM* is reported to range from 1.60 for adults to 3.58 for young children. Consistent with most individualized intelligence tests, the Stanford-Binet–IV demonstrates strong Kuder-Richardson (KR) KR-20 reliabilities, ranging from .95 to .99. In the manual, Thorndike et al. (1986) noted that these values may be somewhat inflated and should be considered an upper estimate of reliability. Test-retest reliability is only slightly less strong but is not reported for the composite score.

For nonexceptional children, the Stanford-Binet–IV correlates .83 with the WISC–Revised. It correlates .80 with the Wechsler Preschool and Primary Scale of Intelligence (WPPSI) and about .91 with the WAIS–Revised and .89 with the Kaufman Assessment Battery for Children.

©American Association on Mental Retardation

COGNITIVE ASSESSMENT SYSTEM

The Cognitive Assessment System (Naglieri & Das, 1997) is an individually administered intelligence test that was designed for use with children from the ages of 5 to 17 years. In contrast with Wechsler and Stanford-Binet scales, the Cognitive Assessment System is based on the assumption that intelligence is multidimensional rather than unidimensional. Its four scales (Planning, Attention, Simultaneous, and Successive) each yield an IQ score, and there is also a Full-Scale IQ score. All four Cognitive Assessment Instrument scale IQ scores have a mean of 100 and a standard deviation of 15. The system derives from the neuropsychological work of Luria and the PASS cognitive processing theory (Das et al., 1994; Naglieri & Das, 1997). The reliability of the standard battery (12 subtests) of the Cognitive Assessment Instrument Full-Scale score has been reported to range from .95 to .97, with a mean reliability of .96. The four Cognitive Assessment Instrument scales have the following average reliability coefficients: .88 (Planning), .88 (Attention), .93 (Simultaneous), and .93 (Successive). These reliability indices are certainly acceptable and comparable to the Wechsler and Stanford-Binet scales. Naglieri and Das (1997) provided factorial validity for their four-factor model of cognitive processes, but not at all ages. The authors also reported strong correlations (.60 to .70), with the Full-Scale IQ on the WISC–III and WPPSI–Revised.

The Cognitive Assessment Instrument was normed on 2,200 American children who were selected to match the general population of the United States on a number of basic characteristics, including gender, race, region, educational classification, and parental education. Recent research (Naglieri & Rojahn, 2001) indicates that this instrument identifies fewer children as having mental retardation (operationalizes in terms of an IQ score of 70 or below) than does the WISC–III. The authors also reported that the instrument identified disproportionately fewer Black children than White children in comparison with the WISC–III.

KAUFMAN ASSESSMENT BATTERY FOR CHILDREN

The Kaufman Assessment Battery for Children (or K–ABC) was developed by Kaufman and Kaufman (1983) to assess the intelligence and achievement of children aged 2.5 through 12.5 years. It yields four global scale scores, with the Mental Processing Scale being essentially equivalent to an IQ score. This Mental Processing Scale was largely derived from Luria's neuropsychological theories, combined with the work of cerebral specialization researchers. It emphasizes sequential and simultaneous problem solving, with an emphasis on the process that is used to obtain answers rather than the answers themselves.

The Mental Processing Scale, like the three other global scales, yields a metric that has a mean score of 100 and a standard deviation of 15. It has yielded split-half reliability coefficients of .90 for preschool children and .94 for school-age children. Concurrent validity has been established via correlation with the WISC–Revised, Stanford-Binet, and other similar scales. The K–ABC was standardized on 2,000 children, with 100 children being drawn to represent each half year from 2.5 years through 12.5 years. The standardization sample was stratified on a variety of demographic variables to ensure representativeness. We note that the standardization sample, by design, included a proportional representation of exceptional children. An additional 615 children were tested in an effort to develop supplementary sociocultural norms. The intent of this effort was to promote less biased assessment for minority children.

TESTS FOR SPECIAL CIRCUMSTANCES

Slosson Intelligence Test

Slosson (1983) designed this instrument to provide an estimate of intelligence that requires little specialized training for the examiner and little time to administer. This short-form test was derived from the 1960 revision of the Stanford-Binet, and concurrent validity estimates with that instrument typically exceed .90. Although somewhat dated, the Slosson Intelligence Test still holds an attraction for practitioners who deal with individuals who have significant cognitive challenges.

The Slosson Intelligence Test employs the concept of a ratio IQ. The derived mental age is compared with an individual's chronological age to estimate IQ. Although this concept of a ratio IQ has generally been abandoned by psychologists, the scores from the Slosson Intelligence Test still tend to correlate well with other types of IQ scores. The Slosson yields an IQ score with a mean of 100 and a standard deviation of 16. The *SEM* varies from 3.02 to 5.91, depending on the age and score of the person tested. For people with IQ scores below 84, four should be a good estimate of the *SEM*. Reliability estimates typically exceed .90. The Slosson Intelligence Test was renormed in 1981, using 1,109 individuals ranging in age from 2 years, 3 months, to 18 years. The sample was collected in New England states.

Bayley Scales of Infant Development

The Bayley Scales of Infant Development–II (Bayley, 1993) was designed to provide measurement of developmental progress of infants. It is not an intelligence test per se, but many diagnosticians, when faced with the task of assessing an individual who appears to have profound impairments of cognition, use the Bayley because of the applicability of the items. The earlier version of the Bayley reported moderate correlations between Bayley scores and scores from the Stanford-Binet–L-M. For the current version, Bayley (1993) reported a .73 correlation between the Bayley Mental Development Index and the Full-Scale IQ score from the WPPSI–R.

The Bayley yields a Mental Development Index that appears much like a deviation IQ score. It has a mean of 100 and a standard deviation of 15. Scores can

©American Association on Mental Retardation

range from 50 to 150 (a range of more than 6 *SDs*). This Mental Development Index was designed to assess sensory-perceptual memory, habituation, problem solving, number concepts, generalization, classification, vocalization, language, and social skills. Reliability coefficients are generally satisfactory for research purposes, but slightly weak for individual diagnostic purposes (Nunnally, 1967).

The Bayley was standardized on 1,700 children, with 100 children selected to represent each of 17 age groups. There were also children in 14 age groups, ranging from 2 months to 30 months. The sample was designed to be representative of the United States population at that time, but few details of the representativeness were presented in the manual.

Comprehensive Test of Nonverbal Intelligence

This instrument, developed by Hamill, Pearson, and Wiederholt (1997), is an individually administered intelligence test that was designed for use with people aged 6 years to 90 years. It was specifically designed to be used to assess intellectual ability of individuals for whom most other intelligence tests are inappropriate or possibly biased. It yields both a composite score and separate subtest scores. The composite score has a mean of 100 and a standard deviation of 15. Test-retest reliability for the total score was in the low .90s, and the correlation with the WISC–III Performance IQ was .90.

The norming sample was 2,901 individuals between the ages of 6 and 89 years. Characteristics of the norm group were stratified to approximate the descriptors presented in the 1990 Statistical Abstract of the United States. Approximately 91% of the norming sample had no known disability.

Leiter International Performance Scale–Revised (Leiter–R)

The Leiter (Roid & Miller, 1997) is a test of intellectual functioning that does not require speech on the part of the examiner or examinee. This instrument is reported to measure fluid intelligence, which is thought to be uninfluenced by education, social background, or family experience. The more recent revised version has added Attention and Memory domains for use in distinguishing individuals who have neuropsychological impairments. The Leiter is designed to be used with individuals aged 2 to 21 years, and it is described as suitable for diagnosing mental retardation and giftedness.

The Leiter–R was standardized on 1,719 children and adolescents as well as on 692 children who represented nine different clinical groups. Overall, the primary standardization group was designed to comply with 1990 Census statistics. The test has yielded reliability (internal consistency) estimates ranging from .88 to .93. Concurrent validity has been established with the WISC–III (r = .85) and the original Leiter (r = .85). There are data suggesting that members of various minority groups score higher on the Leiter–R than on the WISC–III.

Universal Nonverbal Intelligence Test (UNIT)

The UNIT (Bracken & McCallum, 1998) is a relatively new instrument that was designed to measure general intelligence and cognitive ability in children and adolescents. It is specifically designed for use with individuals who may be disadvantaged by more traditional assessment devices that rely on the use of language. The structure and format of the test make it suitable for use with people who have speech, language, or hearing impairments, color-vision deficiencies, different cultural or language backgrounds, and those who cannot communicate verbally. The test is reported to be useful in the diagnosis of both exceptionalities and psychiatric disorders.

The Universal Nonverbal Intelligence Test was standardized using a stratified random sample that matches the U.S. population as reported in 1995 U.S. Census data. Normative data were collected on 2,100 individuals who ranged in age from 5 years through 17 years, 11 months. In selecting the standardization sample, the authors considered the following variables: age, race, sex, Hispanic origin, geographic region, community setting, classroom placement, special-education services, and parental education attainment. Reliability has been reported to range from .93 to .98 for the Full-Scale score, while concurrent validity of the instrument has been established via correlation with the several other intelligence tests.

SUMMARY

Intelligence is a general mental capability that involves several different abilities. However, until more robust instruments based upon one of the many promising multifactorial theories of intellectual abilities are developed and demonstrated to be psychometrically sound, we will continue to rely on a global (general factor) IQ as a measure of intellectual functioning. *Subaverage intellectual functioning,* defined as two or more standard deviations below the mean, is a necessary but insufficient criterion to establish a diagnosis of mental retardation. The assessment of intellectual functioning must rely on sound procedures and may, at times, require information from multiple sources. Testing should be conducted on an individual basis and be carried out in strict guidance of accepted professional practice.

©American Association on Mental Retardation

APPENDIX 4.1
Standard Errors of Measurement (*SEM*) for Intelligence Scales

Tests are listed in alphabetical order.

Test: **Bayley Scales of Infant Development–II**
Ages: **1 month through 42 months**

SEM

Scale	Age in Months																	Avg. *SEM*
	1	2	3	4	5	6	8	10	12	15	18	21	24	27	30	36	42	
Mental	5.62	5.77	6.22	5.13	4.95	4.23	4.69	7.04	5.24	6.19	4.27	4.64	4.16	3.90	5.53	5.06	4.84	5.21
Motor	5.60	6.04	6.06	4.47	5.39	6.02	5.83	5.90	5.94	5.62	5.69	6.46	6.16	5.50	6.86	6.47	7.56	6.01

Note. Data from *Bayley Scales of Infant Development* (2nd ed.), by N. Bayley, 1993, New York: Psychological Corp.

Test: **Cognitive Assessment System**
Ages: **5 years through 17 years, 11 months**

SEM

Full-Scale IQ	Age in Years													Avg. *SEM*
	5	6	7	8	9	10	11	12	13	14	15	16	17	
Basic	5.2	5.6	5.2	5.1	5.6	5.5	6.2	5.5	5.5	5.4	5.6	5.3	5.3	5.4
Standard	2.7	3.1	3.2	3.2	3.2	3.2	3.1	3.0	3.2	3.1	3.1	2.8	3.0	3.1

Note. Data from *Cognitive Assessment System: Interpretive Handbook,* by J. A. Naglieri & J. P. Das, 1997, Itasca, IL: Riverside.

Basic = Basic Battery; Standard = Standard Battery.

(appendix continues)

APPENDIX 4.1 *(continued)*

Test: **Comprehensive Test of Nonverbal Intelligence**
Ages: **6 years through 89 years, 11 months**

SEM

Factor	6	7	8	9	10	11	12	13	14	15	16	17	18	19–29	30–39	40–49	50–59	60–69	70–99	Avg. *SEM*
PNIQ	4.2	4.2	4.2	4.0	4.0	3.7	4.0	3.7	4.0	3.7	3.7	3.7	3.4	4.5	4.0	4.2	4.5	3.4	3.7	4.0
GNIQ	4.0	3.7	3.7	3.4	3.4	3.4	3.0	3.0	3.0	3.0	3.0	3.0	3.4	3.4	3.4	3.4	3.7	3.0	3.0	3.3
NIQ	3.4	3.0	3.0	3.0	2.6	2.6	2.6	2.6	2.6	2.6	2.6	2.6	2.6	3.0	3.0	3.0	3.0	2.6	2.6	2.8

Note. Data from *Comprehensive Test of Nonverbal Intelligence,* by D. Hamill, N. Pearson, & J. Wiederholt, 1997, Austin, TX: Pro-Ed.

PNIQ = Pictorial Nonverbal; GNIQ = Geometric Nonverbal; NIQ = Nonverbal–Full-Scale Score.

Test: **Kaufman Assessment Battery for Children**
Ages: **2 years, 6 months through 12 years, 5 months**

SEM

Factor	2-6 to 2-11	3-0 to 3-11	4-0 to 4-11	5-0 to 5-11	6-0 to 6-11	7-0 to 7-11	8-0 to 8-11	9-0 to 9-11	10-0 to 10-11	11-0 to 11-11	12-0 to 12-5	Avg. *SEM*
Seq. Proc.	5.0	5.0	4.5	4.2	4.5	5.2	4.7	5.2	5.0	5.6	5.4	5.0
Simul. Proc.	6.0	6.0	5.0	4.0	4.0	4.5	4.0	3.7	3.7	4.0	4.0	4.5
Comp.	4.7	5.0	4.0	3.4	3.4	4.0	3.4	3.4	3.4	3.7	3.7	3.8

Note. Data from *Kaufman Assessment Battery for Children,* by A. Kaufman & N. Kaufman, 1983, Circle Pines, MN: American Guidance Service.

Seq. Proc. = Sequential Processing; Simul. Proc. = Simultaneous Processing; Comp. = Mental Processing Composite–Full-Scale Score.

(appendix continues)

©American Association on Mental Retardation

APPENDIX 4.1 *(continued)*

Test: **Leiter International Performance Scale–Revised**

Ages: **2 years through 20 years, 11 months**

SEM

VR Battery	Age in Years			
	2–5	6–10	11–20	Average *SEM*
Full IQ	4.24	4.50	3.97	4.24
IQ Screener	5.20	4.74	4.97	4.97

Note. Data from *Leiter International Performance Scale–Revised,* by G. H. Reid & L. J. Miller, 1997, Wood Dale, IL: Stoelting.

VR = Visualization and Reasoning.

Test: **Stanford-Binet–IV**

Ages: **2 years through 23 years**

SEM

	Age in Years																	
	2	3	4	5	6	7	8	9	10	11	12	13	4	15	16	17	18–23	Avg. *SEM*
Composite SAS	3.58	3.20	2.77	2.77	3.20	2.77	2.77	2.77	2.26	2.26	2.26	1.60	2.26	2.26	2.26	1.60	1.60	2.48

Note. Data from *Technical Manual for Stanford-Binet Intelligence Scale* (4th ed.), by R. Thorndike, E. Hagen, & J. Sattler, 1986, Chicago: Riverside.

SAS = Standard Age Scores.

(appendix continues)

©American Association on Mental Retardation

Test: **Universal Nonverbal Intelligence Test**
Ages: **5 years through 17 years**

SEM

Full-Scale IQ	Age in Years												Avg. *SEM*
	5	6	7	8	9	10	11	12	13	14	15	17	
Abbrev.	5.02	5.25	5.55	4.43	5.05	4.16	4.21	3.78	4.07	4.00	4.18	3.80	4.46
Standard	4.47	4.40	4.52	3.78	4.11	3.85	3.94	3.66	3.77	3.68	3.92	3.68	3.98
Extended	4.05	4.19	4.15	4.09	4.30	4.14	4.14	3.96	4.14	4.07	4.06	3.84	4.09

Note. Data from *Universal Nonverbal Intelligence Test,* by B. Bracken & R. McCallum, 1998, Itasca, IL: Riverside.

Abbrev. = Abbreviated Battery; Standard = Standard Battery; Extended = Extended Battery.

Test: **Wechsler Adult Intelligence Scale–III**
Ages: **16 years through 89 years**

SEM

IQ	Age in Years													Avg. *SEM*
	16–17	18–19	20–24	25–29	30–34	35–44	45–54	55–64	65–69	70–74	75–79	80–84	85–89	
Verbal	2.87	2.49	2.59	2.45	2.46	2.47	2.51	2.35	2.16	2.54	2.59	2.52	3.04	2.55
Performance	4.03	4.09	3.83	3.43	3.96	3.54	3.52	3.27	3.01	3.40	4.04	3.62	3.77	3.67
Full-Scale	2.58	2.38	2.37	2.18	2.32	2.23	2.23	2.07	1.90	2.19	2.47	2.31	2.56	2.30

Note. Data from *Wechsler Adult Intelligence Scale* (3rd ed.), by D. Wechsler, 1997, San Antonio, TX: Psychological Corp., Harcourt Brace.

(appendix continues)

©American Association on Mental Retardation

APPENDIX 4.1 *(continued)*

Test: **Wechsler Intelligence Scale for Children–III**
Ages: **6 years through 16 years, 11 months**

SEM

IQ	Age in Years											
	6	7	8	9	10	11	12	13	14	15	16	Avg. *SEM*
Verbal	3.97	4.24	3.00	3.97	3.35	3.35	3.35	3.67	3.35	3.00	3.35	3.53
Performance	4.50	4.74	4.74	4.50	4.50	4.74	4.50	4.74	4.97	3.67	4.24	4.54
Full-Scale	3.35	3.67	3.00	3.35	3.00	3.35	3.00	3.35	3.35	2.60	3.00	3.20

Note. Data from *Wechsler Intelligence Scale for Children* (3rd ed.), by D. Wechsler, 1991, San Antonio, TX: Psychological Corp., Harcourt Brace.

CHAPTER 5

ASSESSMENT OF ADAPTIVE BEHAVIOR

> *Adaptive behavior* is the collection of conceptual, social, and practical skills that have been learned by people in order to function in their everyday lives.

OVERVIEW

Adaptive behavior assessment can be useful for each of the three functions shown in Table 1.1: diagnosis, classification, and planning supports. It is important to recognize that different measures and methods of assessing adaptive behavior will have advantages and limitations, depending on the specific purposes of assessment. Assessment for diagnosis, for example, requires the use of instruments that (a) are psychometrically sound, (b) address the three areas of adaptive behavior in the definition, and (c) are normed on groups of people with and people without mental retardation. Different assessment instrument characteristics, such as fine breakdowns of skill levels or a focus on specific skill areas, may be important in determining the best methods for measuring adaptive behavior for purposes of classification or planning supports. In this chapter we focus primarily on the assessment of adaptive behavior for the purpose of diagnosing mental retardation.

According to the 2002 AAMR definition (see p. 1), a person with mental retardation has significant limitations both in intellectual functioning *and in adaptive behavior as expressed in conceptual, social, and practical adaptive skills.* The three broad domains of adaptive behavior in the definition represent a shift from the requirement in the 1992 (Luckasson et al.) definition that a person have limitations in at least 2 of the 10 specific skill areas listed in the 1992 definition. The three broader domains of conceptual, social, and practical skills in the new definition are more consistent with the structure of existing measures and with the body of research evidence on adaptive behavior.

The 2002 definition also emphasizes the *expression,* or performance, of relevant skills, rather than the acquisition of skills. Thus it is expected that reasons for limitations in adaptive skills may include (a) not knowing how to perform the skill (acquisition deficit), (b) not knowing when to use learned skills (performance deficit), or (c) other motivational factors that can affect the expression of skills (performance deficit). When an individual has limited intellectual capacity, both acquisition and performance deficits may be attributed to mental retardation. Consistent with this view, most adaptive behavior instruments measure the "skill level a person typically displays when responding to challenges in his or her environment" (Widaman & McGrew, 1996, p. 98).

ADAPTIVE BEHAVIOR AND A DIAGNOSIS OF MENTAL RETARDATION

ASSUMPTIONS ABOUT ADAPTIVE BEHAVIOR RELEVANT TO DIAGNOSIS

In this chapter we address the following assumptions about adaptive behavior that are relevant to a diagnosis of mental retardation:

- Adaptive behavior is a multidomain construct. The domains that have emerged from a long history of factor-analytic studies are consistent with a conceptual model that has three general areas of adaptive skills: conceptual, social, and practical.

- No existing measure of adaptive behavior completely measures all adaptive behavior domains. Adaptive behavior scales place different degrees of emphasis on different domains, evidenced by the number of specific behaviors selected to represent them (Thompson et al., 1999); these differences are partly responsible for variations in the specific dimensions that have emerged from factor-analytic studies.

- For a person with mental retardation, adaptive behavior limitations are generalized across domains of conceptual, social, and practical skills. Because subscale scores on adaptive behavior measures are moderately correlated, however, a generalized deficit is assumed even if the score on only one dimension meets the operational criteria of being two or more standard deviations below the mean. A score of two standard deviations below the mean on a total score from an instrument that measures conceptual, practical, and social skills will also meet the operational definition of a significant limitation in adaptive behavior.

- Some adaptive behaviors are particularly difficult to measure using a rating scale or are not contained on existing standardized instruments. Adaptive skills that may be influenced by levels of gullibility or vulnerability, for example, may be relevant to diagnosis but are not reflected in current adaptive behavior test

©American Association on Mental Retardation

scores. These should still be considered in the overall diagnostic decision process and evaluated by other means. It is assumed that current efforts to develop reliable measures of these skill areas will continue.

- Low intellectual abilities may be responsible for both problems in acquiring adaptive behavior skills (acquisition deficit) and/or with the appropriate use of skills that have been learned (performance deficit).

- Assessment that provides information about typical behavior for the individual requires information that goes beyond what can be observed in a formal testing situation. However, a formal testing situation could be useful to help distinguish acquisition deficits from performance deficits for some behaviors.

- Just as standardized measures of intelligence do not fully reflect what is considered to be intellectual capacity, it is unlikely that a single standardized measure of adaptive behavior can adequately represent an individual's ability to adapt to the everyday demands of living independently. Additional information may be useful in the diagnosis of individuals whose adaptive behavior standardized scores are close to cutoff points. This information should be gathered consistent with the assumptions to the definition (see chap. 1) and the principles of clinical judgment (see chap. 6).

- Problem behavior that is "maladaptive" is not a characteristic or dimension of adaptive behavior, as conceptualized in the 2002 definition of mental retardation, although it often influences the acquisition and performance of adaptive behavior. The presence of problem behavior is not considered to be a limitation in adaptive behavior, although it may be important in the interpretation of adaptive behavior scores (i.e., in clinical judgment) for diagnosis.

- Adaptive behavior must be examined in the context of the developmental periods of infancy and early childhood, childhood and early adolescence, late adolescence, and adulthood. A continuing theme is the importance of the developmental relevance of specific skills within these adaptive areas.

- Adaptive behavior scores must be examined in the context of the individual's own culture that may influence opportunities, motivation, and performance of adaptive skills.

- Limitations in adaptive behavior should be considered in light of the four other dimensions in the 2002 framework of individual functioning (see Figure 1.1): Intellectual Abilities; Participation, Interactions, and Social Roles; Health; and Context.

CONCEPTUAL, SOCIAL, AND PRACTICAL SKILL AREAS OF ADAPTIVE BEHAVIOR

The three domains of adaptive behavior in the 2002 definition are less differentiated than the 10 skill areas that were listed in the 1992 definition, but are more consistent with the conceptual models in the literature that describe major domains of personal competence (Greenspan, 1999a; Greenspan & Driscoll, 1997; Gresham & Elliott, 1987; Thompson et al., 1999). These models are supported by many years of empirical research on the construct of adaptive behavior. This does not mean that factor-analytic studies of adaptive behavior scales have always identified exactly three domains or that the names in the 2002 definition (i.e., *conceptual, social,* and *practical*) have always been assigned to the factors that were found. The number of domains, or factors, that have emerged from factor-analytic studies, in fact, has varied across studies. The variability has been attributed to differences in the array of specific skills assessed by the scales and to the factor-analytic procedures used (Thompson et al., 1999; Widaman & McGrew, 1996). The consistency that has been found for higher order dimensions across measures has, nevertheless, been impressive and supports the three dimensions that are in the current definition (Thompson et al., 1999; Widaman & McGrew, 1996). Table 5.1 illustrates this consistency and confirms that there are existing measures that address the three dimensions of adaptive behavior.

OPERATIONAL DEFINITION OF LIMITATIONS IN ADAPTIVE BEHAVIOR

> For the diagnosis of mental retardation, significant limitations in adaptive behavior should be established through the use of standardized measures normed on the general population, including people with disabilities and people without disabilities. On these standardized measures, significant limitations in adaptive behavior are operationally defined as performance that is at least two standard deviations below the mean of either (a) one of the following three types of adaptive behavior: conceptual, social, or practical, or (b) an overall score on a standardized measure of conceptual, social, and practical skills.

A person with mental retardation is assumed to have significant limitations in multiple dimensions of adaptive behavior. In fact, mental retardation is characterized by deficits in adaptive behavior that are generalized across the domains of conceptual, practical, and social skills. Why, then, does the 2002 operational definition of significant limitations in adaptive behavior require a score of at least two standard deviations below the mean on only one domain?

©American Association on Mental Retardation

TABLE 5.1

Correspondence Between Three Dimensions of Adaptive Behavior and Empirically Derived Factors on Existing Measures

Instrument	Conceptual Skills	Social Skills	Practical Skills
AAMR Adaptive Behavior Scale–School and Community (Lambert, Nihira, & Leland, 1993)	Community self-sufficiency	Personal-social responsibility	Personal self-sufficiency
Vineland Adaptive Behavior Scales (Sparrow, Balla, & Cicchetti, 1984)	Communication	Socialization	Daily living skills
Scales of Independent Behavior–Revised (Bruininks, Woodcock, Weatherman, & Hill, 1991)	Community living skills	Social interaction and Communication skills	Personal living skills
Comprehensive Test of Adaptive Behavior–Revised (Adams, 1999)	Language concepts and academic skills Independent living	Social skills	Self-help skills Home living

Note. All measures shown in this table are considered to have adequate psychometric properties and contain normative data on the general population. The purpose of this table is to illustrate that current adaptive behavior measures provide domain scores that represent the three dimensions of adaptive behavior skills in the 2002 AAMR definition. It is not intended to necessarily endorse these instruments or to exclude other measures that meet the guidelines for diagnosis.

It is important to note that the operational definition of a significant limitation in adaptive behavior requires performance that is at least two standard deviations below the mean on *at least one domain* or on the total score of an instrument that measures all three domains. There are two reasons for what may appear to be an overly inclusive criterion and one that might identify people who have deficits in a single, narrow area rather than the generalized adaptive skill deficit that is assumed to be present in a person with mental retardation. First, correlations among domains of adaptive behavior on standardized instruments tend to vary widely across instruments, with some instruments having low to moderate correlations and others having rather high correlations. Because correlations among domains vary widely across instruments, requiring more than one score to be two standard deviations below the mean will result in the selection of instruments having a large effect on whether a person meets the definitional criterion. By requiring a significant deficit in only one score, the effects of using different measures of adaptive behavior in a diagnosis will be minimized. Furthermore, a score of two standard deviations below the mean on one domain will have a sufficiently broad impact on individual functioning as to constitute a general deficit in adaptive behavior. If it is clear that an individual is functioning in the average or above-average range on the other two domains, clinical judgment should be used to determine whether the deficit is limited to one area of adaptive behavior and is not due to mental retardation. Second, the probability of a person having significant deficits (2 *SDs* below the mean) in two or in all three domains of adaptive behavior is extremely low compared to the probability of scoring two standard deviations or below on only one domain. In fact, simulation studies have demonstrated that the probability of a person scoring two standard deviations below the mean on more than one domain would be so low that almost no one with an IQ in the upper mental retardation range would be identified as having mental retardation (K. F. Widaman, personal communication, November 9, 2001).

Clinicians must also pay attention to the environments addressed by a measure of adaptive behavior. The examination of adaptive skills must be documented within the context of community environments typical of the individual's age peers and culture. If a scale excludes important skill areas, or focuses only on skills observed in one setting (e.g., home, school, or work), reliance on scores from a single instrument would provide a noncomprehensive view of adaptive functioning (Reschly, 1990).

©American Association on Mental Retardation

CUTOFF SCORES

Significant limitations in adaptive behavior are identified by a score of at least two standard deviations below the mean on one or more scores representing conceptual, social, or practical skills on a standardized measure of adaptive behavior or on the total score, taking the standard error of measurement into account. Total scores may also be used to determine eligibility from a comprehensive scale that covers conceptual, social, and practical skill areas. Scales with high reliability and low standard errors of measurement (*SEMs*) are recommended for use in diagnosis. The scale's *SEM* should be taken into consideration when determining whether an individual's adaptive behavior meets the definition of a significant limitation. If a person has a score that does not meet the cutoff but is within one standard deviation of the cut-score, it is advised that the score be reevaluated for reliability or the individual should be reassessed with another measure. If an individual does not have significant limitations in the acquisition and/or performance of adaptive behaviors, then the diagnosis of mental retardation is not applicable.

ADAPTIVE BEHAVIOR VERSUS PROBLEM BEHAVIOR

Adaptive behavior is considered to be conceptually different from maladaptive or problem behavior, even though many adaptive behavior scales contain assessments of problem behavior, maladaptive behavior, or emotional competence (Jacobson & Mulick, 1996; Thompson et al., 1999). Correlational relationships between domains of adaptive behavior and maladaptive behavior are generally low ($r < .25$), with a tendency to be higher in samples of people with more severe forms of mental retardation (Harrison, 1987). There is general agreement that the presence of clinically significant levels of problem behavior found on adaptive behavior scales *does not* meet the criterion of significant limitations in adaptive functioning (Greenspan, 1999a; Jacobson & Mulick, 1996). Therefore, behaviors that interfere with a person's daily activities, or with the activities of those around him or her, should be considered problem behavior rather than the absence of adaptive behavior. We should also recognize, however, that the function of inappropriate, or maladaptive, behavior may be to communicate an individual's needs, and in some cases, may even be considered "adaptive." Recent research on the function of behavior problems in people with severe disabilities (Carr, Horner, & Turnbull, 1999; Durand & Crimmins, 1988; Horner, 2000) demonstrates that such behavior may be an adaptation judged by others to be undesirable but often representing a response to environmental conditions and, in some cases, a lack of alternative communication skills. In the vast majority of cases, this would not apply to people with higher levels of intelligence whose diagnosis is in question.

A BALANCED CONSIDERATION OF INTELLIGENCE AND ADAPTIVE BEHAVIOR CRITERIA IN THE DIAGNOSIS OF MENTAL RETARDATION

Diagnosis should include a balanced consideration of assessments of IQ and adaptive behavior. Relationships between intelligence, adaptive behavior, and mental retardation have been studied since 1850, when Edouard Seguin, who also became the first president of what has become the American Association on Mental Retardation (AAMR), distinguished between "sensibility, intelligence, and will." Seguin believed that all three were necessary when, "to a casual observation, the question may arise whether any default in these particulars exists at all" (cited in Wilbur, 1877, p. 31). Binet and Simon also emphasized the role of personal judgment in diagnosing mental retardation. They stated, "the rest of the intellectual faculties seem of little importance in comparison with judgment" (1916, p. 43, as cited in Greenspan & Granfield, 1992). In his 1936 AAMR presidential address, Edgar Doll was also critical of definitions that based the diagnosis of mental retardation solely on the results of an IQ test. To Doll, mental deficiency was even better understood in terms of social incompetence than of intellectual retardation. Thus in the original concept of mental retardation, adaptive behavior was the central and distinguishing feature of the disability (Greenspan & Granfield, 1992).

In spite of the fact that previous definitions have indicated that intelligence and adaptive behavior should have equal weight in diagnosis, in practice IQ has typically dominated and thus has been overemphasized both in terms of professional decision making and diagnosis (e.g., Furlong & LeDrew, 1985; Harrison, 1987; Reschly & Ward, 1991) and research (e.g., Hawkins & Cooper, 1990; Smith & Polloway, 1979). This dominance of measured IQ has been unfortunate because the earliest conceptions of mental retardation were based on a profile of individuals who were unable to adapt to the demands of everyday life (Biasini, Grupe, Huffman, & Bray, 1999; Greenspan & Driscoll, 1997; Scheerenberger, 1983).

Intelligence test measurement preceded the development of standard measures of adaptive behavior, which may partially explain the shift from the original concept of mental retardation to one that has been more focused on limited intellectual capabilities, as measured by IQ tests. Moreover, adaptive behavior assessment has sometimes been viewed as a mechanism for declassification that occurs when a person who is otherwise considered to have mental retardation (based on IQ) is subsequently determined not to have mental retardation on the basis of adaptive behavior; that is, adaptive behavior has been used as protection against false positives (Harrison & Robinson, 1995; Reschly, 1982). This imbalance between intelligence and adaptive behavior does not represent the current conceptualization of mental retardation.

©American Association on Mental Retardation

RELATIONSHIP OF ADAPTIVE BEHAVIOR DOMAINS TO 1992 SKILL AREAS

A number of professionals involved in the diagnosis of mental retardation expressed concern that the 10 skill areas in the 1992 AAMR (Luckasson et al.) definition were not found on any single standardized measure of adaptive behavior at that time. The requirement that significant limitations be present in at least 2 of the 10 skill areas was particularly problematic when the 10 areas were not known to be internally consistent or independent. The lack of measurement tools and the fact that the 10 areas had not emerged from factor-analytic work on adaptive behavior led the current AAMR Terminology and Classification Committee to reconsider and change this component of the definition criteria.

Since 1992 adaptive behavior scales have been developed or revised that contain items and factors that do represent each of the 10 skill areas in the 1992 definition. The Adaptive Behavior Assessment Scale (Harrison & Oakland, 2000), for example, fits the dimensional structure of the 1992 definition and appears to have promise as a standardized measure of adaptive behavior. Because each of the 10 skill areas listed in the 1992 definition can be conceptually linked to one or more of the three domains (see Table 5.2), a total score on an instrument such as the Adaptive Behavior Assessment Scale can be used to identify significant limitations in adaptive behavior.

The 10 skill areas have been reported to be particularly useful for developing profiles of strengths and weaknesses and for programming supports for people with mental retardation. Measures of the 10 skill areas, and other instruments that may assess conceptual, social, and practical skills, but do not have normative data on the general population, may also be valuable tools for planning supports or educational programming. More information on the use of criterion-referenced measures or support inventories to assist with planning supports is provided in chapter 9.

SPECIAL CONSIDERATIONS IN THE ASSESSMENT OF ADAPTIVE BEHAVIOR

It is essential that the selection of measures and interpretation of adaptive behavior scores address the relevant "Considerations for Assessment" shown on Table 1.1. The following considerations are particularly important in the selection and use of standardized measures of adaptive behavior for a diagnosis of mental retardation:

Table 5.2
Relationships of 1992 and 2002 Adaptive Skill Areas

Adaptive Behavior Skill Areas in 2002 Definition	Representative Skills in 2002 Definition	Skill Areas Listed in 1992 Definition
Conceptual	Language Reading and writing Money concepts Self-direction	Communication Functional academics Self-direction Health and safety
Social	Interpersonal Responsibility Self-esteem Gullibility Naiveté Follows rules Obeys laws Avoids victimization	Social skills Leisure
Practical	Activities of daily living Instrumental activities of daily living Occupational skills Maintains safe environments	Self-care Home living Community use Health and safety Work

SELECTION OF ADAPTIVE BEHAVIOR MEASURES

Purpose of Assessment

The assessment of adaptive behavior can contribute to each of the different functions shown in Table 1.1: diagnosis, classification, and planning for supports. It should be understood that the characteristics of a good assessment for one function (e.g., diagnosis) are not necessarily the same as the characteristics of a good assessment for another (e.g., identifying support needs). Few instruments have the breadth, depth, and psychometric properties to be optimally useful for all purposes. Measures that provide enough detail to assist with programming may be too long to be useful for diagnostic testing, may lack standardization data, or may describe behaviors that do not usually distinguish individuals with from individuals without mental retardation (Nihira, 1999). In the past these differences may have con-

©American Association on Mental Retardation

tributed to confusion about what adaptive behavior is and may have also been responsible for concerns about the relative value of adaptive measures for professional practice. Measures selected for diagnostic purposes should assess adaptive skills that can help discriminate between people with and people without mental retardation.

Technical Adequacy

Regardless of the purpose of diagnosis (e.g., service eligibility, benefits eligibility, legal eligibility), adaptive behavior should be measured with a standardized instrument that provides normative data on people without mental retardation. The fact that adaptive behavior test scores are used to determine whether a person has mental retardation should underscore the importance of selecting measures that do not violate basic technical standards. Such standards have been published by professional organizations with an interest in diagnosis of mental retardation or other disabilities (American Educational Research Association, American Psychological Association, & National Council on Measurement in Education, 1999).

General issues in the assessment of adaptive skills derive in large part from those issues that relate to measurement in any other dimension. Therefore, concerns about validity, reliability, stability of measures, generalization, prediction, and the appropriateness of use are critical in the assessment of mental retardation. Although some available scales have been used for many years, longevity alone does not validate a test's results for diagnostic purposes. Many of the available adaptive behavior scales fall short of appropriate standards for norming (Kamphaus, 1987b) and clarity of the construct of adaptive behavior (Evans, 1991). On the other hand, several measures have been developed and tested in recent years that do meet the criteria of a good test for diagnosis. A review of these is provided at the end of this chapter.

Appropriateness of Measure for the Individual

Professionals not only must select instruments that are technically adequate, they must also be cautious to select ones designed for the particular individual or group (Reschly, 1990). The potential user must employ adaptive skill assessment instruments that are normed within community environments on individuals who are of the same age grouping as the individual being evaluated. The validity of scales normed primarily on individuals in segregated school, work, or living arrangements may be limited to contexts that are useful for programming but are not acceptable for diagnostic purposes.

Purpose of Diagnosis

Diagnosis is performed for a variety of purposes, including special education or other service-system eligibility, legal classifications, and funding. The same measure can be used for different diagnostic purposes as long as it can determine significant deficits in adaptive behavior (i.e., 2 *SDs* from the *M* on a cognitive, social, or practical skill domain or on a total score). For example, if the Vineland Adaptive Behavior Scales or the AAMR Adaptive Behavior Scale is determined to be an appropriate measure of adaptive behavior for an individual in the diagnosis of mental retardation for special education eligibility, it should also be appropriate in the diagnosis of mental retardation for that individual for legal purposes. (Readers are cautioned, however, to confirm that the same definition is used in both situations.)

Evaluating New Instruments

Professionals are advised to remain current with the literature in the field in order to be aware of newly published instruments. At the same time, there is benefit in exercising a healthy caution toward tools that may lack documentation of their appropriateness for use with individuals who have mental retardation. Tests may use current trends and popular buzz words without demonstrating that they adhere to the standards for these concepts. The key point is that new instruments may not offer the advantage that established tools can; that is, exposure to careful professional scrutiny and the availability of a literature base on their validity. Nevertheless, new measures that report strong psychometric data should be seriously considered.

Multimethod Approaches to Measurement

As Sattler (1988) stated, "no one instrument can measure all of the relevant domains of adaptive behavior" (p. 376). Although every effort must be made to select an instrument that is appropriate for the age and status of the person being assessed, clinicians must recognize that adaptive behavior instruments are imperfect measures for distinguishing individuals with and those without mental retardation as they face the everyday demands of life. For example, information about levels of credulity and gullibility, as they affect adaptive behavior, could provide key information for a diagnosis of mental retardation. Greenspan (1999a) argued that the victimization of people with mental retardation, observed in social and economic exploitation, is "a more central (and generally more subtle) problem that goes to the heart of why people with mental retardation are considered to need the label" (p. 69). Because there are no standardized measures that assess adaptive skills related to credulity and gullibility, these characteristics should be considered in the clinical judgment of adaptive behavior limitations.

In spite of the focus on typical rather than maximal behavior, some authors have also urged that naturalistic and controlled observation be used to assess the acquisition of certain behaviors, such as economic and domestic skills (McCarver & Campbell, 1987; Taylor & Ivimey, 1982). Observations, interviews, or other methods of assessment to gather information about adaptive behavior may complement, but ordinarily should not replace, standardized measures (see chap. 6).

©American Association on Mental Retardation

SELECTION OF RATERS OR THIRD-PARTY INFORMANTS

Those who use most current adaptive behavior scales to gather information about typical behavior rely primarily on the recording of information obtained from a third person who is familiar with the individual being assessed. Thus assessment typically takes the form of an interview process, with the respondent being a parent, teacher, or direct-service provider rather than from direct observation of adaptive behavior or from self-report of typical behavior (Voelker et al., 1990). It is critical that the interviewer and informant or rater fully understand the meaning of each question and response category in order to provide valid and reliable information to the clinician. It is also essential that people interviewed about someone's adaptive behavior be well-acquainted with the typical behavior of the person over an extended period of time, preferably in multiple settings. In some cases it may be necessary to obtain information from more than one informant. The consequences of scores to the rater, informant, or individual being rated should also be taken into consideration, as well as the positive or negative nature of the relationship between the rater or informant and the person being assessed (Evans & Bradley-Johnson, 1988; Harrison & Robinson, 1995; Reschly, 1990). Observations made outside the context of community environments typical of the individual's age peers and culture warrant severely reduced weight.

CLINICAL JUDGMENT

Chapter 6 contains a general discussion of clinical judgment and diagnosis. Here we address issues of clinical judgment that are specific to adaptive behavior measurement. Adaptive behavior measures can provide very useful information about the extent to which an individual responds to the demands of everyday life. Nevertheless, the interpretation of standardized adaptive behavior scores, especially in connection with assessments of intellectual ability in the diagnosis of mental retardation, requires clinical judgment involving each of the following factors.

The Individual's Physical Condition and Mental Health

Individuals who exhibit specific sensory, motor, or communicative limitations can present special difficulties for those interpreting adaptive behavior scores. For purposes of diagnosis, it is important to identify influences on levels of adaptive behavior related to physical handicaps, medical conditions, and emotional health. Evaluators must be able to distinguish limitations in adaptive behavior from problems associated with sensory, emotional, or physical conditions.

Opportunities or Experiences and Participation or Interactions

Opportunities to participate in community life, including limited opportunities resulting from emotional or physical health or residential placement, must be considered in decisions about significant limitations in adaptive behavior (Hill, 1999). A person whose opportunities to learn adaptive skills have been restricted in comparison to age peers may have acquisition or performance deficits that are unrelated to mental retardation. For example, a person who has not been provided opportunities to make purchases may lack the adaptive skills needed for shopping. Likewise, a person who has not been taught to use money will not have this skill, regardless of his or her potential to understand the concept and use the skill when needed. Finally, if a person possesses certain skills assessed on an adaptive behavior measure but rarely or never has an opportunity to use them, this should be considered in the interpretation of scores. If these factors, which also contribute to individual functioning (see Figure 1.1), are considered to contribute to lowered scores on adaptive behavior measures, this should be taken into account when scores are interpreted.

Multiple Data Sources
The addition of different sources of data provides a basis for more informed professional judgment by providing a context within which to evaluate the meaning of a score obtained from a standardized measure of adaptive behavior. This approach is the preferred option to the sole reliance on a single measure of adaptive skills and to a single evaluator or rater. It emphasizes the importance of *convergent validity*, or the consistency of information obtained from different sources and settings. The importance of such a focus is emphasized by the fact that some specific adaptive skills are not sufficiently addressed by current scales. Gresham and Elliott (1987) noted, for example, that a comprehensive social skills assessment would require direct observations of behavior, sociometric tools, and role-plays or interviews.

Relevant Context or Environments
One would assume that adaptive behavior is evaluated in relation to contexts typical of the individual's age peers. However, in some cases, typical behavior is observed in "atypical" environments, such as residential or educational programs that primarily serve people with disabilities. This disconnect must be taken into account in the clinical interpretation of scores. A second issue is that some raters will have no information about the individual's typical performance in settings other than those where they interact with the person. For example, in the Classroom edition of the Vineland Adaptive Behavior Scales (Sparrow, Balla, & Cicchetti, 1984), teachers are asked to designate whether they have actually observed each behavior or whether, due to contextual limitations (e.g., behaviors that may only be displayed outside of schools), they are estimating typical behavior on the basis of what they know about the person. Too many estimates should constitute a warning that scores may not reflect adaptive behavior across contexts. Thus the reliability of ratings that are not based on personal observation of typical behavior must be cautiously evaluated.

 ©American Association on Mental Retardation

Sociocultural Considerations

A diagnosis of mental retardation must take into account the sociocultural context of the individual. The key challenges are to identify sociocultural circumstances that might differ from those of the norm group, to examine the individual's performance in relation to others of the same age and culture, and to evaluate the expectations and opportunities of the individual's culture that might influence an adaptive behavior score. Behavioral expectations may differ across cultural groups, along with education and training in adaptive skills. Assessments, therefore, must consider relevant ethnic or cultural factors.

Even if a standardization sample matches the governmental census proportion (which is psychometrically appropriate), this does not necessarily mean that norms applied to a person from that ethnic group would adequately reflect typical expectations for that person (Tassé & Craig, 1999). This issue, which some believe is not relevant for basic behaviors contained on adaptive behavior scales (e.g., individuals in all ethnic or socioeconomic groups are expected to perform daily living skills with increasing independence as they get older), is getting more attention in recent years. Because it would be impossible to obtain many standardization samples to represent all cultural variations in the United States, this may need to be dealt with in the clinical interpretation of scores rather than the actual scoring procedure, as Mercer suggested 30 years ago (Mercer, 1973).

MEASURES OF ADAPTIVE BEHAVIOR

There has never been a shortage of adaptive behavior scales. Meyers, Nihira, and Zetlin (1979) reported the existence of more than 200 measures of adaptive behavior. In spite of the numbers, however, none of these measures was normed on nonhandicapped samples, and most could not demonstrate sufficient evidence of reliability and validity to justify use in diagnosis Since then, the attention to adaptive behavior measurement has resulted in the development and refinement of several measures that have excellent psychometric properties, including impressive norms on samples of people with and people without disabilities (Bruininks, McGrew, & Maruyama, 1988; McGrew & Bruininks, 1989; Thompson et al., 1999; Widaman, Borthwick-Duffy, & Little, 1991; Widaman & McGrew, 1996).

Best practices in the assessment of adaptive behavior should always be considered in the selection of a measure for a specific individual. Manuals containing best practices are published by the National Association of School Psychologists, the American Psychological Association, and other professional organizations, members of which assess adaptive behavior for purposes of diagnosis. In addition, users must follow the administration, scoring, and interpretation instructions found in the measure's standardization manual.

The information that follows about specific instruments is intended to assist

© American Association on Mental Retardation

readers as they develop procedures consistent with the current conceptualization and operational definition of mental retardation. Its purpose is not to endorse or recommend that specific instruments be used for the assessment of adaptive skills in the diagnostic process to the exclusion of others. In fact, there may be other instruments in existence, or under development or revision, that also meet the criteria for a good diagnostic measure of adaptive behavior. The descriptions that follow are provided to illustrate the features of adaptive behavior scales that are important in the selection of a measure for a particular individual. The instruments described include the revised Vineland Adaptive Behavior Scales (Sparrow et al., 1984), the AAMR Adaptive Behavior Scale–School and Community (Lambert, Nihira, & Leland, 1993), the Scales of Independent Behavior–Revised (Bruininks, Woodcock, Weatherman, & Hill, 1991), the Comprehensive Test of Adaptive Behavior–Revised (Adams, 1999), and the Adaptive Behavior Assessment Scale (Harrison & Oakland, 2000).

VINELAND ADAPTIVE BEHAVIOR SCALES

The revised Vineland Adaptive Behavior Scales (VABS) (Sparrow et al., 1984) consists of three scales: (a) a Survey form (Vineland–S), (b) an Expanded form (Vineland–E), and (c) a Classroom form (Vineland–C). The first two forms use a conversation data-gathering format during interviews with parents or guardians. Norms on children without handicaps are available from birth to 18 years, 11 months, based on a standardization sample of 3,000 cases that were stratified on age, gender, ethnicity, parental education, geographic region, and community size and that were generally consistent with United States Census data. Vineland–E is intentionally longer and more detailed in its collection of information on specific skill deficiencies. This version can contribute to both purposes of measuring adaptive behavior (i.e., diagnosis and planning of supports). Data from reliability and validity studies of Vineland–S are very good, especially in light of the flexible conversation format for obtaining rating information. Vineland–C is appropriate for children aged 3 to 12 years and is completed by the teacher in a relatively brief period of time. Teachers are asked to record when they estimate behaviors so it is not an unknown threat to reliability and validity. Standardization testing of children and adults without disabilities from birth to age 70-plus on a new revision of the Vineland is being conducted at this time.

AAMR ADAPTIVE BEHAVIOR SCALES (ABS)

There are two versions of the ABS: (a) a School and Community version (ABS–S:2) (Lambert, Nihira, & Leland, 1993), and (b) a Residential and Community version (ABS–RC:2) (Nihira et al., 1993). The ABS–S:2 is used to identify students who are significantly below their peers in adaptive functioning for diagnostic purposes

©American Association on Mental Retardation

and to assess the effects of intervention programs. Behavior domains measure personal independence and personal responsibility in daily living, including pre-vocational or vocational activity. The second part of the ABS–S:2 relates to problem behavior. This measure was standardized on samples composed of individuals with and those without mental retardation. Standard scores, age-equivalent scores, and percentile rank scores can be converted from raw scores on the adaptive behavior subscales and three factor scores for individuals aged 3 to 21 years. The ABS–S:2 provides norms through age 21 and includes items appropriate for school settings that may not be relevant to adult environments.

The Residential and Community version, ABS–RC:2, was developed to be appropriate for individuals through 79 years of age, but norms are not available for adults with typical functioning. Because standard scores and percentile ranks do not indicate relative standing to people without developmental disabilities, the ABS–RC:2 does not fit the psychometric criteria proposed in this 2002 manual for a diagnosis of mental retardation. It has a long history, however, of providing excellent information for planning supports and assessing change in individual functioning over time.

SCALES OF INDEPENDENT BEHAVIOR

The Scales of Independent Behavior–Revised (SIB–R) (Bruininks et al., 1991) is a component of the Woodcock-Johnson Psycho-Educational Battery and has three forms: the Full-Scale, the Short Form, and the Early Development Form. A Problem Behavior Scale is included in each form. The SIB–R provides a wide array of scores for diagnosis and planning supports. For diagnosis, scores on Social Interaction and Community Skills, Personal Living Skills, and Community Living Skills are consistent with the social, practical, and conceptual domains in the current definition. A fourth SIB domain score, Motor Skills, can contribute information about the Health dimension in the conceptual model of individual functioning in Figure 1.1.

The SIB manual addresses many of the issues that make the interpretation of adaptive behavior scores especially challenging in the diagnosis of mental retardation, including: physical disability, use of adaptive equipment, alternative communication methods, tasks no longer age-appropriate, partial performance of multi-part tasks, and lack of opportunity due to environment or safety and cognitive ability to understand social expectations for performing behaviors. Guidelines regarding these special conditions suggest that individuals should be rated according to what they actually do (or would do if age-appropriate) rather than giving "credit" for lack of opportunity, overprotective environments, adaptive equipment, or physical disability or denying credit if tasks are performed well with the assistance of adaptive equipment and/or medication (Hill, 1999). The Checklist of Adaptive Living Skills (CALS) (Bruininks & Moreau, 1991) is part of the same assessment battery. It is a criterion-referenced measure of adaptive living skills that is useful for program planning but would not be appropriate for diagnostic purposes.

COMPREHENSIVE TEST OF ADAPTIVE BEHAVIOR–REVISED

The Comprehensive Test of Adaptive Behavior–Revised (CTAB–R) (Adams, 1999) is used to evaluate the ability to function independently in different environments. Norms that include standardization samples of children, adolescents, and adults in schools, community-based programs, and residential facilities are available for the domains of Self-Help Skills, Home Living Skills, Independent Living Skills, Social Skills, Sensory and Motor Skills, and Language Concepts and Academic Skills. With the current scoring system that does not clearly correspond to the domains of conceptual, practical, and social skills, a total score on CTAB–R would be appropriate for diagnosis of mental retardation.

A Parent or Guardian Survey is available to provide information for any section of the CTAB–R for which the rater (usually teacher) feels additional input is necessary for an accurate response. The rater waits for the Parent or Guardian Survey to be returned before completing these sections. This instrument also contains items that are gender-specific. Specific guidelines are provided in the examiner's manual for testing students with visual, physical, or language disabilities.

ADAPTIVE BEHAVIOR ASSESSMENT SYSTEM

The Adaptive Behavior Assessment System (ABAS) (Harrison & Oakland, 2000) is a new adaptive behavior measure developed by using the 1992 AAMR 10 adaptive skill domains as the a priori domains of adaptive behavior. As shown in Table 5.2, the 10 skill domains from the 1992 definition address the conceptual, practical, and social skill areas in the current definition. Although the ABAS does not provide broader domain scores that are consistent with the three skill areas in the 2002 definition, the use of a total score on the ABAS would be appropriate for diagnostic purposes. Norms are available for children, aged 5 and older, as well as adults. Publication of norms for children from birth to 5 years is expected soon. This measure also has two adult forms, including a self-report and a report by others. Although too new to have been critiqued by users, the ABAS appears to have good psychometric properties and potential for use in the diagnosis of mental retardation.

SUMMARY

In summary, adaptive behavior is the collection of conceptual, social, and practical skills that have been learned by people in order to function in their everyday lives. Throughout this chapter the following aspects of adaptive behavior — as it relates

©American Association on Mental Retardation

to assessment and the diagnosis of mental retardation — have been stressed:

- Limitations in adaptive behavior affect both daily life and the ability to respond to life changes and environmental demands.

- Limitations in adaptive behavior should be considered in light of the four other dimensions of the 2002 definition: Intellectual Abilities; Participation, Interactions, and Social Roles; Health; and Context.

- The presence or absence of adaptive behavior can have different relevance, depending on whether it is being considered for purposes of diagnosis, classification, or planning supports.

- For diagnosis, significant limitations in adaptive behavior should be established through the use of standardized measures normed on the general population, including people with disabilities and people without disabilities. On these standardized measures, significant limitations in adaptive behavior are operationally defined as performance that is at least two standard deviations below the mean of either (a) one of the following three types of adaptive behavior: conceptual, social, or practical, or (b) an overall score on a standardized measure of conceptual, social, and practical skills.

CHAPTER 6
DIAGNOSIS AND CLINICAL JUDGMENT

Mental retardation is a disability characterized by significant limitations both in intellectual functioning and in adaptive behavior as expressed in conceptual, social, and practical skills. This disability originates before age 18.

Five assumptions are essential to the application of this definition:

1. Limitations in present functioning must be considered within the context of community environments typical of the individual's age peers and culture.

2. Valid assessment considers cultural and linguistic diversity as well as differences in communication, sensory, motor, and behavioral factors.

3. Within an individual, limitations often coexist with strengths.

4. An important purpose of describing limitations is to develop a profile of needed supports.

5. With appropriate personalized supports over a sustained period, the life functioning of the person with mental retardation generally will improve.

OVERVIEW

A diagnosis of the presence of mental retardation under the 2002 definition requires a finding that the person's intelligence and adaptive behavior are significantly below average and that the combination was present during the developmental period. Typically this requires the administration of an individualized assessment of intelligence, an individualized assessment of adaptive behavior, and a determination made through review of documents and interviews with relevant observers that the disability was present before the age of 18.

Making a diagnosis of mental retardation can be challenging in some cases and may require the application of clinical judgment. Clinical judgment is often required when (a) the individual comes from a cultural and/or linguistic background that differs significantly from the mainstream; (b) earlier information is lacking or incomplete; (c) for security or medical reasons, the individual's adaptive behavior functioning cannot be assessed consistent with this 2002 definition and assumptions; (d) standardized assessment procedures are not appropriate because the individual has multiple disabilities, sensory motor limitations, and/or behavioral challenges that limit the use or valid interpretation of standardized instruments; (e) there is a risk of practice effects due to repeated use of the same instrument outside of recommended time intervals; (f) the individual uses a language, dialect, or communication system that differs significantly from that of the instrument's normative populations; (g) the individual is very young and has potentially limited language and/or performance skills; (h) difficulties arise in selecting informants and validating informant observations; (i) direct observation of the individual's actual performance has been limited and additional direct observation is necessary; and (j) difficulties arise when attempting to determine whether the age of onset criterion has been met, which is frequently problematic for older individuals. Each of these situations may require the use of *clinical judgment* to make decisions and/or to integrate the input from an interdisciplinary team whose function is to blend the multidimensional assessment and contextual information.

In addition, certain of the assumptions essential to the application of the 2002 definition of mental retardation anticipate clinical judgment. For example, neither Assumption 1 ("Limitations in present functioning must be considered within the context of community environments typical of the individual's age peers and culture") nor Assumption 2 ("Valid assessment considers cultural and linguistic diversity as well as differences in communication, sensory, motor, and behavioral factors") could be properly addressed without the exercise of competent clinical judgment.

Clinical judgment can be problematic, especially if disconnected from direct observations by trained professionals and relevant testing data. As stated by Salvia and Ysseldyke (1991),

> Judgments represent both the best and worst of assessment data. Judgments made by conscientious, capable, and objective individuals can be an invaluable aid in the assessment process. Inaccurate, biased, subjective judgment can be misleading at best and harmful at worst. (p. 26)

Fortunately, as tools for assessment have improved, and as more individuals with mental retardation have attended school and received increasingly appropriate evaluations during the developmental period, the need for widespread use of clinical judgment in the diagnosis of mental retardation has been reduced.

©American Association on Mental Retardation

CLINICAL JUDGMENT DEFINED

Clinical judgment is a special type of judgment rooted in a high level of clinical expertise and experience; it emerges directly from extensive data. It is based on the clinician's explicit training, direct experience with people who have mental retardation, and familiarity with the person and the person's environments. Thus clinicians who have not gathered extensive relevant assessment data should not claim clinical judgment. Clinical judgment should *not* be thought of as a justification for abbreviated evaluations, a vehicle for stereotypes or prejudices, a substitute for insufficiently explored questions, an excuse for incomplete or missing data, or a way to solve political problems. Rather, it should be viewed as a tool of clinicians with training and expertise in mental retardation and ongoing experiences with — and observations of — people with mental retardation and their families.

CLINICAL JUDGMENT GUIDELINES

As discussed in chapters 4 and 5 and summarized in Table 1.1 ("Framework for Assessment"), the function of diagnosis is influenced by a number of factors. The following clinical guidelines, which will enhance any application of clinical judgment, are based primarily on the factors listed in Table 1.1.

1. Ensure a match between the assessment measures used and the evaluation's purpose.

2. Review the appropriateness and psychometric characteristics of the measures selected in terms of the person's age and gender, cultural group, primary language, means of communication, and sensori-motor limitations.

3. Be sensitive to the instrument's stated qualifications needed by the examiner and the examiner's characteristics and potential for bias.

4. Apply the instrument consistent with the directions.

5. Use currently published professional practices and ethical standards.

6. Select informants who know the person well and can give reliable and valid information.

7. Consider, in the interpretation of tests or scales, the individual's opportunities and experiences as they relate to participation, interactions, and social roles.

8. In the interpretation of test scores, be sensitive to physical and mental health factors that influence an individual's behavior.

9. Use members of the interdisciplinary team, including the individual, as partners.

10. Follow the diagnostic guidelines presented in this manual (chaps. 4 & 5) for defining significant limitations in intelligence and adaptive behavior.

The continued recognition of the potential risks and benefits of clinical judgment in this 2002 manual is consistent with cautionary statements, standards, and guidelines found in all the major professional groups concerned with testing (see, e.g., American Educational Research Association, American Psychological Association, & National Council on Measurement in Education, 1999; American Psychiatric Association, 1994; American Psychological Association, 1992, 1999).

SUMMARY

In summary, clinical judgment is a special kind of judgment rooted in a high level of clinical expertise and experience; it emerges directly from extensive data. The use of clinical judgment may be required in a number of situations (e.g., those summarized at the beginning of the chapter) and is also anticipated in at least two of the assumptions essential to the application of the 2002 definition of mental retardation. Although this chapter has been focused on the use of clinical judgment in diagnosis, clinical judgment may also be required in the classification and supports planning functions. Similar emphasis must be placed on competent and thorough analysis that is rooted in data and observation and avoids pitfalls, such as shortcuts and stereotypes.

©American Association on Mental Retardation

PART 3
CLASSIFICATION

CHAPTER 7
CLASSIFICATION SYSTEMS

The purposes of classification include grouping for service reimbursement or funding, research, services, and communication about selected characteristics. Multiple classification systems may be used so that the multiple needs of researchers, clinicians, and practitioners can be met. Such classification systems can be based, for example, on the intensities of needed supports, etiology, levels of measured intelligence, or levels of assessed adaptive behavior.

OVERVIEW

Any system by which a person is diagnosed as having mental retardation and classified according to some level consists of a series of formalized rules specifying the characteristics that a person needs to possess in order to be so diagnosed and classified. (Luckasson et al., 1992, p. 23)

A major purpose of this manual is to specify the diagnostic and classification rules for mental retardation considered most valid and useful by professionals and advocates in the field. Over the years, the American Association on Mental Retardation (AAMR) definition and classification systems have historically led the field and been subsequently adopted in large part by other classification systems.

This chapter contains an analysis of classification by intensities of needed supports and other current diagnostic and classification systems, focusing on their coverage of mental retardation. Additional diagnostic and classification categories frequently applied to people with mental retardation will also be described. For example, the World Health Organization's (WHO) *International Classification of Diseases (ICD),* which contains codes for the various levels of mental retardation, is the accepted international system for identifying diseases and physical conditions, including those that may be associated with mental retardation (Medicode, 1998). Another WHO classification system with relevance to mental retardation is the *International Classification of Functioning, Disability, and Health (ICF)* (WHO,

2001).This system classifies functioning in terms of Body Functions and Structures, Activities, Participation, and Contextual Factors. Analogously, the *Diagnostic and Statistical Manual of Mental Disorders (DSM–IV–TR)* (American Psychiatric Association, 2000) contains a definition and codes for levels of mental retardation but is primarily used to classify a wide variety of "mental" disorders, some of which are often associated with mental retardation.

In this chapter special attention is directed toward classification systems based on individual characteristics essential to the diagnosis of mental retardation (i.e., intellectual and adaptive functioning), of closely related concern (e.g., etiology), and of importance in service delivery (e.g., health status and support need category). Eligibility criteria and classifications used in public mental retardation programs are described. Finally, eligibility and classification tied to funding is addressed.

PURPOSES OF CLASSIFICATION

All classification systems have as their fundamental purpose the provision of an organized schema for the categorization of various kinds of observations. Such organization is essential for the advancement of any science in the acquisition of knowledge. Further, classification can enhance communication and establish agreement in an area of study. More particularly, classification may be a component of determining eligibility for services and benefits. It is important that any classification system be updated periodically to incorporate new findings and accommodate changing concepts and philosophies. The major classification systems of relevance to the field of mental retardation are reviewed next with these purposes and criteria of classification systems in mind.

MAJOR CLASSIFICATION SYSTEMS

CLASSIFICATION BY INTENSITIES
OF NEEDED SUPPORTS

In 1992 the AAMR proposed a new classification system based on the intensities of supports needed by individuals with mental retardation. The 1992 System (Luckasson et al.) was a significant departure from previous classification systems in that individuals with mental retardation were *not* divided into yet smaller subgroups based on their IQ ranges (the older mild, moderate, severe, and profound classifications). Rather, in 1992, what was classified was their intensities of needed supports. Thus an individual's needs in specified areas might be classified as intermittent, limited, extensive, or pervasive (ILEP), irrespective of his or her IQ (see chap. 9). The ILEP classification system reflected the shift to a functional definition, emphasized the importance of the interaction of supports to functioning, and

©American Association on Mental Retardation

provided a way to classify and organize critical information about what people needed. This 2002 manual maintains this strong commitment to a supports-based classification system and also explains the use of multiple classification systems.

Implementing an ILEP system and classifying by intensities of needed supports requires consideration of several factors about the supports needed by each individual (Luckasson, Schalock, Snell, & Spitalnik , 1996). These might include the factors of (a) time duration (how long a support is needed), (b) time frequency (how often a support is needed), (c) settings in which the support is needed, (d) resources required for the supports (e.g., cost, personnel, expertise), and (e) the degree of intrusiveness in one's life. Chapter 9 contains a full discussion of supports, their application to people with mental retardation, and classification by intensities of needed supports.

INTERNATIONAL CLASSIFICATION OF DISEASES

Although the origins of medical classification date back to the ancient Egyptians and Greeks (Temkin, 1965), not until 17th-century England was diagnostic coding used to gather statistical information (Medicode, 1998). Undoubtedly the major contribution to medical classification has been the publications by the WHO of statistical listings of diseases and conditions for tracking morbidity and mortality. The ninth edition of the *International Classification of Diseases (ICD–9)* (WHO, 1977) is the one in use today in the United States. The United States National Center for Health Statistics developed a modification of the *ICD–9*, focusing on clinical descriptions accompanying the groupings of diseases and conditions. This effort is the *International Classification of Diseases (9th rev.), Clinical Modification (ICD–9–CM)* (Medicode, 1998).

The *ICD–9–CM* classification levels and coding of mental retardation is found in Table 7.1. Although many of the terms in subcategories, such as *mental subnormality* and *deficiency,* in this coding classification are considered archaic and stigmatizing by many, they are still in use in some parts of the international community. Also of concern is the categorization of the condition solely on the basis of IQ. The AAMR definition of mental retardation includes intellectual limitations and adaptive functioning and stipulates onset during the developmental period. Nevertheless, virtually all governmental and insurance benefit plans, as well as most service delivery systems, require use of these codes. Further, the most valuable function of the system is the standard classification of diseases and conditions, some of which play an etiological role (e.g., Down's syndrome, Code 758.0) or are frequently associated with certain syndromes (e.g., heart murmurs, Code 785.2).

Work began on another revision of the *ICD* in 1983. The title of the system's 10th edition has been expanded to the *International Statistical Classification of Diseases and Related Health Problems (ICD–10)* (WHO, 1993). This revision reflects

TABLE 7.1
ICD–9–CM **Classification of Mental Retardation**

Mental Retardation (317–319)
Use additional code(s) to identify any associated psychiatric or physical condition(s).

317.0	**Mild mental retardation** High-grade defect IQ 50 to 70 Mild mental subnormality
317.1	**Other specified mental retardation**
317.1.1	**Moderate mental retardation** IQ 35 to 49 Moderate mental subnormality
317.2	**Severe mental retardation** IQ 20 to 34 Severe mental subnormality
317.3	**Profound mental retardation** IQ under 20 Profound mental subnormality
317.4	**Unspecified mental retardation** Mental deficiency NOS Mental subnormality NOS

Note. ICD–9–CM = International Classification of Diseases (9th rev.) Clinical Modification (6th ed.) (Medicode, 1998).

NOS = Not otherwise specified.

the further extension of the scope of classification beyond diseases and injuries to also include medical procedures and disablement. Although already in widespread use internationally, the *ICD–10* is not scheduled for implementation in the United States until 2004.

The *ICD–10* retains the traditional *ICD* structure (a single-variable-axis classi-

©American Association on Mental Retardation

fication design) but replaces the previous numeric coding scheme with an alphanumeric one. This expands the coding structure and permits future revisions without disrupting the coding system. For example, all the endocrine, nutritional, and metabolic diseases are E codes (e.g., Code E70.0–classical phenylketonuria), whereas mental and behavioral disorders (where mental retardation is included) are F codes.

The *ICD–10* is basically a tabular classification list built around 21 chapters covering a wide area from "infectious and parasitic diseases" to "factors influencing health status and contact with health services." Each classification item is labeled with a four-character alphanumeric code. Mental retardation is categorized in chapter 5, "Mental and Behavioral Disorders." The *ICD–10* is being used internationally in health care, especially in physical health services.

The *ICD–10* description of mental retardation is as follows:

A condition of arrested or incomplete development of the mind, which is especially characterized by impairment of skills manifested during the developmental period, skills which contribute to the overall level of intelligence, i.e., cognitive, language, motor, and social abilities. Retardation can occur with or without any other mental or physical condition. Degrees of mental retardation are conventionally estimated by standardized intelligence tests. These can be supplemented by scales assessing social adaptation in a given environment. These measures provide an approximate indication of the degree of mental retardation. The diagnosis will also depend on the overall assessment of intellectual functioning by a skilled diagnostician. Intellectual abilities and social adaptation may change over time, and, however poor, may improve as a result of training and rehabilitation. Diagnosis should be based on the current levels of functioning. (pp. 369–370)

Table 7.2 contains the *ICD–10* coding for mental retardation. Although the *ICD–10* description of mental retardation represents a slight improvement over the *ICD–9–CM* in terms of breadth, it still has significant limitations when considered in relationship to the AAMR system. Some of the language continues to be archaic and stigmatizing. It emphasizes classification by IQ scores, with adaptive behavior assessment presented as an optional supplement. An emphasis is placed on mental age scores, although their use in current practice is quite limited. Finally, the functional expectations described are quite minimal, especially for individuals in the moderate and severe categories.

It needs to be emphasized that the *ICD–10* is not an in-depth diagnostic manual but, rather, a system for assigning statistical codes to identified health conditions. Because the *ICD* is widely used in the medical field, it is often used by professionals to identify mental retardation and enter the diagnosis in health-care data systems. The *ICD–10* is not intended and is not suitable for assessment goals or for the determination of supports.

TABLE 7.2
ICD–10 Coding for Mental Retardation

**Mental Retardation
(F70–F79)**

The following fourth-character subdivisions are for use with categories F70–F79 to identify the extent of impairment of behavior:

.0   **With the statement of no, or minimal, impairment of behavior**

.1   **Significant impairment of behavior requiring attention or treatment**

.8   **Other impairments of behavior**

.9   **Without mention of impairment of behavior**

Use additional code, if desired, to identify associated conditions such as autism, other developmental disorders, epilepsy, conduct disorders, or severe physical handicap.

F70   **Mild mental retardation**
Approximate IQ range of 50 to 69 (in adults, mental age from 9 to under 12 years). Likely to result in some learning difficulties in school. Many adults will be able to work and maintain good social relationships and contribute to society.

F71   **Moderate mental retardation**
Approximate IQ range of 35 to 49 (in adults, mental age from 6 to under 9 years). Likely to result in marked developmental delays in childhood, but most can learn to develop some degree of independence in self-care and acquire adequate communication and academic skills. Adults will need varying degrees of support to live and work in the community.

F72   **Severe mental retardation**
Approximate IQ of 20 to 34 (in adults, mental age from 3 to under 6 years). Likely to result in continuous need of support.

F73   **Profound mental retardation**
IQ under 20 (in adults, mental age below 3 years). Results in severe limitation in self-care, continence, communication, and mobility.

F78   **Other mental retardation**

F79   **Unspecified mental retardation**

Note. ICD–10 = International Statistical Classification of Diseases and Related Health Problems (10th ed.) (World Health Organization, 1993).

©American Association on Mental Retardation

INTERNATIONAL CLASSIFICATION OF FUNCTIONING, DISABILITY, AND HEALTH (ICF)

The *ICD–10* is a member of a broader family of WHO health-related classifications. Another member of the family is the *International Classification of Functioning, Disability, and Health (ICF)*, published in 2001. The ICF is a revised version of the *International Classification of Impairments, Disabilities, and Handicaps (ICIDH)* (WHO, 1980).

As a classification instrument, it is complementary to the *ICD–10*, which represents a classification of health conditions, diseases, and disorders. The *ICF*, however, extends beyond the medical perspective and includes a societal and environmental perspective. The *ICF* is oriented toward human functioning and health.

A multipurpose instrument, the *ICF* provides: (a) a conceptual framework for the understanding of health-related states of functioning and disability; (b) a common language to improve communication about disability among users from different backgrounds, such as clinicians, health-care workers, researchers, policy makers, and people with disabilities; and (c) a classification and systematic coding system that permits statistical comparison of data across countries, health-care disciplines, and time.

The *ICF* conceives functioning as an interactive person-environment process. *Functioning* is used as an umbrella term for neutral or nonproblematic states of functioning, whereas *disability* is used as a term for problems in functioning. The *ICF* takes a neutral stand with regard to etiology, but conceives human functioning and disability in relation to both the person's health condition and to contextual (environmental and personal) factors.

Functioning is conceptualized along three basic dimensions representing the perspectives of the body, the individual, and society. Figure 7.1 illustrates a process model of human functioning and disability. It is essential to note the complex interactions among the components. For example, a significant limitation of intelligence (Body Functions component) may be a "cause" of serious limitations in adaptive skills (Activities component). When community participation of an individual is restricted (e.g., he or she lives in an institutional setting; has no job; does not go on outings in the community), one experiences "participation restrictions." These might be more related to environmental circumstances, such as lack of appropriate community resources, lack of support, nonaccepting attitudes of others in the community, or lack of transportation, than to the limitations in adaptive skills or intelligence.

It should be noted that the *ICF* model allows for many different patterns and directions of interactions. This is an important aspect of the conception of disability: A disability can never be explained by the mere presence of a primary impairment (e.g., significant limitations in intellectual functioning) and should always be understood within a frame of physiological and psychological as well as social and

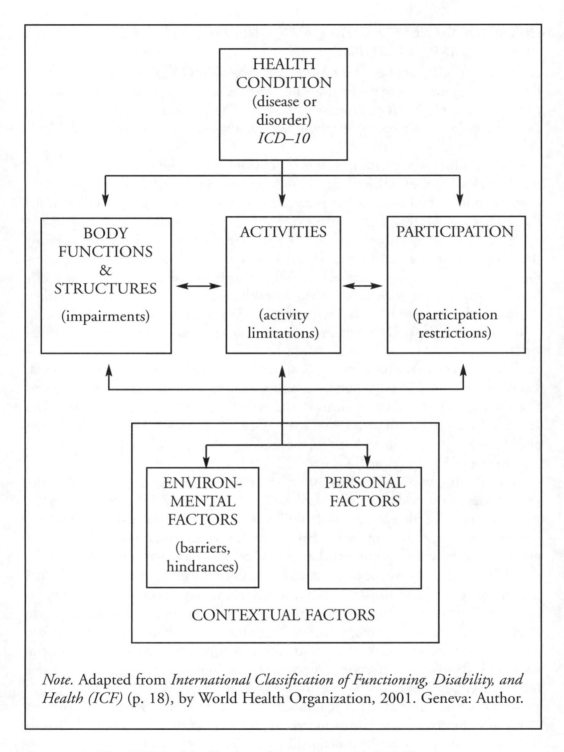

Note. Adapted from *International Classification of Functioning, Disability, and Health (ICF)* (p. 18), by World Health Organization, 2001. Geneva: Author.

Figure 7.1. The *ICF* model of human functioning and disability.

©American Association on Mental Retardation

societal conditions, both past and present. Appropriate supports in any of three dimensions can influence the state of functioning of an individual and, hence, the nature and degree of disability.

Because the *ICF* System is useful in the understanding of mental retardation as a disability, the correspondence between its basic concepts and the multidimensional model of the AAMR 2002 System will now be highlighted and discussed in reference to the *ICF* model shown in Figure 7.1.

Body Functions and Structures

These represent the perspective of the physiological and psychological functions of the body. They comprise Body Functions (the physiological and psychological functions of body systems) and Body Structures (anatomic parts of the body, such as organs, limbs, and their components). *Impairments* are problems in body function or structure, such as a significant deviation or loss. In the context of mental retardation, it is important to note that intellectual and cognitive functions are subdomains of the Body Functions and Structures component of human functioning.

Activities

Activities refer to the execution of tasks or actions by an individual. Difficulties an individual may have in the execution of an activity are referred to as *activity limitations.*

Participation

Participation, which refers to an individual's involvement in real life situations, denotes the degree of involvement, including society's response to the individual's level of functioning. Problems that an individual may have in the manner or extent of involvement in life situations are *participation restrictions.* Restrictions should be understood as interaction problems resulting from hampered availability or accessibility of resources, accommodations, and/or services, relative to the impairments and limitations of the person. Participation restrictions are disadvantages that limit the fulfillment of social roles that are typical (considering age, gender, and culture) for the individual.

Activities and Participation refer to the same domains or life areas. The difference between the dimensions of Activities and Participation is in the individual or societal perspective that is taken. So, although they are represented as distinctive dimensions of functioning in the general diagram, both perspectives are combined in one single list of domains and subdomains in the classification system.

Health Conditions

The *ICF* also provides a frame of reference for the description of human functioning in relation to health conditions. *Health,* however, should be viewed according to the WHO definition, comprising physical, psychological, and social well-being, and not just the absence of disease. Actually, the *ICD–10* (WHO, 1993) represents a separate framework in which health conditions can be identified that affect the functioning of the individual. However, the use of the *ICF* does not presuppose a clearly identified disease or etiology. Thus it is can be used even without reference to the *ICD–10*.

Contextual Factors

Contextual factors represent the complete background of an individual's life that may affect the state of functioning. Contextual factors comprise two domains: Environmental (as external influences) and Personal (as internal influences) factors.

Environmental factors include the physical, social, and attitudinal environments in which people live and conduct their lives. They refer to the environment that the individual shares with others in his or her family, community, culture, and nation. Environmental factors can have a positive or a negative influence on the person's participation as a member of society, on his or her performance of activities, or on the individual's body functions and structure. Positive aspects of the environment are regarded as facilitators of functioning; negative factors are seen as barriers. In the *ICF,* Environmental factors are focused on two levels:

- *Individual level:* the immediate personal environment, including settings such as home, school, and workplace; it includes material features as well as people, supports and relationships, and values and attitudes.

- *Services and systems level:* the formal and informal social structures, organizations and services in the community, and settings including, for example, housing services, communication, transportation, health and education services, Social Security, and governmental agencies that are relevant to service provision for the individual. This level also includes the overarching approaches and systems established in a culture, subculture, or on the level of a nation that set the pattern for the service level and the individual level; it includes laws, regulations, ideologies, and health and educational systems.

Personal factors are the individual background of a person's life, composed of features that are not part of the individual's health condition or functional state. Personal factors include age, race, gender, educational background, fitness, lifestyle, habits, coping styles, social background, and past and current experiences. Personal factors are not classified further in the *ICF.* However, they may influence the functioning of the individual with a health condition as well as the outcome of interventions.

©American Association on Mental Retardation

COMPARISON OF *ICF* AND AAMR SYSTEMS

The relation between the AAMR and the *ICF* systems can be described at different levels. Discussed here are the levels of (a) construct or concept, (b) definition of mental retardation, and (c) assessment. Next, the similarities and differences between the two systems will be briefly described.

The AAMR construct of mental retardation and the *ICF* focus on *human functioning* as a person-environment interaction. Both systems are similar in their ecological conception of functioning and disability. Both systems also present a dynamic concept of disability that does not imply a permanent state of being and recognizes positive and negative aspects of functioning: limitations as well as strengths. Both systems use similar dimensions or basic concepts that are relevant to the understanding and the assessment of intellectual disability as a problem in human functioning. Both systems are driven by a positive orientation toward improving the lives of people with disabilities.

Both systems have a multiparadigmatic background; that is, they do not rely on a singular objective or subjective worldview and they attempt to integrate medical, psychological, and social models of disability (Imrie, 1997; Mercer, 1992; Rioux, 1997). Both systems are directed toward convergence of models rather than toward divergence, and they both move in the direction of an integrated biopsychosocial model (WHO, 2001). A consequence of the multiparadigmatic nature of the *ICF* and the AAMR systems, though, is complexity. Both systems come with challenges for rethinking disability and redesigning assessment and service practices. Because classification systems rely on models and paradigms that are subject to change, the concepts of mental retardation and disability will continue to change as well with our ongoing understanding of related relevant constructs.

The AAMR definition of mental retardation comprises a statement and three requirements (Luckasson & Reeve, 2001), as illustrated in Table 7.3. The statement places the definition in the realm of human functioning. From the perspective of the *ICF,* the initial statement is referring to all three dimensions of functioning and disability as represented in the *ICF* (Figure 7.1). The limitations referenced in the first requirement correspond to an impairment of the *ICF* body functions, in particular to the domain of intellectual functions (Code b117). The limitations of the second requirement correspond to the *ICF* components of Activities and Participation. Execution of daily life activities clearly requires the presence of specific adaptive skills. Although the *ICF* does not make a distinction among conceptual, social, and practical adaptive skills, the classification of activities and participation includes an extensive list of activities that can be related to areas of adaptive skills. It may be concluded that the core concepts and criteria of the AAMR 2002 System fit the frame of reference of functioning and disability of the *ICF.*

©American Association on Mental Retardation

TABLE 7.3
Structure of the AAMR 2002 Definition of Mental Retardation

AAMR Definition	Component
Statement	Mental retardation is a disability
First requirement	Significant limitations in intellectual functioning
Second requirement	Significant limitations in adaptive behavior as expressed in conceptual, social, and practical adaptive skills
Third requirement	Originates before age 18

The AAMR 2002 system adopts a multidimensional model of mental retardation that includes five interrelated dimensions: Intellectual Abilities (Dimension I); Adaptive Behavior (II); Participation, Interactions, and Social Roles (III); Health (including etiology) (IV); and Context (V). These five dimensions are compatible with the basic concepts of the *ICF* and are relevant to understanding human functioning and disability in general (Figure 7.1). The relation between the five AAMR dimensions and the five basic concepts of the *ICF* model is shown in Figure 7.2.

The *ICF* itself is not an assessment instrument; it is a general conceptual tool for creating models of disability and a classification tool that is primarily intended for statistical purposes. However, because of its structure and extensive classification system, the *ICF* is also relevant to the construction of disability assessment instruments and procedures in various fields of disability. The structure and guidelines of the AAMR assessment process are more finely tuned to the needs of the field of mental retardation. The philosophy behind the multidimensional AAMR assessment process, however, is compatible with the *ICF* multidimensional approach to disability in general. Therefore, the various *ICF* classification components and their subdomains may be relevant for classification purposes as well as for the establishment of assessment procedures and guidelines in the context of mental retardation.

For example, in assessment the *ICF* classifications of Global Mental Functions and Specific Mental Functions (both part of the Body Functions classification) can be used to further describe limitations in intellectual abilities in AAMR Dimension I (Intellectual Abilities). Because the *ICF* components of Activities and Participation refer to performance and involvement in daily life settings, the accompanying classification items of these components may also be used in the AAMR Dimen-

©American Association on Mental Retardation

ICF → AAMR ↓	Health Condition	Body Functions & Structures	Activities	Participation	Contextual Factors
Dimension I: Intellectual Abilities		*			
Dimension II: Adaptive Behavior			*		
Dimension III: Participation, Interactions, & Social Roles				*	
Dimension IV: Health	*	*			
Dimension V: Context					*

Figure 7.2. Relation between the five AAMR dimensions of functioning and the five basic concepts of the *ICF* (World Health Organization, 2001).

sions II (Adaptive Behavior) and III (Participation). As for Dimension IV (Health, including etiology), the *ICF* component of Body Functions and Structures offers useful assessment items and classification categories. Within the same AAMR Dimension IV, the *ICD–10* can be used to classify etiology. The *ICF* Contextual Factors classification can be used as a checklist for assessment and classification related to the AAMR Dimension V (Context).

In conclusion, the AAMR theoretical model is compatible with the *ICF* process model of disability. In general, this may have useful implications for procedures and instruments in the assessment of mental retardation (i.e., the analysis of strengths and limitations and the need for support), although specific applications need more study.

The relevance of the *ICF* to the assessment of disability has been recognized by the American Psychological Association (APA) in its collaborative project with the WHO that eventually will lead to a *Procedural Manual and Guide for a Standardized Application of the International Classification of Functioning, Disability, and Health (ICF)* (Cohen, 2001). This project aims at a systematic grouping of assessment instruments and clinical guidelines along the structure of the *ICF* and might be useful in the context of mental retardation as well.

The classification categories of the various parts of the *ICF* can serve as (additional) checklists for clinicians in the assessment process and as an organizing frame for the development of future assessment instruments and methods. However, because of the elaborateness of the full *ICF*, a straightforward application of the detailed classification items might result in an impractical inventory and multitude of "problems," especially for people with severe limitations (Kraijer, 1993). For the same reason, the use of the *ICF* as a coding instrument in mental retardation should be restricted to the more general levels of the classification of impairments, activity limitations, and participation restrictions, unless a specific purpose is served (e.g., research on the prevalence of specific impairments in people with multiple disabilities). The use of the *ICF* as an assessment aid, therefore, should always be made with professional discretion.

Similarities and differences between the AAMR 2002 System and the *ICF* model of functioning, disability, and health are summarized in Table 7.4. Although the AAMR 1992 System and the *ICF* System are highly compatible (Buntinx, in press), that compatibility has been enhanced in the AAMR 2002 model of mental retardation. Compatibility may be understood in terms of content validity; the theoretical constructs and the process models of both systems are congruent. This points to a common paradigmatic background of the AAMR 2002 construct of mental retardation and the WHO construct of disability. Therefore, the *ICF* may serve as an interpreting interface between different disciplines and stakeholders involved in the assessment and service provision to people with mental retardation.

DIAGNOSTIC AND STATISTICAL MANUAL OF MENTAL DISORDERS

It was not until after World War II that the *International Classification of Diseases (ICD–6)* (WHO, 1948) contained a separate section for mental disorders (including categories for disorders of intelligence). A variant of the *ICD–6* was published in 1952 by the American Psychiatric Association as the first edition of the *Diagnostic and Statistical Manual: Mental Disorders (DSM–I)*. It included expanded descriptions of diagnostic categories and focused on clinical, rather than statistical, use. Subsequently the development of the *DSM–II* (1968) was coordinated with that of the *ICD–8* (1969). Similarly, the *DSM–III* (1980) development was coor-

©American Association on Mental Retardation

TABLE 7.4

Similarities and Differences Between the AAMR 2002 System and the *ICF* Model of Functioning, Disability, and Health

Similarities

- Both focus on human functioning as a whole.

- *Functioning* is defined as the person-environment interaction on different levels (physiological, psychological, and social), placing both systems in the realm of ecological theory (Landesman-Ramey, Dossett, & Echols, 1996).

- Both have multiparadigmatic background (biopsychosocial).

- They have compatible process models.

- There is congruence between adaptive skill areas and Activities and Participation domains.

- They share a common approach to assessment of the functioning of the person as a whole within the context of both the person's capacities and the expectations and supportive resources of the environment.

Differences

- The *ICF* is a general model of disability, whereas the AAMR System is specific to mental retardation.

- The *ICF* reflects a professional, objective view of functioning and disability, whereas the AAMR 2002 System includes subjective aspects of functioning (e.g., personal appraisal, personal satisfaction issues, and a strong orientation toward supports).

- The *ICF* has been constructed as a result of consensus procedures involving international professional as well as consumer views on disability and functioning. In addition to field consultation, the AAMR 2002 System is more oriented toward including empirically validated views within the conceptual model of mental retardation.

Note. ICF = International Classification of Functioning, Disability, and Health (World Health Organization, 2001).

dinated with that of *ICD–9* (1977). However, *DSM–III* (1980) introduced explicit diagnostic criteria and a multiaxial classification system, features not found in *ICD–9,* with its continuing emphasis on basic health statistics. Subsequent modifications, rather than revisions, were made to both systems: *ICD–9–CM* (Medicode,

©American Association on Mental Retardation

1998) and *DSM–III–R* (1987). Coordinated development continued with *ICD–10* and *DSM–IV*. However, as noted earlier, the *ICD–10,* although initially published in 1993, has yet to be implemented in the United States. The *DSM–IV* was published in 1994 by the American Psychiatric Association and implemented shortly thereafter.

The *DSM–IV* multiaxial system comprises five domains of potential information about an individual. Axis I includes all the clinical mental disorders except for personality disorders and mental retardation, which are included on Axis II. Axis III is used for reporting general medical conditions. The coding on all three axes is consistent with *ICD–9–CM*. Axis IV is used for describing psychosocial or environmental problems that may influence the diagnosis and treatment of an individual due to the resulting stress (e.g., housing problems). A judgment of an individual's overall level of functioning is reported on Axis V. This is typically based on an assessment using the Global Assessment of Functioning (GAF) scale, which addresses psychological, social, and occupational functioning. However, this assessment should not be considered synonymous with the standardized adaptive behavior assessments used in diagnosing mental retardation.

Although the coding system is identical (see Table 7.1), the treatment of mental retardation in *DSM–IV* is significantly different from that of *ICD–9–CM* (or *ICD–10*). The most notable exception is *DSM–IV's* clear adoption of the 1992 AAMR diagnostic criteria (i.e., significantly subaverage intellectual functioning, limitations in adaptive skills, and onset prior to age 18 years). Recommendations regarding IQ cutoff scores are comparable, and the equal importance of adaptive functioning as a diagnostic criterion is emphasized. Further, the *DSM–IV* adopts the criterion of significant limitations in 2 of the 10 adaptive skill areas introduced in the 1992 AAMR System.

A major distinction between the *DSM–IV* and the 1992 AAMR System is the retention in *DSM–IV* of a severity classification based on IQ ranges. Actually, this particular classification dates back to the fifth edition of an AAMR manual on terminology and classification (Heber, 1959). The IQ ranges and accompanying descriptions or labels (mild, moderate, severe, and profound) are based on standard deviation ranges (from 2 to 5+) below the theoretical average IQ score of 100. An unspecified category (Code 319) is also included in the *DSM–IV* (and *ICD–9–CM*) for those instances in which mental retardation is presumed but a valid intellectual assessment cannot be achieved (e.g., because of uncooperativeness). The extent to which this latter category should be used for individuals simply because they are significantly impaired and cannot be successfully tested by standard intelligence tests is an area of debate within the field.

The *DSM–IV* provides a discussion of issues involved in making a diagnosis of mental retardation as well as relevant clinical information. The issues of IQ cutoff scores, measurement error, adaptive functioning, and marked variations in areas of ability are raised as considerations. The descriptions of functional expectations for

©American Association on Mental Retardation

individuals at various severity (IQ) levels include developmental information and prevalence estimates. The terminology and labels used are more current than in the case of the *ICD*. A listing of the most common associated mental disorders (coded on Axis I) is provided, as is a summary of major etiological factors.

The point is made that an exclusion criterion does not apply to a diagnosis of mental retardation; that is, the diagnosis should be made if the basic three criteria are met, regardless of and in addition to the identification of other disorders. Thus having a diagnosis of a pervasive developmental disorder such as autism would not preclude a diagnosis of mental retardation as well.

DEVELOPMENTAL DISABILITIES DEFINITION

Although the category of developmental disabilities is broader than that of mental retardation, it is of particular relevance because many people with mental retardation fit within it. Further, many state mental retardation service systems have expanded their eligibility criteria to include this larger group.

The original federal definition of this category was only slightly broader than mental retardation. The definition in the Developmental Disabilities Services and Facilities Construction Act of 1970 (Pub. L. 91–517) was that:

> The term developmental disability means a disability attributable to mental retardation, cerebral palsy, epilepsy or another neurological condition of an individual found by the Secretary to be closely related to mental retardation or to require treatment similar to that required for mentally retarded individuals, which disability originates before such individual attains age 18, which has continued or can be expected to continue indefinitely, and which constitutes a substantial handicap to such individual. (p. 1325)

A 1975 amendment (Developmentally Disabled Assistance and Bill of Rights Act, Pub. L. 94–103) added autism as a qualifying condition. However, there was growing dissatisfaction because the definition excluded many individuals whose disabilities were similar but were associated with some other etiology. An expanded noncategorical and functionally based definition was adopted in 1978 (Rehabilitative, Comprehensive Services, and Developmental Disabilities Amendments, Pub. L. 95–602). With only slight changes, the revised definition is still in effect. According to the Developmental Disabilities Assistance and Bill of Rights Act of 2000 (DD Act; Pub. L. 106–402),

> The term 'developmental disability' means a severe, chronic disability of an individual 5 years of age or older that —
>
> (A) is attributable to a mental or physical impairment or a combination of mental and physical impairments;
>
> (B) is manifested before the individual attains age 22;

©American Association on Mental Retardation

(C) is likely to continue indefinitely;

(D) results in substantial functional limitations in three or more of the following areas of major life activity: (i) self care, (ii) receptive and expressive language, (iii) learning, (iv) mobility, (v) self-direction, (vi) capacity for independent learning, and (vii) economic self-sufficiency; and

(E) reflects the individual's need for a combination and sequence of special, interdisciplinary, or generic services, individualized supports, or other forms of assistance that are of lifelong or extended duration and are individually planned and coordinated. (§ 102(8)(A))

The major differences between the AAMR definition of mental retardation and the governmental definition for developmental disabilities are the later age of onset criterion and absence of reference to IQ for developmental disabilities. One might assume considerable overlap in the AAMR's criterion of limitations in adaptive skills and the DD Act (2000) functional limitations of major life activities.

However, several groups (including the Arc of the U.S.) have taken a stand in opposition to adoption of the developmental disability criteria in place of current mental retardation criteria for program and funding eligibility. The expressed concern is that most individuals with mental retardation (approximately one half) would no longer be eligible for services because they would not meet the functional limitation criterion in the developmental disabilities (DD) definition (Larson et al., 2001). Lubin, Jacobson, and Kiely (1982) reported that only 78.8% of individuals receiving mental retardation services in New York State would qualify under the DD definition. Further, only 41.5% of those classified with mild mental retardation would qualify.

The state of Ohio recently revised their eligibility criteria, widening from mental retardation to the broader developmental disability group (except for people with a sole diagnosis of mental illness). They developed objective criteria for what constitutes a substantial functional limitation in the seven areas of major life activity. In a report of the results of this process, Reardon and Hitzing (1994) observed that 90% of the adults with mental retardation who applied for services were deemed eligible as compared to 81% of the adults with other developmental disabilities. The corresponding figures for children were 88% and 77%, respectively. With regard to level of retardation, the findings were that all applicants with severe or profound mental retardation were deemed eligible. Some individuals with moderate mental retardation were determined ineligible (3% of the adults and 6% of the children). In the case of those with a sole diagnosis of mild mental retardation (i.e., no other type of developmental disability present), 23% of the adults and 38% of the children did not meet the objective Ohio DD criteria. Overall, 86% of the adult applicants and 84% of the children, regardless of type of disability, were determined eligible.

©American Association on Mental Retardation

The findings of the New York and Ohio studies do suggest that some individuals with mental retardation, especially in the mild range, would not be determined eligible for services if the DD criteria were adopted. However, the Ohio study indicates that the impact might be even larger for types of disabilities other than mental retardation. The Ohio study also made use of assessment instruments that are more objective than is typically the case when a determination of the existence of a developmental disability is being made. Seltzer (1983) observed that the operational clarity of the DD definition is weak, especially regarding measurement of the functional limitation areas. This results in reliability and validity problems when clinicians have to make judgments without clear guidelines.

Thus there is a direct relevance and applicability of the DD definition for people with mental retardation in those states where the eligible population has been expanded to include the broader developmental disability group. Further, Medicaid regulations affecting the intermediate care facilities for the mentally retarded (ICF-MRs) and related Waiver (home and community-based services) programs have adopted a variant of the DD definition for eligibility purposes. An applicant may qualify for these programs on the basis of a diagnosis of mental retardation or because of the existence of a "related condition." As defined in the Code of Federal Regulations (CFR), *related condition* is

a severe and chronic disability that:

(A) is attributable to:

    (i) cerebral palsy or epilepsy; or

    (ii) any other condition, other than mental illness, found to be closely related to mental retardation because the condition results in impairment of general intellectual functioning or adaptive behavior similar to that of persons with mental retardation, and requires treatment or services similar to those required for those persons with mental retardation;

(B) is manifested before the person reaches age 22; and

(C) is likely to continue indefinitely; and

(D) results in substantial functional limitation in three or more of the following areas of major life activity:

    (i) self-care;

    (ii) understanding and use of language

    (iii) learning;

    (iv) mobility;

    (v) self-direction; and

    (vi) capacity for independent living. (Title 42, § 435.1009)

© American Association on Mental Retardation

Rather than being primarily functional-based, as the DD Act (1994) definition has evolved, the above definition emphasizes the necessity of having an identifiable impairment or medical condition, In fact, state Medicaid plans usually have a listing of qualifying medical conditions (*ICD–9–CM* codes). Second, this definition specifically excludes mental illness as a sole qualifying condition. Third, here there is an emphasis on any of the other conditions impacting the individual in a way similar to mental retardation. Fourth, the seventh DD Act (1994) criterion, economic self-sufficiency, is deleted. The reasoning is that a person is unlikely to be economically self-sufficient and yet remain eligible for Medicaid funding.

SOCIAL SECURITY

The Social Security Administration (SSA) has two separate income support programs for people with disabilities. The first, Social Security Disability Insurance (SSDI), is normally used as income support for workers who become disabled after having worked and paid FICA taxes for at least 10 years. Further, unmarried dependent children of such workers who have a qualifying disability that began before age 22 are also eligible as long as the child continues to have a disability. Health-care coverage for SSDI recipients is provided by Medicare. The second program, Supplemental Security Income (SSI), provides income support for people with limited income and resources. However, even middle-income families may be eligible for SSI benefits for a child who has disabilities by use of a deemed income formula that considers income, number of children, children with disabilities, and other factors. Health-care coverage for SSI recipients is provided by Medicaid.

For Social Security purposes, *disability* is defined as (Social Security Administration, 2001):

> the inability to engage in any substantial gainful activity by reason of any medically determinable physical or mental impairment(s) which can be expected to result in death or which has lasted or can be expected to last for a continuous period of not less than 12 months. (p. 29)

State agencies (Disability Determination Services [DDS]) make the decisions regarding presence of a disability for SSA.

The SSA regulations contain a Listing of Impairments that includes examples of common impairments that may qualify as a disability. However, a diagnosis alone is not sufficient. There must be evidence that the impairment is severe enough to prevent the person from accomplishing substantial gainful activity or, in the case of a child, causing severe functional limitations. *Substantial* is further defined as work activity involving significant physical or mental duties and that is productive. *Gainful activity* is further defined as work generally performed for pay or profit, full or part time.

In making disability determinations, a DDS team (physician and disability ex-

118   ©American Association on Mental Retardation

aminer) reviews the application and conducts what is called a Sequential Evaluation Process. For adults (ages 18 and above), the first step is to determine whether the person is currently performing *substantial gainful activity* (generally defined as earnings over a set amount: $700 monthly in 2001). If the person is not engaged in substantial gainful activity, the second step is to determine whether a severe physical or mental impairment exists (i.e., one that limits ability to do basic work activities). Examples of these activities include lifting, speaking, following instructions, using judgment, and adjusting to changes. If the person meets the severe impairment criterion, the third step is to determine whether there is an impairment or condition found on the SSA Listing of Impairments (mental retardation being one such impairment). In some instances, unlisted impairments may be judged sufficiently severe to also warrant a disability determination.

For children, the substantial gainful activity criterion is also applied as the first step. The second step of determining the existence of a severe impairment, however, focuses on identification of more than a minimal functional limitation in self-care, school performance, or relations with peers and family members. If there is a severe impairment in functioning and an accompanying diagnosis or impairment on the Listing of Impairments, a disability determination will usually be made.

These Social Security eligibility criteria could be met for many individuals with mental retardation. For others, however, financial status or lack of severe functional limitations may lead to an ineligible determination.

MEDICAID (ICF-MR AND WAIVERS)

Similar to Social Security disability determinations, Medicaid eligibility, especially for the ICF-MR and related Waiver programs, is subject to financial eligibility criteria and existence of functional limitations and need for services. Nationally, these specific Medicaid programs provide the majority of funding for services to people with mental retardation and some other disability groups. The financial eligibility criteria will not be addressed here, but they are similar to those for Social Security.

The eligibility criteria relating to functional limitations are specified in the Medicaid State Plans submitted for approval by each state to the federal Center for Medicare and Medicaid Services (CMS), formerly the Health Care Financing Administration (HCFA). The Medicaid program for ICF-MR and related Waivers is restricted to individuals with mental retardation or related conditions (as described earlier in the section "Developmental Disabilities"). Although the state plans and other state regulations generally adopt a definition of mental retardation consistent with that of the AAMR, there is considerable variability across states in actual IQ cutoff scores, role of adaptive behavior, and the operational definitions of related conditions.

As in all Medicaid programs, a determination of "medical necessity" is an important element in eligibility. Eligibility for the ICF-MR or a related Waiver program requires that a physician certify that (a) the medical regimen of the individual needs to be under the supervision of a medical doctor; (b) the health status of the individual will not prevent participation in the active treatment that is part of the ICF-MR program; (c) the individual has mental retardation and/or a related condition; and (d) the individual requires ICF-MR care. The Medicaid Waiver referenced here is actually a "waiver" of ICF-MR services; that is, the physician certifies that ICF-MR (i.e., institutional) services will be necessary unless the individual receives the community-based Waiver services. Most individuals with appropriately diagnosed mental retardation, and many with qualifying related conditions, are likely to be determined eligible for these Medicaid programs if there is a documented need for the services and the financial criteria are met.

STATE MENTAL RETARDATION PROGRAMS AND FUNDING CLASSIFICATIONS

Although most states have attempted to maximize the use of federal Medicaid funds for mental retardation programs, the required state funding match imposes some limits on the degree of expansion. Further, some individuals require very specific or limited services. For these, state-only general revenue funding may be used rather than Medicaid. In other cases, Medicaid funding for an individual might be restricted to purely medical services (as a result of SSI or SSDI eligibility). Some states have also restricted state funding to the population with mental retardation rather than to the broader developmental disabilities group.

In an effort to better manage both state general revenue and federal Medicaid expenditures, many states have been attempting to develop classification systems that can be used objectively and fairly to allocate resources. Such funding classifications are not entirely new. For example, in the early 1970s when the ICF–MR program was first beginning, many states established reimbursement levels differing by "level of care." *Level of care* was often defined by IQ categories (mild through profound) and similar adaptive behavior level categories (I through IV) (Grossman, 1973), with greater funding available to those with lower levels of functioning.

More recent approaches still rely heavily on the assumption that those individuals with more extensive functional limitations will require greater support resources. However, the explicit influences of special medical needs and challenging behaviors are specifically being incorporated into the funding classifications. Further, type of residential setting and availability of natural, unpaid supports are being recognized as key factors.

One particular adaptive behavior instrument, the Inventory for Client and Agency Planning (ICAP) (Bruininks, Hill, Weatherman, & Woodcock, 1986), has been adopted by a number of states for funding classification purposes. The ICAP includes a unique measure called the Service Level. It is an index of the degree of

©American Association on Mental Retardation

supervision likely to be needed by an individual based on adaptive skill limitations and challenging behaviors. Descriptive categories are as follows: (a) total personal care and intense supervision, (b) extensive personal care and/or constant supervision, (c) regular personal care and/or close supervision, (d) limited personal care and/or regular supervision, and (e) infrequent or no assistance for daily living. Some research evidence (Campbell & Heal, 1995) indicates that ICAP measures are good predictors of service costs. Other similar measures being used for funding classification include New York's Developmental Disabilities Profile (Brown et al., 1986) and the North Carolina Support Needs Assessment Profile (Hennike, Myers, Realon, & Thompson (1999). Another such instrument, the Supports Intensity Scale, is under development by an AAMR Ad Hoc Committee (see Thompson et al., in press).

The critical importance of this type of classification will likely generate much more research on the most important variables predicting service and support costs and the most effective and efficient means of measuring these variables. A functional classification system will be a logical product.

SUMMARY

In this chapter we have summarized the major classification systems, besides AAMR's, with which researchers, clinicians, program administrators, or advocates in the area of mental retardation should be familiar. The purposes of any classification system, including, for example, meaningful organization, consistency, communication, generalizability, predictability, consistency with a desired theoretical framework, and contribution to positive portrayal, should guide the use of these systems.

The *ICD* System is the one in most widespread use and is essential for many eligibility and funding uses. Although its classification system for mental retardation has some limitations, it is the primary source for etiological classification, especially of a biological nature. The *ICF* broadens the classification perspective of the *ICD* and is likely to become of increasing interest in the field of mental retardation. The *DSM* is intended to accompany the *ICD* and expands the classification of mental disorders. Its treatment of mental retardation is generally consistent with AAMR's. Social Security and Medicaid eligibility criteria are key to income support and program funding for people with mental retardation and related conditions. Finally, sophisticated funding classification systems based on individual characteristics and settings will likely be a major new area of development in the field.

©American Association on Mental Retardation

CHAPTER 8
ETIOLOGY AND PREVENTION

Etiology is a multifactorial construct composed of four categories of risk factors (biomedical, social, behavioral, and educational) that interact across time, including across the life of the individual and across generations from parent to child. The intent of this approach to etiology is to describe all of the risk factors that contribute to the individual's present functioning. This then allows providers to identify strategies for supporting the individual and family so that these risk factors might be prevented or ameliorated through primary, secondary, or tertiary strategies.

OVERVIEW

In this chapter we describes the multifactorial nature of the etiology of mental retardation and present a new approach to classification of etiology based on biomedical, social, behavioral, and educational risk factors. Also discussed is the diagnostic assessment process, which incorporates new research advances and research about behaviors that are associated with specific etiologies. The role of prevention is then reconceptualized to form a linkage among etiology, prevention, and support.

IMPORTANCE OF ETIOLOGY

Consideration of the etiology of mental retardation is an important aspect of diagnosis and classification for several reasons:

1. The etiology may be associated with other health-related problems that may influence physical and psychological functioning.

2. The etiology may be treatable, which could permit appropriate intervention to minimize or prevent mental retardation.

3. Accurate information is needed for the design and evaluation of programs to prevent specific etiologies of mental retardation.

4. Comparison of individuals for research, administrative, or clinical purposes may depend on formation of maximally homogeneous groups composed of individuals with the same or similar etiologies.

5. The etiology may be associated with a specific behavioral phenotype that allows anticipation of actual, potential, or future functional support needs.

6. Identification about the etiology facilitates genetic counseling and promotes family choice and decision making, including preconception counseling.

7. Individuals and families can be referred to other people and families with the same etiologic diagnosis for desired information and support.

8. Knowing the etiology facilitates self-knowledge and life planning for the individual.

9. When adults in crisis present to service providers, understanding the condition's etiology may clarify clinical issues.

10. Clarification of social, behavioral, and educational risk factors that contribute to the etiology of mental retardation offers opportunities for prevention of disability.

Performing a diagnostic evaluation to determine the etiology of mental retardation may be questioned by some providers. They may argue that the cost of testing is excessive and that the results will not change the individual's treatment. If the parents do not plan to have any more children, they may argue that testing for an inherited disorder is pointless. When the individual with mental retardation is an adult, the parents may no longer have any interest in finding the etiology. Adult service providers may feel that the etiology is irrelevant to development of the individual's plan of supports and services. These objections can be answered by considering the just listed reasons for establishing the etiology, and the cost of diagnostic testing can often be justified in specific situations. For example, knowing that an adult with cognitive decline has Down syndrome should alert the provider to look for hypothyroidism or depression. Knowing that a child with cognitive decline has Angelman syndrome should alert the provider to look for subclinical seizures. Knowing that an individual with new neurological findings has tuberous sclerosis should alert the provider to look for the characteristic brain tumor associated with this diagnosis. Knowing that an adult man has fragile X syndrome should alert the provider to offer genetic testing to the man's sisters who may be carriers and could have affected sons. Knowing that a child has a particular condition allows the family to search the Internet and to contact other families affected by this diagnosis, thereby learning more about it than their health care provider may know. These examples illustrate why testing to establish the etiologic diagnosis may be important for many individuals with mental retardation.

©American Association on Mental Retardation

In some situations, an etiology cannot be determined at the present time. It is important to remember that an inability to determine an etiology does not necessarily mean that there is no etiology. Similarly, an inability to determine an etiology does not necessarily mean there is no mental retardation.

MULTIFACTORIAL NATURE OF ETIOLOGY

This chapter builds on the approach to etiology described in the 1992 American Association on Mental Retardation (AAMR) manual (Luckasson et al.). In that manual, etiology was conceptualized as a multifactorial construct composed of four categories of risk factors (biomedical, social, behavioral, and educational) that interact across time, including across the life of the individual and across generations from parent to child. This construct replaced prior historical approaches that had divided the etiology of mental retardation into two broad types: mental retardation of biological origin and mental retardation due to psychosocial disadvantage (Grossman, 1983). McLaren and Bryson (1987) had noted in their review of epidemiological studies of mental retardation that as much as 50% of the population of individuals with mental retardation have more than one causal risk factor. Furthermore, mental retardation often reflects the cumulative or interactive effects of more than one risk factor. Similarly, Scott (1988) observed that from a public health perspective, the data do not support separating the etiology of mental retardation into biological and psychosocial categories. He proposed a multiple risk-factor approach that would include factors from both categories that may interact to cause mental retardation. Thus the historical distinction between biological and psychosocial types may be blurred in many cases (Rowitz, 1986). The Institute of Medicine of the National Academy of Sciences also noted that multiple risk factors converge to predispose an individual to the disabling process and that risk factors interact at different stages of the disabling process (Institute of Medicine, 1991).

The two-group approach (biological and cultural-familial) has been defended on the basis of developmental theory (Hodapp, Burack, & Zigler, 1990). Different developmental pathways have been associated with mental retardation of biological origin (due to identified biological disorders) compared to those with mental retardation for which no organic etiology is apparent (due to cultural-familial factors or psychosocial disadvantage). The former group tends to have lower IQ scores compared to the latter. The latter group comprises much of what has been termed *mild mental retardation.* Hodapp et al. recommended a biological or genetic classification of etiology, in which there is either a demonstrated biological cause or there is not. This approach is not inconsistent with the risk-factor model described here. In fact, the risk-factor approach can be seen as a fine tuning of the developmental (two-group) approach. Mental retardation of biological origin can be seen as involving individuals for whom biomedical risk factors predominate, whereas mental

©American Association on Mental Retardation

retardation of cultural-familial origin can be seen as involving individuals for whom social, behavioral, or educational risk factors predominate. The two-group distinction is often blurred in real life, however. The multiple-risk-factor model correctly reflects that biomedical risk factors may be present in people with mild mental retardation of cultural-familial origin, and social, behavioral, and educational risk factors may be present in people with severe mental retardation of biological origin. For example, individuals with the same biomedical etiology (e.g., Down syndrome) often vary widely in functioning, presumably as the result of other modifying risk factors. The multiple-risk-factor model for the etiology of mental retardation shown in Table 8.1 appears to be a more comprehensive explanation of the many interacting causes of impaired functioning in people with mental retardation.

The multifactorial approach to etiology expands the list of causal factors in two directions: types of factors and timing of factors. The first direction expands the types or categories of factors into four groupings:

- biomedical: factors that relate to biologic processes, such as genetic disorders or nutrition;

- social: factors that relate to social and family interaction, such as stimulation and adult responsiveness;

- behavioral: factors that relate to potentially causal behaviors, such as dangerous (injurious) activities or maternal substance abuse;

- educational: factors that relate to the availability of educational supports that promote mental development and the development of adaptive skills.

Table 8.1 lists risk factors for mental retardation by category and by time of occurrence of the risk factor in the life of the individual with mental retardation. This table represents a new approach to classification of etiology. Unlike classification systems based primarily on biomedical conditions (e.g., the World Health Organization's *International Classification of Diseases*), the classification system outlined in Table 8.1 explicitly adopts a multifactorial approach to etiology of mental retardation. It incorporates biomedical risk factors but places them in context by including other risk factors that may be of equal or greater importance in determining the individual's level of functioning.

Mental retardation is a disability characterized by impaired functioning. The cause of mental retardation is whatever causes this impairment in functioning. A biomedical risk factor may be present, but by itself it does not cause mental retardation. Any risk factor causes mental retardation only when it results in impaired functioning sufficient to meet the criteria for diagnosis described in chapters 4 and 5. Table 8.1 emphasizes that the impairment of functioning that is present when an individual meets the criteria for a diagnosis of mental retardation usually reflects the presence of several risk factors that interact over time. Thus the search for the

126

©American Association on Mental Retardation

TABLE 8.1
Risk Factors for Mental Retardation

Timing	Biomedical	Social	Behavioral	Educational
Prenatal	1. Chromosomal disorders 2. Single-gene disorders 3. Syndromes 4. Metabolic disorders 5. Cerebral dysgenesis 6. Maternal illnesses 7. Parental age	1. Poverty 2. Maternal malnutrition 3. Domestic violence 4. Lack of access to prenatal care	1. Parental drug use 2. Parental alcohol use 3. Parental smoking 4. Parental immaturity	1. Parental cognitive disability without supports 2. Lack of preparation for parenthood
Perinatal	1. Prematurity 2. Birth injury 3. Neonatal disorders	1. Lack of access to birth care	1. Parental rejection of caretaking 2. Parental abandonment of child	1. Lack of medical referral for intervention services at discharge
Postnatal	1. Traumatic brain injury 2. Malnutrition 3. Meningoencephalitis 4. Seizure disorders 5. Degenerative disorders	1. Impaired child-caregiver 2. Lack of adequate stimulation 3. Family poverty 4. Chronic illness in the family 5. Institutionalization	1. Child abuse and neglect 2. Domestic violence 3. Inadequate safety measures 4. Social deprivation 5. Difficult child behaviors	1. Impaired parenting 2. Delayed diagnosis 3. Inadequate early intervention services 4. Inadequate special-educational services 5. Inadequate family support

©American Association on Mental Retardation

etiology of mental retardation in a particular individual must consist of a search for all of the risk factors that may result in impaired functioning for that individual.

The second direction describes the timing of the occurrence of causal factors according to whether these factors affect the parents of the person with mental retardation, the person with mental retardation, or both. This aspect of causation is termed *intergenerational* to describe the influence of factors present during one generation on the outcome in the next generation. This concept of intergenerational effects must be distinguished from the historical pseudoscientific concept that mental retardation due to psychosocial, cultural, or familial factors was due to weak genes in the family (Scheerenberger, 1983). That idea was related to the now discredited eugenics movement that sought to sterilize individuals with mental retardation to prevent their reproduction. The modern concept recognizes that reversible environmental factors in the lives of some families may be related to the etiology of mental retardation. Current ideas about intergenerational effects stress their origin in preventable and reversible influences of adverse environments and how understanding these effects should lead to enhanced individual and family supports. Table 8.2 diagrams these intergenerational effects and their linkage to efforts at prevention. The link between etiology and prevention is discussed in more detail later in this chapter.

ETIOLOGIC DIAGNOSIS

MEDICAL HISTORY

Diagnostic assessment begins with a complete history and physical examination to uncover all of the potential risk factors that may be present in each of the four categories shown in Table 8.1. The medical history begins at conception and includes detailed information about the prenatal, perinatal, and postnatal periods. Information needed about the *prenatal period* includes maternal age, parity, and health (including maternal infections such as hepatitis, HIV, rubella, cytomegalovirus, group B streptococcus, etc.); the adequacy of maternal nutrition; the amount and quality of prenatal care (including results of prenatal screening, ultrasound examinations, and amniocentesis if performed); maternal use of drugs, alcohol, and other substances; maternal exposure to potential toxins or teratogens (e.g., lead or radiation); and occurrence of any significant maternal injuries during the pregnancy. Information needed about the *perinatal period* includes growth status at birth (gestational age at birth, birth weight, length, and head circumference); labor and delivery experiences (including onset, duration, route of delivery, presence of fetal distress prior to delivery, Apgar scores after birth, need for resuscitation); and the occurrence of any neonatal disorders after birth (e.g., seizures, infections, respiratory distress, brain hemorrhage, and metabolic disorders). Information needed about the

©American Association on Mental Retardation

TABLE 8.2
Risk Factors and Prevention Activities for Different Recipients of Service:
A Multifactorial and Intergenerational Model of Mental Retardation Etiology and Prevention

RISK FACTOR CATEGORY	PRIMARY PREVENTION ACTIVITIES			PRIMARY AND SECONDARY PREVENTION ACTIVITIES		TERTIARY PREVENTION ACTIVITIES
	Child	Teenager	Parent-to-be	Newborn	Child	Adult
BIO-MEDICAL	Lead screening Nutrition	Nutrition	Prenatal care and screening Nutrition	Metabolic screening	Nutrition Lead screening	Physical and mental health care Prevention of obesity
SOCIAL	Prevention of domestic violence	Family support	Emotional and social support	Promotion of parent-child interaction	Family support Avoidance of abuse	Community inclusion
BEHAVIORAL	Acceptance	Mature self-care	Avoidance of substance abuse (or treatment of substance abuse)	Parental acceptance of child	Avoidance of accidents and injuries	Exercise and fitness Leisure activities
EDUCATIONAL	Social skills	Sexuality	Parenting	Referral of at-risk newborn for services	Early intervention Special education	Employment

©American Association on Mental Retardation

postnatal period includes the history of any significant head injuries, infections, seizures, and toxic and metabolic disorders (e.g., lead poisoning, significant malnutrition or growth impairment), and any indication of loss of previously acquired developmental skills, which could indicate the presence of a progressive or degenerative disorder.

A detailed family history is necessary to identify potential genetic etiologies (Curry et al., 1997). A detailed three-generation pedigree is recommended that includes information about the health status, medical and psychological disorders, and level of functioning of all known relatives. In particular, relatives who were affected by conditions that may be associated with mental retardation (e.g., autism) or who were diagnosed with mental retardation should be noted. Additional records concerning these individuals may be requested to provide further details. The occurrence of mental retardation in other family members does not necessarily imply a genetic mechanism, however. Multiple individuals in a family may be affected by fetal alcohol syndrome, for example, or mental retardation in a relative may be due to childhood infections or head trauma. Results of genetic testing performed previously on any relatives should be sought and examined for completeness because testing performed more than 5 to 10 years earlier may have missed conditions diagnosable with current methods.

PSYCHOLOGICAL EVALUATION

The psychosocial evaluation includes detailed information about the individual, family, school or work setting, and community or cultural milieu. Information about the psychosocial environment is needed to evaluate possible social, behavioral, and educational risk factors that may have contributed to the occurrence of mental retardation. When an intergenerational perspective is used, information is needed about the parents' social, educational, and psychological history. Information is also needed about the structure, stability, and functioning of the immediate and extended family of the person with mental retardation. Information about the roles and expectations of the person with mental retardation and relatives within the extended community or culture may also be useful. The sociocultural milieu in which the individual develops is important because it may influence the psychosocial environment, including the local community; the country of origin; and specific ethnic, cultural, or religious factors that may affect environmental experiences and interactions.

The developmental history of the individual with mental retardation includes early milestones, such as the age when the person started walking or talking. The age at entry into the educational system, the adequacy of the educational experience, and the duration of formal education should also be noted. The occurrence of other mental disorders, such as attention deficit hyperactivity disorder, specific learning disability, or anxiety disorder, should be noted, because this may provide

©American Association on Mental Retardation

clues to a behavioral phenotype associated with a specific etiology.

Evaluation of the psychosocial environment may not yield any relevant information about causal factors in a particular individual. Even when the etiology appears straightforward, however, psychosocial factors may prove to be contributory. Reflecting the multiple-risk-factor model of causation, known biomedical factors may be affected by social, behavioral, or educational factors. The ultimate etiology of mental retardation in such cases reflects the interaction of all of these factors. For example, whether or not an individual with fetal alcohol syndrome develops mental retardation may be influenced by environmental influences in early childhood, and the individual's level of functioning will likely reflect the adequacy of educational interventions.

PHYSICAL EXAMINATION

The physical examination serves several distinct purposes. The usual purpose is to assist in the diagnosis of a medical problem, such as pneumonia or back pain, for which the individual has sought attention and that may require specific medical treatment. The purpose considered in this chapter is to assist in the identification of the etiology of mental retardation. A single physical examination may serve both purposes, but the conceptual distinction between them needs to be retained.

The physical examination may provide evidence of an obvious etiology, such as Down syndrome. More often, however, it will provide only supportive evidence for an etiology suspected from other data (e.g., spastic diplegia associated with a history of premature birth), or it will not provide any useful information about etiology at all. For most individuals whose etiology of mental retardation is obscure or unknown, the physical examination may well be normal or noncontributory. Thus one cannot expect to discover the etiology solely from the physical examination in most cases. Physical examination is necessary, but it is only one component in the diagnostic assessment and, in many cases, will not be the most important component.

Information needed from the physical examination includes measurements of growth (height, weight, and head circumference), which should be plotted against age on graphs that are appropriate for the individual's status. Additional measurement of specific body structures (e.g., the distance between the eyes or the arm span) also may be useful (Jones, 1997). Detailed examination of the head, eyes, ears, nose, throat, glands, heart, blood vessels, lungs, abdomen, genitalia, spine, extremities, and skin should be conducted. Any major or minor malformations should be noted (Jones, 1997). A detailed neurologic examination should include evaluation for any focal or generalized deficits (Haerer, 1992; Paine & Oppe, 1966). Specific neurologic findings will rarely indicate the etiology directly but certain findings (e.g., hypotonia, tremor, or ataxia) could be important clues to the etiology. In some instances, examination of parents, siblings, or other relatives may be helpful.

All of the data derived from the history and physical examination is then evaluated to determine whether additional laboratory testing is indicated. Table 8.3 provides a guide to evaluation of these data (Luckasson et al., 1992). In some cases the diagnosis may be fairly obvious, as, for example, when the child meets all of the clinical criteria for fetal alcohol syndrome. In most cases however, the available data are sufficient only to provide clues or ideas about the etiology that warrant further investigation. When the etiology is not obvious, it is often helpful to list the most likely possibilities. This list, which is often referred to as the differential diagnosis of the problem, can be considered as a series of hypotheses regarding possible etiologies. For example, the clinical finding of microcephaly (i.e., small head) may suggest several hypotheses, such as cerebral malformation or birth injury. Clinicians can then identify a strategy for testing each hypothesis to increase or decrease the probability of it being correct. In the example of microcephaly, a hypothesis of cerebral malformation might be tested by looking for other malformations, performing neuroimaging (i.e., CT or MRI scanning of the brain), or pursuing genetic testing for a chromosome disorder. A hypothesis of birth injury might be tested by examining birth records and determining whether the head circumference was normal at birth. This example is not intended to be a complete analysis of the possible causes of microcephaly. It is described here only to illustrate the process of generating and testing hypotheses regarding possible etiologies.

The purpose of evaluating several competing hypotheses is to optimize the probability of making the correct diagnosis. In some cases, the evaluation of these hypotheses will consist of obtaining additional historical information or more extensive physical examination. In many cases, however, the evaluation will necessitate the performance of properly selected laboratory tests and procedures. Table 8.3 suggests some laboratory tests and procedures that might be helpful in evaluating the hypotheses listed in the table. This table should not be considered complete or prescriptive, because the evaluation must be tailored to the facts in an individual case. The clinician is responsible for identifying the appropriate hypotheses, devising strategies for testing them, and evaluating the results of whatever tests and procedures are performed.

The American College of Medical Genetics has published recommendations for the etiologic evaluation of a person with mental retardation (Curry et al., 1997). These guidelines are generally valid but need to be updated in light of subsequent research, especially regarding the availability of DNA testing for microdeletion syndromes and for specific disorders (e.g., Rett syndrome) whose gene abnormality has been identified more recently. Computerized databases exist that provide a list of possible etiologies when all of the available clinical data for a particular individual are entered. These databases are updated continually and are generally used by clinical geneticists. Indeed, the pace of genetic research is such that any guidelines will be outdated by the time they are published, and referral to a clinical geneticist is

©American Association on Mental Retardation

TABLE 8.3
Hypotheses and Strategies for Assessing Etiologic Risk Factors

Onset	Hypothesis	Possible Strategies
Prenatal	Chromosomal disorder	1. Extended physical examination 2. Referral to clinical geneticist 3. Chromosomal and DNA analysis
	Syndrome disorder	1. Extended family history and examination of relatives 2. Extended physical examination 3. Referral to clinical geneticist
	Inborn error of metabolism	1. Newborn screening using tandem mass spectrometry 2. Analysis of amino acids in blood, urine, and/or cerebrospinal fluid 3. Analysis of organic acids in urine 4. Blood levels of lactate, pyruvate, very long chain fatty acids, free and total carnitine and acylcarnitines 5. Arterial ammonia and gases 6. Assays of specific enzymes in cultured skin fibroblasts 7. Biopsies of specific tissue for light and electron microscopy and biochemical analysis
	Cerebral dysgenesis	1. Neuroimaging (CT or MRI)
	Social, behavioral, and environmental risk factors	1. Intrauterine and postnatal growth 2. Placental pathology 3. Detailed social history of parents 4. Medical history and examination of mother 5. Toxicological screening of mother at prenatal visits and of child at birth 6. Referral to clinical geneticist
Perinatal	Intrapartum and neonatal disorders	1. Review of maternal records (prenatal care, labor, and delivery) 2. Review of birth and neonatal records

(table continues)

©American Association on Mental Retardation

TABLE 8.3 *(continued)*

Onset	Hypothesis	Possible Strategies
Postnatal	Head injury	1. Detailed medical history 2. Skull X-rays and neuroimaging
	Brain infection	1. Detailed medical history 2. Cerebrospinal fluid analysis
	Demyelinating disorders	1. Neuroimaging 2. Cerebrospinal fluid analysis
	Degenerative disorders	1. Neuroimaging 2. Specific DNA studies for genetic disorders 3. Assays of specific enzymes in blood or cultured skin fibroblasts 4. Biopsies of specific tissue for light and electron microscopy and biochemical analysis 5. Referral to clinical geneticist or neurologist
	Seizure disorders	1. Electroencephalography 2. Referral to clinical neurologist
	Toxic-metabolic disorders	1. See "Inborn error of metabolism" in Prenatal category 2. Toxicological studies 3. Lead and heavy metal assays
	Malnutrition	1. Body measurements 2. Detailed nutritional history 3. Family history of nutrition
	Environmental and social disadvantage	1. Detailed social history 2. History of abuse or neglect 3. Psychological evaluation 4. Observation in new environment
	Educational inadequacy	1. Early referral and intervention records 2. Review of educational records

©American Association on Mental Retardation

often the best way to ensure an up-to-date evaluation of genetic etiologies.

Mental retardation begins before age 18, but individuals with mental retardation may first present a need for services during adulthood. If the diagnosis of mental retardation was not made previously, it may be difficult to gather all of the relevant information needed to make the diagnosis in an adult. This is also true for assessment of the etiology of mental retardation in such cases. Much of the information described earlier, such as details of the pregnancy, birth history, early developmental milestones, and family functioning during childhood, as well as details of the family history or pedigree, may simply be unavailable. Similar problems often arise when individuals present in need of services following immigration from another country. The physical examination becomes more important as the clinician looks for clues about the etiology. The list of possible hypotheses or differential diagnosis becomes longer and more tentative when the available data are limited. Laboratory tests and procedures are often needed to examine these hypotheses. In the end many risk factors may be more suspected than confirmed, and a degree of uncertainty or imprecision about the etiologic diagnosis may be expected.

FORMULATION OF THE ETIOLOGIC DIAGNOSIS

This formulation of the etiologic diagnosis follows from the multifactorial model shown in Table 8.1. For each category (biomedical, social, behavioral, and educational), all relevant risk factors should be identified and listed. In addition, the presence of interactions among risk factors should be noted (Coulter, 1996). An example of how to do this for a specific individual is as follows:

- Biomedical risk factors might include the presence of fetal alcohol syndrome with congenital heart disease.

- Social risk factors might include family poverty, homelessness, and inadequate parenting skills.

- Behavioral risk factors might include parental substance abuse and abuse or neglect of the child with mental retardation.

- Educational risk factors might include lack of adequate early intervention services.

- Interactions between risk factors might include (a) maternal poverty and substance abuse, causing lack of prenatal care and fetal alcohol syndrome, and (b) homelessness, causing lack of adequate early intervention services.

The intent of this multifactorial approach to etiology is to describe all of the risk factors that contribute to the individual's present functioning. This then allows providers to identify strategies for supporting the individual and the family so that these risk factors might be prevented or ameliorated.

ETIOLOGY AND BEHAVIORAL PHENOTYPES

Using an etiological label, such as fetal alcohol syndrome or fragile X syndrome, has desirable and undesirable effects. For example, identifying an individual as having fetal alcohol syndrome tells us a great deal about that person's actual, potential, and future support needs. We can assume that the person's mother drank alcohol during the pregnancy, which would reflect behavioral risk factors for mental retardation. This may also reflect significant social risk factors, such as parental dysfunction. The presence of these risk factors results in needs for family supports or adoption if adequate family support is not feasible. Individuals with fetal alcohol syndrome often have special nutritional needs because of the growth impairment that is a constant aspect of the condition. The prudent physician will search for other biomedical conditions that can be associated with fetal alcohol syndrome, such as congenital heart disorders that will require medical management. Once a diagnosis of fetal alcohol syndrome is made, the child's educational risks will be apparent, and professionals in the educational system will need to assess and identify any needs for educational supports. These will likely change as the individual grows up, so potential support needs can be anticipated. Psychological difficulties are commonly identified in individuals with fetal alcohol syndrome, so these too can be anticipated, diagnosed promptly, and treated before they become disabling.

These benefits of an etiological diagnosis must be balanced with a sensitive and humane understanding of the person as an individual. Etiology is not destiny, and an individual with fetal alcohol syndrome may or may not have any or all of the conditions commonly associated with the diagnosis. For example, although many individuals with fetal alcohol syndrome will have mental retardation, some will have normal intelligence. Each person must be seen as a unique individual with actual and potential strengths as well as needs for support. The benefit of being able to predict this profile of needed supports, based on an etiological diagnosis, needs to be balanced against the risk of unfair expectations that the person has aspects of the etiology that may or may not be present.

In general, greater diagnostic precision is preferred because an etiological diagnosis conveys more information than a solely functional diagnosis. If an individual has fetal alcohol syndrome and functions within the range of mental retardation, a diagnosis of fetal alcohol syndrome (with mental retardation) is preferred to a diagnosis of mental retardation alone. In fact, information about risks or expectations for actual and potential functioning is part of the etiological diagnosis, as was shown with the diagnosis of fetal alcohol syndrome. Similarly, information about risks and expectations for functioning is part of other etiologic diagnoses such as Down syndrome, Angelman syndrome, Williams syndrome, or Prader-Willi syndrome. This information is often referred to as the *behavioral phenotype* of the condition (Dykens, Hodapp, & Finucane, 2000). Research has identified behavioral

©American Association on Mental Retardation

phenotypes for a small number of etiologies, using careful studies and analyses of the behaviors of individuals with each etiologic diagnosis. Some of these associations are shown in Table 8.4. Once an etiologic diagnosis is made, information can be sought about whether a behavioral phenotype has been described. Research studies on behavioral phenotypes may be flawed by methodological issues, such as small sample size, retrospective design, or inadequate analysis; therefore, this information needs to be scrutinized for its validity and reliability.

Knowledge of the behavioral phenotype is not the same as a functional diagnosis. The behavioral phenotype provides only a general sense of what can be expected, based on data about other individuals with the same diagnosis. The behavioral phenotype is an aspect of the etiologic diagnosis, much as a specific DNA deletion is an aspect of the etiologic diagnosis. The functional diagnosis is an aspect of the individual, much as height, eye color, or gender are aspects of the individual. A functional diagnosis provides specific information about how a particular individual is functioning at a certain place and time. This functional diagnosis is specific to the individual (not the etiology) and is tailored to the individual's needs for supports. If an individual functions within the range of mental retardation, then that individual will need to have a complete multidimensional assessment of current functioning and needed supports (see chap. 9).

If a behavioral phenotype is known, this information may be useful for all of the team members, including teachers, therapists, counselors, and family members. Team members must understand that for a given individual, some, all, or none of the behaviors may be expressed and that the extent of expression may depend on the context of time and place. This information may be useful in planning the nature and extent of needed treatment and supports. Although medication may be indicated for some behaviors (e.g., attention deficit hyperactivity disorder or anxiety), prescription of medication is not the sole purpose of identifying the behavioral phenotype.

PREVENTION AS A FORM OF SUPPORT

Table 8.2 shows how opportunities for prevention exist at multiple levels. In general, three types of prevention can be identified:

- *Primary prevention* involves prevention of the condition that would otherwise result in mental retardation. For example, prevention of maternal alcohol use during pregnancy will prevent mental retardation caused by fetal alcohol syndrome.

- *Secondary prevention* involves actions to prevent an existing condition from resulting in mental retardation. For example, dietary management for an individual born with phenylketonuria (PKU) will prevent mental retardation caused by PKU, even though the individual will always have the genetic abnormality associated with PKU.

©American Association on Mental Retardation

TABLE 8.4

Behavioral Phenotypes of Selected Genetic Disorders

Etiologic Diagnosis	Behavioral Manifestations That Are Often Present
Down syndrome	1. Better performance on visuo-spatial tasks than on verbal or auditory tasks 2. Adaptive behavior strength relative to intelligence 3. Pleasant and sociable personality 4. Depression common in adulthood
Williams syndrome	1. Strengths in language, auditory memory, and facial recognition 2. Limitations in visuo-spatial functioning, perceptual-motor planning, and fine-motor skills 3. Strength in theory of mind (interpersonal intelligence) 4. Friendliness with impaired social intelligence 5. Anxiety disorders common at all ages
Fragile X syndrome	1. Verbal skills better than visuo-spatial skills 2. Relative strengths in daily living and self-care skills 3. Frequent association with inattention, hyperactivity, and autistic-like behaviors 4. Anxiety disorders common at all ages
Prader-Willi syndrome	1. Impaired satiety, food-seeking behavior, and obesity 2. Strength in visual processing and solving jigsaw puzzles 3. Obsessive-compulsive disorders and impulse control disorders common at all ages 4. Occasional psychosis in adults
Velocardiofacial syndrome	1. Verbal skills better than nonverbal skills 2. Inattention and hyperactivity common in children 3. Schizophrenia and mood disorders more common in older adolescents and adults
Rubinstein-Taybi syndrome	1. Inattention and impulsivity common in children 2. Friendliness and interest in music 3. Occasional association with mood disorders, tics, and obsessive-compulsive disorders

(table continues)

©American Association on Mental Retardation

TABLE 8.4 *(continued)*

Etiologic Diagnosis	Behavioral Manifestations That Are Often Present
Smith-Magenis syndrome	1. Delayed speech acquisition 2. Relative weakness in sequential processing 3. Sleep disorders common 4. Frequent stereotyped and self-injurious behaviors 5. Impulse control disorders common in children
Angelman syndrome	1. Bouts of inappropriate laughter are characteristic in younger individuals 2. Generally happy disposition at all ages 3. Hyperactivity and sleep disorders in younger individuals

- *Tertiary prevention* involves actions to minimize the severity of functional impairments associated with the etiology or to prevent secondary conditions (Pope, 1992) that may be caused by the diagnosis or develop later during life. For example, early corrective surgery for congenital heart defects in an individual with Down syndrome will prevent later functional impairments. This level of prevention is also relevant for older adults, who may benefit from strategies to prevent obesity, diabetes, heart disease, and osteoporosis.

In general, knowledge about etiology is necessary to develop effective programs for the prevention of mental retardation. One cannot prevent what one does not understand. Past efforts to prevent mental retardation may have been unsuccessful in part because prevention was conceived too narrowly (Coulter, 1991). The multifactorial and intergenerational model of etiology shown in Table 8.2 leads to a broader approach to prevention that emphasizes opportunities for support.

Prevention as a form of support builds on the interactive or ecological understanding of what mental retardation is and what causes it (Coulter, 1992). It reflects an ecological understanding of how the interaction between individuals and their environments results in mental retardation, as well as an ecological understanding of how risk factors from multiple categories interact across a lifetime to result in mental retardation. Mental retardation is not a disease like cancer or diabetes that can be prevented by single-target, one-dimensional strategies. Rather, mental retardation describes a particular state of functioning in a particular context of time and place that results from these ecological interactions. Prevention efforts can be developed that address each of these etiological risk factors and contextual factors that result in impaired functioning. These efforts could potentially interrupt or reverse the disabling process (Coulter, 1996).

©American Association on Mental Retardation

The linkage between etiology, prevention, and support is demonstrated in Table 8.5. The first step is to describe the etiologic risk factors present in a particular case as well as the interactions among them. This table shows the etiologic risk factors that might be identified in the case of a child with fetal alcohol syndrome. The next step is to describe prevention strategies that address each identified risk factor and the interactions among them. Table 8.5 also shows how prevention strategies might be identified that would provide individual and family supports for a child with fetal alcohol syndrome. Many of these prevention strategies can be accomplished at the local or personal level and thus become part of the system of supports for that individual.

TABLE 8.5
Relating Etiology to Prevention and Support

Category	Risk Factors Present	Prevention Supports
Biomedical	1. Fetal alcohol syndrome 2. Congenital heart disease	1. Nutritional support 2. Medical and surgical treatment of heart disease
Social	1. Family poverty 2. Homelessness 3. Inadequate parenting skills	1. Family support 2. Parental job training 3. Parenting skills development
Behavioral	1. Parental substance abuse 2. Child abuse or neglect	1. Treatment for alcoholism 2. Domestic violence prevention
Educational	1. Lack of adequate early intervention services	1. Enrollment in early intervention
Interactions among risk factors	1. Maternal poverty and substance abuse causing lack of prenatal care and fetal alcohol syndrome 2. Homelessness causing lack of adequate early intervention services	1. Treatment for alcoholism and job training promotes good prenatal care and avoidance of alcohol use during pregnancy 2. Family support and job training results in stable home and enrollment in local early intervention program

©American Association on Mental Retardation

The World Health Organization (WHO) defines *health* as a state of complete physical, mental, and social well-being. As a form of individual support, prevention can enhance well-being in all of these aspects in order to improve the person's health, life functioning, and satisfaction. This permits a shift in perspective when thinking about prevention. Rather than thinking about prevention solely from the perspective of program providers, prevention as a form of support involves thinking about prevention from the perspective of the individual. From this perspective, wellness (or individual well-being) is the individual's experience of prevention. Furthermore, the ultimate measure of the success of prevention efforts is the extent to which they enhance personal well-being.

SUMMARY

In this chapter the multifactorial nature of the etiology of mental retardation was described, and a new approach to classification of etiology based on biomedical, social, behavioral, and educational risk factors was presented. The diagnostic assessment process that incorporates new research advances as well as research about behaviors that are associated with specific etiologies was also discussed. The role of prevention was then reconceptualized to form a linkage between etiology, prevention, and support.

PART 4

SUPPORTS

CHAPTER 9

SUPPORTS AND THEIR APPLICATION TO PEOPLE WITH MENTAL RETARDATION

Supports are resources and strategies that aim to promote the development, education, interests, and personal well-being of a person and that enhance individual functioning. Services are one type of support provided by professionals and agencies. Individual functioning results from the interaction of supports with the dimensions of Intellectual Abilities; Adaptive Behavior; Participation, Interactions, and Social Roles; Health; and Context. The assessment of support needs can have different relevance, depending on whether it is done for purposes of classification or planning supports.

OVERVIEW

The concept of supports is integral to understanding and implementing the 2002 AAMR *Definition, Classification, and Systems of Supports.* Since the mid-1980s the supports paradigm has made at least two significant impacts on education and habilitation programs. First, the level or intensity of a person's support needs is being used as the basis for agency and systems planning and reimbursement patterns. Second, the supports orientation has brought together the related practices of person-centered planning, personal growth and development opportunities, community inclusion, and empowerment. Although the concept of supports is by no means new, *what is new is the belief that the judicious application of supports can improve the functional capabilities of individuals with mental retardation.* This belief is exemplified in the current emphasis on supported employment, supported living, and inclusive education. The importance of supports is that they hold the promise of providing a more natural, efficient, and ongoing basis for enhancing personal outcomes.

Our purpose in this chapter is to discuss the concept of supports and their application to people with mental retardation. Throughout the chapter, readers need to keep the following four key aspects of supports and the supports paradigm clearly in mind:

- Individual functioning results from the interaction of supports with the dimensions of Intellectual Abilities; Adaptive Behavior; Participation, Interactions, and Social Roles; Health; and Context.

- The primary purpose for providing supports to people with mental retardation is to enhance personal outcomes related to independence, relationships, contributions, school and community participation, and personal well-being.

- The assessment of support needs can have different relevance, depending on whether it is done for purposes of classification or planning of supports.

- Services are one type of support provided by professionals and agencies.

The current conceptual and practical interest in the use of supports extends across disciplines and rehabilitation areas, including education, families, employment, medicine, and community living. This emphasis on supports and systems of supports is consistent with both psychological and social concepts. Psychologically, the concept of supports is in harmony with the notion of *the zone of proximal development,* defined as the distance between the individual's independent and assisted problem-solving levels. As discussed by Vygotsky (1986) and Scharnhorst and Buchel (1990), an individual's functioning can be increased significantly by inquiring about the tasks the person can solve as compared with the tasks the person could solve with the help of a more capable member of society. Socially, the concept of supports is also consistent with the 19th-century concept of *communitarianism,* which involves tempering the excesses of individualism with an assertion of the rights of others in the larger society (H. Turnbull & Brunk, 1990).

The continued use of supports and the supports paradigm is occurring at the same time as the fields of education and habilitation are experiencing a significant shift in thinking characterized by:

- a focus on person-centered planning, which emphasizes personal growth and development, choices, decisions, and empowerment;

- an ecological approach to disability that stresses the power of person-environmental interactions and the reduction of functional and activity limitations through person-centered support strategies;

- a quality revolution that emphasizes personal well-being, quality of life, and valued outcomes; and

- the provision of services and supports in natural environments, based on the principles of inclusion and equity.

146   ©American Association on Mental Retardation

Although a popular topic, the concept of supports is by no means a new one. What has emerged over the past decade, however, is a better understanding of supports and their use in reducing the mismatch between environmental demands and the person's capabilities (Schalock, 1995). In this chapter our current understanding of the supports paradigm is organized in reference to: a supports model, the ecological and egalitarian basis of supports, key factors in operationalizing supports, the supports assessment and planning process, the provision of supports, and the evaluation of supports.

SUPPORTS MODEL

Figure 9.1 presents a supports model that reflects current understanding and use of supports for persons with mental retardation. The following are key aspects of the model (moving from top to bottom):

- The model is based on an ecological approach to understanding behavior that depends on evaluating the discrepancy between a person's capabilities and skills and the adaptive skills and competencies required to function in an environment.

- The idiosyncratic risk and protective factors of physical and psychological health, environment and its demands, and related disabilities may influence the supports that improve individual functioning.

- The discrepancy between skills and requirements is evaluated in terms of nine potential support areas: human development, teaching and education, home living, community living, employment, health and safety, behavioral, social, and protection and advocacy.

- The intensity of needed supports is determined for each of these nine support areas.

- Supports have various functions that act to reduce the discrepancy between a person and his or her environmental requirements. These support functions are teaching, befriending, financial planning, employee assistance, behavioral support, in-home living assistance, community access and use, and health assistance.

- The sources of these support functions can be either natural or service based. Thus services should be considered as a type of support provided by agencies and/or professionals.

- The desired personal outcomes from the use of supports include enhanced independence, relationships, contributions, school and community participation, and personal well-being.

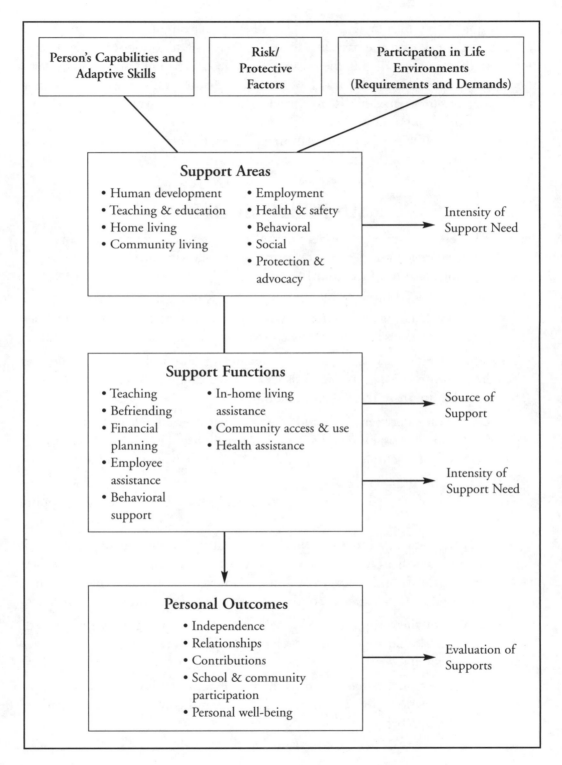

Figure 9.1. Supports model for people with mental retardation.

©American Association on Mental Retardation

THE ECOLOGICAL AND EGALITARIAN BASIS OF SUPPORTS

Contextualism, or the context within which supports are given, is a critical concept in understanding the current use of supports, the supports paradigm, and the influence of external factors on one's behavior. Contextualism has three central themes that are relevant to supports and their application to people with mental retardation. First is the appreciation of the milieu, circumstances, environment, or perspective within which behavior occurs. In this regard, the context of current education and habilitation programs includes more than just the immediate setting; one needs to consider the larger cultural and historical setting that allows or invites the occurrence of an event and renders it socially acceptable and timely. Second, a central part of contextualism is its dynamic nature; reality is ongoing and changing and involves the environment being transformed by its members, who are, in turn, transformed by the environment. The third contextual theme is that the person is an active determiner of his or her own development. These three themes are evident in the ecological and egalitarian bases of supports discussed next.

THE ECOLOGICAL BASIS OF SUPPORTS

There is clear evidence dating back to the 1980s that the successful adjustment of people with disabilities to their environments is related to both person-specific behavioral capabilities and setting-specific performance requirements (e.g., Landesman-Dwyer, 1981; Romer & Heller, 1983; Schalock & Jensen, 1986). These results are consistent with a social-ecological model proposing that a person's growth, development, and adjustment depend on both (a) the measurement and programming of person- and setting-specific factors and (b) the facilitation of congruence between individuals and their environments. Facilitating that congruence involves determining the profile of needed supports for a particular person and their intensity, and providing the supports to enhance the individual's functioning.

This social-ecological model is consistent with the current concept of disability that views the disabling process as a relationship among pathology, impairments, and one's environment (Institute of Medicine, 1991; World Health Organization [WHO], 2001). For example, and as discussed more fully in chapter 7, the *International Classification of Functioning, Disability, and Health* (WHO, 2001) provides a description of human functioning along three dimensions: Body Function and Structures (the human organism as a whole, including physiological and psychological aspects), Activities (the complete range of actions, behaviors, and routines performed by the individual), and Participation (areas of life in which the individual is involved and to which the individual has access). *Disability,* which is an umbrella term referring to problems in functioning in these three dimensions, is impacted

©American Association on Mental Retardation

significantly by two contextual variables: Personal and Environmental Factors. Thus the evolving conception of disability has changed not only the way in which services and supports are provided to people with mental retardation, but also our very understanding of the disabling process in the following ways:

- Disability is the expression of limitations in individual functioning within a social context and represents a substantial disadvantage to the individual.

- Disability is neither fixed nor dichotomized; rather, it is fluid, continuous, and changing, depending on the person's functional limitations and the supports available within the person's environment.

- One lessens a person's disability by providing interventions, services, or supports that focus on prevention, adaptive behaviors, and role status.

THE EGALITARIAN BASIS OF SUPPORTS

Egalitarianism is the belief in human equality, especially with respect to social, political, and economic rights. Since the 1960s we have seen the emergence of the egalitarian movement from both a legal and service-delivery perspective. Legally we have seen that people with mental retardation must have a right to the following (A. Turnbull & Turnbull, 2000; H. Turnbull & Turnbull, 2000): (a) free and appropriate public education, (b) community-based services, and (c) freedom from discrimination solely on the basis of disability. Programmatically we have seen the egalitarian movement reflected in services and supports based on:

- The concept of *person-centered planning*, which operates according to several general principles (Butterworth, Steere, & Whitney-Thomas, 1997): (a) the individual is a part of shaping the planning process and formulating plans; (b) emphasis is placed on the involvement of family members and friends in planning and reliance on personal social relationships as the primary source of individual support; (c) a primary focus is on the preferences, talents, and dreams of the individual rather than on needs or limitations; (d) a vision of the lifestyle the individual would like to have, and the goals needed to achieve it, are unrestricted by current resources or services; and (e) a broad implementation approach uses supports for the individual that are as local, informal, and generic as possible.

- The power of *self-advocacy* and *personal empowerment* that is forcing the following significant changes in the service delivery system (Ficker-Terrill, in press): (a) *control* — people with disabilities controlling their money and resources; (b) *choices* — people with disabilities selecting who will provide their services and supports; (c) *dignity and respect* — customer service programs designed as partnerships; (d) *personal goals* — people with disabilities realizing goals that are important to them and using their control over their resources to reach these goals; and (e) *individual rights* — people with disabilities being able to vote and having a durable power of attorney and will.

©American Association on Mental Retardation

- *Personal-referenced outcomes* or aims that reflect an individual's rights, values, and preferences and that involve both community inclusion and community participation (Schalock, 2001).

The net result of these legal and service-delivery trends has been to stress the role that appropriate supports can play in a person's life. The development of community and school-based services and supports is intended to allow people with mental retardation to live closer to the typical parameters of society, to offer an increased range of participation in those communities, and to lay the foundations for participatory citizenship. As we continue to understand better the distinction between "living in the community" and "being part of the community," it is apparent that "community" is an experience, not a location. More specifically, community is the experience of sharing one's life with others, with community presence being a precondition (Rapley, 2000).

OPERATIONALIZING SUPPORTS

DEFINITION

The 2002 AAMR System defines *supports* in much the same way as in the 1992 System. Specifically, supports are

> resources and strategies that aim to promote the development, education, interests, and personal well-being of a person and that enhance individual functioning.

Key aspects of this definition indicate that supports (a) pertain to resources and strategies; (b) enable people to access resources, information, and relationships within integrated environments; (c) result in increased integration and enhanced personal growth and development; and (d) can be evaluated in reference to their outcomes. Three additional aspects of supports need to be considered in operationalizing supports: the sources of supports, support functions, and the intensity of needed supports.

SOURCES OF SUPPORTS

In the 1992 AAMR System (Luckasson et al.) four sources of supports were proposed: oneself, other people, technology, and services. The 2002 System suggests that the sources of support are either natural (including oneself and other people) or service based (i.e., currently available education and habilitation services that are used to augment natural supports). The distinction between these two sources of support is that:

- *Natural supports* are resources and strategies provided by people or equipment in a given environment that (a) potentially lead to desired personal and performance outcomes; (b) are typically available and culturally appropriate in the respective environment; and (c) are supported by resources from within the environment, facilitated to the degree necessary by human service coordination (Butterworth, Hagner, Kiernan, & Schalock, 1996).

- *Service-based supports* are the same resources and strategies, but are provided by people or equipment that are typically not part of the person's "natural environment." Such people include teachers, academically trained and certified health and habilitation professionals, direct-care staff or professionals, and/or paid volunteers.

These issues are discussed further in chapter 11.

SUPPORT FUNCTIONS AND SUPPORT ACTIVITIES

The previous discussion of the changing conception of disability and the ecological perspective indicates that the discrepancy between the person's behavioral capabilities and his or her environment's performance requirements could be reduced through the judicious use of supports. This judicious use is guided by the eight support functions and corresponding activities summarized in Table 9.1. As shown in the table, the proposed support functions are (as in the 1992 manual) teaching, befriending, financial planning, employee assistance, behavioral support, in-home living assistance, community access and use, and health assistance.

SUPPORTS INTENSITIES

The intensity of needed supports varies across people, life situations, and life stages. Hence, supports should be viewed as varying potentially in both duration and intensity. The following four intensities have value in the planning, implementation, and evaluation of supports (Luckasson et al., 1992, 1996):

- *Intermittent:* Supports on an "as needed basis," characterized by their episodic (person not always needing the support[s]) or short-term nature (supports needed during life-span transitions, e.g., job loss or acute medical crisis). Intermittent supports may be high or low intensity when provided.

- *Limited:* An intensity of supports characterized by consistency over time, time-limited but not of an intermittent nature, may require fewer staff members and less cost than more intense levels of support (e.g., time-limited employment training or transitional supports during the school-to-adult period).

- *Extensive:* Supports characterized by regular involvement (e.g., daily) in at least some environments (e.g., school, work, or home) and not time-limited nature (e.g., long-term support and long-term home living support).

- *Pervasive:* Supports characterized by their constancy, high intensity, provision across environments, potentially life-sustaining nature. Pervasive supports typically involve more staff members and intrusiveness than do extensive or time-limited supports.

©American Association on Mental Retardation

TABLE 9.1
Support Functions and Representative Activities

Support Function[a]	Representative Activities		
Teaching	Supervising Giving feedback Organizing the learning environment	Training Evaluating Supporting inclusive classrooms	Instructing Collecting data Individualizing instruction
Befriending	Advocating Car pooling Supervising Instructing	Evaluating Communicating Training Giving feedback	Reciprocating Associating & disassociating Socializing
Financial planning	Working with SSI- Medicaid Advocating for benefits	Assisting with money management Protection and legal assistance	Budgeting Income assistance & planning/ considerations
Employee assistance	Counseling Procuring/using assistive technology devices	Supervisory training Job performance enhancement	Crisis inter- vention/ assistance Job/task accom- modation and redesigning job/work duties
Behavioral support	Functional analysis Multicomponent instruction Emphasis on antece- dent manipulation	Manipulation of ecological & setting events Teaching adaptive behavior	Building envir- onment with effective consequences

[a] The support functions and activities may need to be modified slightly to accommodate individuals of different ages.

(table continues)

©American Association on Mental Retardation

TABLE 9.1 *(continued)*

Support Function[a]	Representative Activities		
In-home living assistance	Personal maintenance/ care Transfer & mobility Dressing & clothing care Architectural modifications	Communication devices Behavioral support Eating & food management Housekeeping	Respite care Attendant care Home-health aides Homemaker services
Community access and use	Carpooling/rides program Transportation training Personal protection skills	Recreation/leisure involvement Community awareness opportunities Vehicle modification	Community use opportunities & interacting with generic agencies Personal pro-tection skills
Health assistance	Medical appointments Medical interventions Supervision Med Alert devices	Emergency procedures Mobility (assistive devices) Counseling appointments Medication taking	Hazard awareness Safety training Physical therapy & related activities Counseling interventions

As discussed in the following section, needed supports and their intensity can be based on a three-step assessment process: (a) identifying relevant support areas, (b) identifying relevant support activities for each support area, and then (c) determining for the individual the level of support needs in each relevant support activity. The intensity of needed supports is determined based on either a simple summation of the assessed frequency, daily support time, and/or type of support or on the basis of other decision rules determined by the supports provider and/or funder.

©American Association on Mental Retardation

SUPPORTS ASSESSMENT AND PLANNING PROCESS

Recently considerable work has helped identify the life activity (support) areas and support activities around which support assessment and support provision should focus. For example, the literature in this area (approximately 1,500 sources) has recently been summarized as part of the work of the AAMR Supports Intensity Assessment Committee, whose charge was to integrate the supports literature and develop a supports assessment system (Thompson, Hughes, Schalock, & Silverman, in press). This section of the chapter relies heavily on the work of this committee, even though a *generic* supports assessment and planning process is presented. The Support Assessment and Planning Process Model presented in Table 9.2 depicts a four-step process for the assessment of an individual's needed supports and the development of an individualized supports plan.

TABLE 9.2
Support Assessment and Planning Process Model

Step 1: Identify Relevant Support Area
Human development
Teaching & education
Home living
Community living
Employment
Health & safety
Behavioral
Social
Protection & advocacy

Step 2: Identify Relevant Support Activities for Each Support Area
The individual's interests and preferences
Activities in which the person does or most likely will participate
Settings in which the person does or most likely will participate

Step 3: Evaluate the Level or Intensity of Support Needs
Frequency
Daily support times
Types of support

(table continues)

TABLE 9.2 *(continued)*

> **Step 4: Write the Individualized Supports Plan to Reflect the Individual**
> The individual's interests and preferences
> Needed support areas and activities
> Settings in which the person does or most likely will participate
> Activities in which the person does or most likely will participate
> Specific support functions that address identified support needs
> An emphasis on natural supports
> Persons responsible for providing the support function(s)
> Personal outcomes
> A plan to monitor the provision of supports and their outcomes

STEP 1: IDENTIFY RELEVANT SUPPORT AREAS

First, a number of potential support areas are identified for assessment. A thorough review of the supports literature (Thompson et al., in press) suggests the appropriateness of the nine areas listed in Table 9.3: human development, teaching and education, home living, community living, employment, health and safety, behavioral, social, and protection and advocacy.

STEP 2: IDENTIFY RELEVANT SUPPORT ACTIVITIES FOR SUPPORT AREA

Second, and as shown in Table 9.3, a number of support activities are identified for each of the nine support areas. The majority of the activities listed in Table 9.3 are the result of two tasks undertaken by the AAMR Supports Intensity Assessment Committee: (a) a thorough literature review, in which a number of potential support activities were identified; and (b) an aggregation of these potential support activities into each of the nine support areas by a panel of 50 experts in the field of mental retardation or developmental disabilities (Thompson et al., in press).

STEP 3: EVALUATE THE LEVEL OR INTENSITY OF SUPPORT NEEDS

Third, specific support activities are selected for evaluation using two criteria: (a) Planning supports requires input from the person and all individuals (including other team members) who are important to the person and who have knowledge of him or her; and (b) the person's future is the time reference of the evaluation efforts; that is, supports assessment and provision need to focus on what supports the person desires and would need in a more inclusive, integrated, and productive environ-

©American Association on Mental Retardation

ment, not simply to maintain the person where he or she is currently. The intensity of needed supports can be determined using a 5-point Likert scale based on a simple summation of the assessed *frequency* (e.g., less than monthly, monthly,

---

TABLE 9.3

Support Areas and Representative Support Activities

Human Development Activities
> Providing physical development opportunities that include eye-hand coordination, fine-motor skills, and gross-motor activities
> Providing cognitive development opportunities related to coordinating sensory experiences, representing the world with words and images, reasoning logically about concrete events, and reasoning in more realistic and logical ways
> Providing social-emotional developmental activities related to trust, autonomy, initiative, mastery, and identity

Teaching and Education Activities
> Interacting with trainers or teachers and fellow trainees or students
> Participating in training or educational decisions
> Learning and using problem-solving strategies
> Operating technology for learning
> Accessing training or educational settings
> Learning and using functional academics (e.g., reading signs, counting change)
> Learning and using health and physical education skills
> Learning and using self-determination skills
> Receiving transitional services

Home-Living Activities
> Using the restroom/toilet
> Laundering and taking care of clothes
> Preparing and eating food
> Housekeeping and cleaning
> Dressing
> Bathing and taking care of personal hygiene and grooming needs
> Operating home appliances and technology
> Participating in leisure activities within the home

(table continues)

©American Association on Mental Retardation

TABLE 9.3 *(continued)*

Community-Living Activities
    Using transportation
    Participating in recreation or leisure activities in the community
    Using services in the community
    Going to visit friends and family
    Participating in preferred community activities (e.g., church, volunteer)
    Shopping and purchasing goods
    Interacting with community members
    Using public buildings and settings

Employment Activities
    Accessing or receiving job or task accommodations
    Learning and using specific job skills
    Interacting with coworkers
    Interacting with supervisors or coaches
    Completing work-related tasks with acceptable speed and quality
    Changing job assignments
    Accessing and obtaining crisis intervention and assistance
    Accessing employee assistance services

Health and Safety Activities
    Accessing and obtaining therapy services
    Taking medications
    Avoiding health and safety hazards
    Receiving home health care
    Ambulating and moving about
    Communicating with health-care providers
    Accessing emergency services
    Maintaining a nutritious diet
    Maintaining physical health
    Maintaining mental health or emotional well-being
    Following rules and laws
    Receiving respiratory, feeding, skin care, seizure management, ostomy
        care, and other exceptional medical needs

(table continues)

©American Association on Mental Retardation

TABLE 9.3 *(continued)*

Behavioral Activities
   Learning specific skills or behaviors
   Learning or making appropriate decisions
   Accessing and obtaining mental health treatments
   Accessing and obtaining substance abuse treatments
   Making choices and taking initiatives
   Incorporating personal preferences into daily activities
   Maintaining socially appropriate behavior in public
   Learning or using self-management strategies
   Controlling anger and aggression
   Increasing adaptive skills and behaviors

Social Activities
   Socializing within the family
   Participating in recreation or leisure activities
   Making appropriate sexuality decisions
   Socializing outside the family
   Making and keeping friends
   Associating and disassociating from people
   Communicating with others about personal needs
   Using appropriate social skills
   Engaging in loving and intimate relationships
   Offering assistance and assisting others

Protection and Advocacy Activities
   Advocating for self and others
   Managing money and personal finances
   Protecting self from exploitation
   Exercising legal rights and responsibilities
   Belonging to and participating in self-advocacy or support organizations
   Obtaining legal services
   Making suitable choices and decisions
   Using banks and cashing checks

weekly, daily, hourly or more frequently), *daily support time* (e.g., none, less than 30 minutes, 30 minutes to less than 2 hours, 2 hours to less than 4 hours, 4 hours or more), and/or *type of support* (e.g., none, monitoring, verbal or gestural prompt, partial physical assistance, full physical assistance) for each relevant support activity.

©American Association on Mental Retardation

STEP 4: WRITE THE INDIVIDUALIZED SUPPORTS PLAN TO REFLECT THE INDIVIDUAL

Data from the assessment of frequency, daily support time, and/or type of supports result in a support needs profile and guide the development of an individualized supports plan. The profile is based on the information obtained from Step 3 and indicates the life areas and support activities in which a person needs supports to enhance personal functioning and achieve personal goals. In addition, sources of support can be identified, distinguishing between natural and service-based supports. Thus the support needs profile will guide the person's planning team in the development of an individualized supports plan such as that described next.

THE PROVISION OF SUPPORTS

The provision of supports cuts across individuals and age groups, as reflected in individualized plans related to families, children, and adults. The generic term *individualized supports plan* (ISP) will be used in this section of the chapter to discuss the provision of supports, with special reference to the individualized family service plan (IFSP), individualized education program (IEP), individualized transition plan (ITP), and individualized habilitation plan (IHP). The operationalization of the ISP will be discussed in reference to implementation guidelines, changed staff roles, and support standards.

INDIVIDUALIZED SUPPORTS PLAN

A planning team needs to apply information from Step 3 (evaluate the level or intensity of support needs) and prioritize preferences in regard to life experiences and goals. An ISP is completed when the team has identified (a) the individual's interests and preferences, (b) the needed support areas and activities, (c) the settings the person is most likely to be in as well as the activities in which the individual will participate, (d) the specific support functions that will address the identified support needs, (e) natural supports available to the person, (f) valued personal outcomes, and (g) a plan mechanism to monitor the provision and personal outcomes of the support provided.

For very young children identified as having developmental delays or specific disabilities, the Individuals With Disabilities Education Act Amendments of 1997 (IDEA) (Pub. L. 105–17) requires that educational planning be centered upon the family's preferences for its child while also reflecting the knowledge and ideas of other members of the team — the teacher, physical and occupational therapists, speech and language pathologist, social worker, nurse, and any other professionals designated to provide needed services and supports. These IFSPs address both child and family needs and strengths through team-generated goals and objectives for

©American Association on Mental Retardation

learning and improvement as well as by specifying services and supports based on current child and family functioning.

When children reach their preschool years, around 2 to 3 years old, educational services under IDEA continue to be individualized and planned by teams but are more child-centered in their focus. These IEPs are designed for students with disabilities from the preschool years through early adulthood, age 21 or older, or as long as the individual is found eligible for services under IDEA. Eligibility may be granted with a label of mental retardation or developmental delay (a label that typically applies from preschool to age 8) or may be established based on developmental delay plus the presence of an etiology associated with the disability (e.g., Down syndrome, fragile X, cerebral palsy, or autism). IEPs begin with a definition of the individual's present level of functioning (i.e., his or her unique needs, strengths, and characteristics). The team then determines a set of educational services that will address the individual's needs and characteristics and defines when these services will begin and what their frequency, location, and duration will be. Finally, the team works to write goals and objectives for the individual's academic and social accomplishments whose quarterly measurement serves as indicators of whether the services are effective and appropriate (Bateman & Linden, 1998; Giangreco, 2001).

When students reach the age of 14 years (or younger if appropriate), IEPs must include a statement of their vocational and transition service needs; this part of the IEP is called the ITP. At least by age 16, the ITP must address transition services that include the interagency linkages between the school and adult services. By definition *transition services* are "a coordinated set of activities," not a loose plan, that is aimed at fostering movement from school to postschool life. Services may include instruction, related therapy services, community experiences and instruction, development of employment skills, and adult living skills. Basic daily living skills and job assessment may be a part of ITPs. For students with the most severe disabilities, ITPs may include a focus on basic daily living and community-use skills, job assessment, and training in actual work or volunteer settings. Thus the focus of the IEP expands during the teen years and early 20s to include the transition to adult activities: higher education (for some students), adult life, and work.

The IFSP and the IEP are regarded as "a firm, legally binding commitment of resources" (Bateman & Linden, 1998, p. 60) by a school system and, therefore, must be team generated and written with careful deliberation. When these documents describe IEPs and needed supports and services matched to a particular student's many unique needs, the team has a valuable guide for helping students achieve meaningful improvements. Program plans, as required by IDEA (1997), serve similar functions, as do profiles of individualized supports, although there are several important differences. First, IEPs, in contrast to IFSPs and profiles of support, do not address family needs nor do they define services and supports that extend beyond the student's educational needs. IFSPs do address family supports, but these documents do not broadly include medical supports pertinent during the first 2 years of life. Second, IEPs do not focus on medical and health issues that are separate from educational success. Thus profiles of support may be needed to complement educational plans during the school years so that needed supports related to families and to health and etiology are fully addressed. Profiles of support are designed by teams that include the individual with mental retardation, family members (depending on the age of the person), a school representative, and professionals from community service agencies who serve as the case managers and brokers of community supports beyond the public school. These profiles are written to complement rather than duplicate any existing IEP.

When individuals with mental retardation are no longer eligible for public schools services under IDEA (1997), they typically seek eligibility from an adult community service agency. Most adults service agencies require the development and use of an IHP to guide program goals for individuals with disabilities who are over the age 21. Profiles of support are based on the individual's assessed strengths, needs, and preferences and supplement an IHP as reflected in the individually referenced goals, objectives, and programmatic or habilitation activities.

Different types of individualized plans (e.g., IFSP, IEP, ITP, IHP) should *not* be viewed as being different from an ISP. For example, the requirements of designing an IEP described in IDEA (1997) are both consistent with and strongly confirm the elements of the supports models shown in Figure 9.1 and Table 9.2 (A. Turnbull & Turnbull, 2000; H. Turnbull & Turnbull, 2000). Instead of writing different documents, teams need to simply track their process by:

- operating according to person-centered planning (or family-centered planning when young children are involved);

- identifying needed support areas and activities, very similar to goals and objectives;

- developing a document that reflects team consensus;

- reflecting an ecological perspective (disability view as fluid and changing, depending on the person's functional limitations and the supports available, the egalitarian movement, and the ecological perspective);

- specifying outcome categories that are appropriate for the person;

- identifying needed supports and their functions, emphasizing natural supports, and specifying the intensities predicted as being necessary;

- providing a plan for providing those supports;

- providing a plan for evaluating personal outcomes that are monitored regularly and lead to improvements in the services and supports provided.

©American Association on Mental Retardation

IMPLEMENTATION GUIDELINES

In addition to the support standards summarized later in this section, five suggested guidelines will assist in the successful development, implementation, and monitoring of the ISP:

- The provision of supports must be tailored to an individual's needs and preferences.

- People need access to flexible support systems.

- Some supports are more important than others.

- Support needs assessment must guide the development and revision of an ISP.

- When assessing a person's support needs and developing an ISP, the person's cultural, ethnic, linguistic, and economic characteristics must be considered in addition to factors related to physical, psychological, and functional status.

CHANGED STAFF ROLES IDENTIFIED

The effective and efficient provision of individualized supports requires a rethinking of staff roles. Specifically, staff roles are shifting to a supports provision orientation, with changing staff roles that involve:

- planner role: responsible for analyzing the services that the person is seeking and assisting the individual in developing a plan to achieve the identified outcome;

- community resource role: responsible for having knowledge of community resources in order to assist the individual in accessing and obtaining needed service-based and natural supports;

- consultant role: responsible for entering into a consultant relationship with the person and providing recommendations based on knowledge and expertise;

- technician role: responsible for staying versed in current assistive technologies and strategies to ensure skill acquisition and maintenance.

SUPPORT STANDARDS

In addition to the implementation guidelines previously discussed, a number of standards should guide the provision of supports. Following are the more important of these standards:

- Supports occur in regular, *integrated environments*.

- Support activities are performed primarily by *regular* people working, living, educating, or recreating within integrated environments.

- Support activities are *person referenced*.

- Supports are *coordinated* through someone such as a supports manager.

- *Outcomes* from the use of supports are evaluated against quality indicators and measured based on individual values.

- The use of supports can *fluctuate* during different stages of one's life.

- Supports should be *ongoing* and should not be withdrawn unless the service or supports provider continues to monitor the person's current and future intensities of needed support.

THE EVALUATION OF SUPPORTS

Evaluation theory and strategies have undergone tremendous changes over the past 30 years. Historically, an experimental approach has been used to evaluate the effects of treatments applied to large groups, with the major purpose being hypothesis testing or theory building. According to some (e.g., Schorr, 1997), this traditional approach to evaluation, which requires experimental and control conditions, is overreliant on a biomedical, experimental model and more suited to large group evaluation of treatment effects than to understanding the impact of social and human service programs on individuals. Group design, controlled conditions, and statistical analyses do not fit well with the current service delivery system, with its emphasis on equity, empowerment, individualized supports, inclusion, and personal growth and development. Thus the purpose and focus of the evaluation of supports should be on whether personal outcomes related to independence, relationships, contributions, school and community participation, and personal well-being have been enhanced. An evaluation model that fulfills this criterion is presented in Figure 9.2. As shown, there are three components to this model: Outcome Categories, Key Indicators, and Measures.

OUTCOME CATEGORIES

The aim of providing supports is to achieve noticeable improvement in one or more personal outcomes: independence, relationships, contributions, school and community participation, and personal well-being. Selecting one or more outcome categories that are relevant to a given person is the first component for planning evaluation. For example, consider a young woman now out of school who is unemployed and has too much spare time; her support needs and outcome category focus mainly on community participation and personal contribution.

KEY INDICATORS

When outcomes are applied to a given person, they can be operationalized to suit that person's needs. This second component requires specifying measurable aspects or "indicators" of each outcome category. Exemplar indicators for each personal

©American Association on Mental Retardation

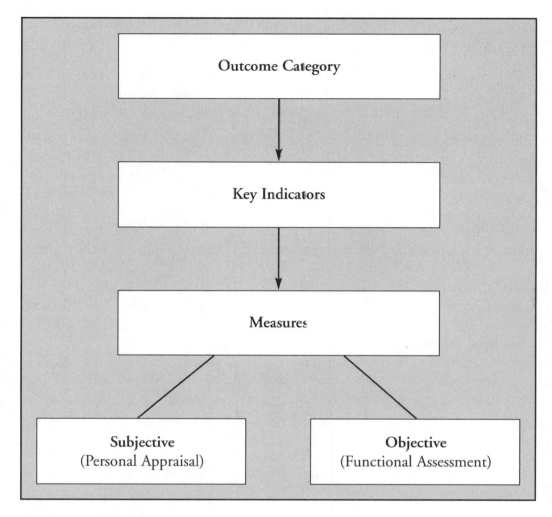

Figure 9.2. Supports evaluation model.

outcome category shown in Figure 9.1 are listed in Table 9.4. As an example, the young woman whose need for supports in community participation and productivity may focus on two outcome indicators: becoming more contributory several days a week by engaging in two volunteer activities and three hobbies that reflect her personal interests.

MEASURES

Good methodological practices use multiple measures and analyze both subjective and objective data. *Personal appraisal* is an example of using *subjective data* to evaluate effects; this approach may draw data from personal interviews, surveys, or focus groups. *Functional assessment* exemplifies the use of *objective data* gathered through rating scales, observation, objective behavioral measures, and status indicators (e.g., education, living, employment status).

Personal Appraisal

The personal appraisal component of the Supports Evaluation Model addresses the subjective nature of life experiences. The typical dependent measure used in this type of evaluation is the person's stated level of satisfaction. Its advantages include the fact that (a) satisfaction is a commonly used aggregate measure of individual life domains and demonstrates a trait-like stability over time; (b) there is an extensive body of research on levels of satisfaction across populations and clinical conditions; and (c) satisfaction as a dependent variable allows one to assess the relative importance of individual and environmental factors to one's assessed level of satisfaction. Its major disadvantages are that satisfaction measures (a) provide only a global measure of perceived well-being; (b) are potentially sensitive to response preservation; (c) are usually dependent on self-report, which may be difficult for the person; and (d) may not correlate with objective measures of the same key indicator.

Functional Assessment

Not to be confused with functional assessment of problem behavior, this measurement approach applied to a supports model addresses the objective nature of one's life and life experiences and is generally organized around the concepts of adaptive behavior and role status. *Adaptive behavior* is the collection of conceptual, social, and practical skills that have been learned by people in order to function in their everyday lives. In general, adaptive behavior also refers to those behaviors that are required for successful adaptation to or functioning in different major life-activity areas, such as home and community living, school or work, and health and wellness. *Role status* refers to a set of valued activities that are considered normative for a specific age group. Examples include one's living arrangement, employment status, education level, community participation, recreation-leisure patterns, and health status. For example, for youth, attending school is a valued, age-specific activity, whereas for high school graduates and adults, living and working in the community are valued activities.

Thus the evaluation of supports necessitates thinking beyond the immediacy of providing supports and causes one to ask several fundamental questions:

- What, if any, personal outcomes appear to have resulted from the supports that were provided to this person?

- Are these the desired outcomes?

- Are other outcomes affected? Are the effects reflected as changes in the relevant key indicators or in other indicators?

 ©American Association on Mental Retardation

TABLE 9.4
Key Indicators for Personal Support Outcome Categories

Outcome Category	Indicators
Independence	Autonomy Choices Decisions Personal control Self-direction Personal goals
Relationships	Intimacy Affection Family Interactions Friendships Mentors
Contributions	Employment status Vocational activities Volunteerism Ownership Possessions Hobbies
School and community participation	School presence Community presence School activities Community activities School involvement Community involvement Acceptance Role status
Personal well-being	Emotional well-being Interpersonal relations Material well-being Personal development Physical well-being Self-determination Social inclusion Rights

©American Association on Mental Retardation

SUMMARY

Readers who have worked in the fields of education or habilitation during the past decade or longer will appreciate the significant changes that have occurred during that time. For example, during the 1990s, we experienced significant shifts from: services to supports, programming to opportunity development, passive to active consumer roles, process to outcomes, the individual to the individual and the environment, categorical to noncategorical, a deficiency model to a growth model, dependency to interdependency, and normalization to personal well-being.

The supports paradigm has revolutionized how we provide education and habilitation services to people with mental retardation and closely related disabilities. Our purpose in this chapter was to update the concept of supports found in the 1992 AAMR *Mental Retardation: Definition, Classification, and Systems of Supports* manual (Luckasson et al.) and to discuss our current understanding of supports from a number of perspectives. Throughout the chapter, supports were defined as:

> resources and strategies that aim to promote the development, education, interests, and personal well-being of a person and that enhance individual functioning.

The future of the supports paradigm is bright, and this simple concept has already been influential in the introduction of profound changes in the lives of many individuals. But we are not there yet, for the emerging supports strategies involving person-centered planning, self-determination, positive behavior support, facilitating natural supports, and community building are in various stages of implementation. Thus a number of challenges remain before us, including: the existence of a philosophy or mission emphasizing inclusive environments, flexible funding and service delivery policies, family and consumer input and direction, and attention to outcomes and performance goals. Successfully meeting these challenges, which will necessitate a change in our thinking about and application of the 2002 System, is discussed more fully in chapters 11 and 12.

©American Association on Mental Retardation

CHAPTER 10
PHYSICAL AND MENTAL HEALTH

Health is a state of complete physical, mental, and social well-being. For the majority of individuals with mental retardation, physical and mental health concerns are similar to those of the general population.

OVERVIEW

In this chapter the impact of physical and mental health on assessment, classification, and supports is discussed. The World Health Organization (WHO) model of the disabling process and the *International Classification of Diseases (ICD–10)* (WHO, 1993) and *Diagnostic and Statistical Manual of Mental Disorders* (4th ed.– Transition; *DSM–IV–TR*) (American Psychiatric Association, 2000) systems for classification of physical and mental disorders are briefly reviewed in this context. The prevalence of common physical and mental health disorders among people with mental retardation is summarized later in tables, with the readers' attention directed to the importance of a multidisciplinary analysis of behavior for making accurate psychiatric diagnostic assessments. The impact of general and specific health concerns on assessment of intelligence, adaptive behavior, and support needs is also discussed. Self-determination in health care is described briefly, along with specific supports and support strategies for health maintenance.

HEALTH CLASSIFICATION

Health is defined by the WHO (1993, 2001) as a state of complete physical, mental, and social well-being, not just the absence of disability. This definition emphasizes the positive aspect of health. Physical health is not more important than mental health or social health; all are necessary for optimal well-being. Health, in this sense, is a goal in itself and is not just the absence of disability. Health and disability are distinct, although related, concepts. Disability is the result of a complicated process that involves a number of interacting factors and is defined in this manual as "the expression of limitations in individual functioning within a social context and represents a substantial disadvantage to the individual."

Evolving concepts about how people become disabled reflect new attitudes, knowledge, and social policy. In the past, a purely "medical model" related disability directly and primarily to the existence of a medical illness or injury. In that model, anyone who had a specific condition (e.g., Down syndrome) was disabled to the same degree (moderate mental retardation) and could be treated the same way (early institutionalization). This view is no longer tenable. Recent researchers examining the social construction of illness (see, e.g., Aronowitz, 1998) have identified the extensive impact that societal attitudes, roles, and policies have on the ways that individuals experience health disorders.

In 1980 the WHO developed a model that described how an intrinsic condition (e.g., a disease) can affect organ or body functioning (impairment), which may then influence individual performance or behavior (disability) and put the individual at a social disadvantage (handicap). The system was called the *International Classification of Impairments, Disabilities, and Handicaps* or *ICIDH* (WHO, 1980). In 1991 the Institute of Medicine (IOM) developed a similar model of the disabling process that described how a medical condition (e.g., heart disease) could cause impaired function of an organ (e.g., a heart attack), which could then result in impaired functioning of the whole person (e.g., inability to work), who might then become disabled (unable to support his or her family). In that model, the functional impairment only became a disability when the individual could no longer perform expected social roles. Note that handicap in the *ICIDH* had a comparable meaning to disability in the IOM system. Both models of the disabling process also emphasized how multiple physical, social, and behavioral risk factors may converge at different stages of the life cycle to predispose an individual to the disabling process.

Current thinking has revised these models while retaining the concept that disability reflects a complex interaction among health disorders, functional impairments, and social roles. The *ICIDH–2* (WHO, 2000a, 2000b) notes that a health condition (disease or disorder) affects body function and structures (impairments), functioning of the individual (activity limitations), and social roles (participation restrictions). Furthermore, interactions among these three areas are influenced by personal and environmental factors that provide the context for human functioning. For this reason, the *ICIDH–2* has been renamed the *International Classification of Functioning, Health, and Disability,* or *ICF.* The *ICF* was described in greater detail in chapter 7.

For the purposes of tracking prevalence of medical conditions, the *International Classification of Diseases (ICD)* was developed by the WHO. Now in its 10th edition (1993), *ICD* presents a comprehensive descriptive coding system for physical health, including mental health. Differences between European and American colleagues in the understanding about mental illnesses led to a separate diagnostic

©American Association on Mental Retardation

system being developed in the United States. The *DSM* reflects the clinical and research consensus of psychiatrists and is used internationally. Since the mid-1980s, *ICD* and *DSM* have developed diagnostic criteria that are very similar, at least for the major psychiatric disorders. The *DSM* includes a descriptive time duration and severity of symptom criterion for each disorder's collection of symptoms.

Within the framework provided by these models, the *ICF* is used to classify the impact on functioning and disability, and the *ICD* is intended to classify specific health disorders. In the United States, physical health disorders are classified using the ninth edition of the *ICD*. (The 10th edition of the *ICD* is used in other countries.) Mental health disorders are classified in the United States using the *DSM–IV–TR* (American Psychiatric Association, 2000). Publication by the WHO of the new *ICF* occurred in 2001. These systems will likely become the dominant classification systems of the near-term future: The *ICD* and *DSM* will be used to classify specific physical and mental health conditions, including the etiologies of mental retardation, whereas the *ICF* will be used to classify individual impairments and disabilities, placing an individual within a functional context.

HEALTH ASSESSMENT

For the majority of individuals with mental retardation, physical and mental health concerns are similar to those of the general population. Getting an infectious disease depends upon exposure and general immunological health. Healthy habits, such as regular exercise, eating a well-balanced diet, learning new facts, having meaningful social connections, feeling productive, and getting appropriate routine health evaluations, are the best predictors of good health and longevity. In other words, mental retardation per se does not directly predispose a person to particular physical or mental illnesses.

However, having mental retardation can influence how an individual's health and well-being are evaluated, treated, supported, and even thought of by people around them (Spitalnik & White-Scott, 2001). Mannerisms and behavioral differences from "the norm" in an individual with mental retardation may cause people to distance themselves from the individual and to miss important clues that are being communicated. When direct verbal communication is not possible, physical changes in a person's habits or routines are important clues to something "not being right." Generally, a medical concern is the most likely cause of a new disturbance in routine behaviors (see later section, "Difficult Behaviors").

PHYSICAL HEALTH DISORDERS

Comprehensive physical exams need to be conducted at least annually in people who cannot reliably communicate the state of their bodies' health, and this applies across the lifespan. A practical and detailed summary of physical and mental health care needs of individuals with mental retardation is available in a report prepared for Special Olympics, Inc. (Horwitz, Kerker, Owens, & Zigler, 2000).

Based on that report, some of which is summarized in Table 10.1, the most common causes of death for people with mental retardation were cardiovascular disease, respiratory illness, and cancer. Cardiovascular disease affects 6.7% to 55.2% of individuals with mental retardation, and the rate of illness increases with increasing age. Cerebrovascular disease and stroke affects 2.8% to 9.0% of older people with mental retardation. Respiratory illnesses affect 1.5% to 5.1% of adults living in the community and up to 33% of those living in institutions. Cancer affects 7.4% to 34% of individuals with mental retardation, which is comparable to the general population. Leukemia is more common in people with Down syndrome. Gastrointestinal cancers are found more often in all people with chronic reflux disorder (gastroesophogeal reflux disorder or GERD). Within the population having mental retardation, the prevalence of diabetes is 1.6% to 9.1%, comparable to the general population. It is more common in obese individuals. Obesity is more common among individuals with mental retardation compared to the general population and affects 29.5% to 50.5% of this population throughout their lifespan. Oral health disorders are more common among children and adults with mental retardation compared to the general population and include higher rates of dental caries (24% to 56%) and gingivitis (60% to 90%). This is a typical secondary medical condition brought on by irregular or incomplete attention to brushing teeth after eating on a daily basis. Poor dental hygiene is fostered by excessive dryness of the mouth, which may be caused by the anticholinergic side-effects of medications, including antiallergy and antidepression medications. Seizure disorders are also more common with a rate of 8.8% to 32%.

MENTAL HEALTH DISORDERS

The prevalence of mental health disorders among individuals with mental retardation is difficult to estimate due to problems in sampling and diagnosis. In general, mental health disorders are much more prevalent in this population compared to the general population. Overall estimates suggest a prevalence of approximately 7% to 26% in individuals in the general population and 9% to 74% in individuals with mental retardation — two- to three-fold higher rates among people with mental retardation (Dosen & Day, 2001).

The types of mental health disorders are the same in people with and people without mental retardation. The behavioral manifestations of psychiatric illness are likely to differ from individual to individual. The incidence of anxiety and stress disorders is greater in the population with mental retardation compared with the population of people without mental retardation who are of similar age. The most

©American Association on Mental Retardation

TABLE 10.1

Prevalence of Common Physical Health Disorders in People With Mental Retardation

Disorder	%
Cardiovascular disease	6.7–55.2
Respiratory illness	
Community-based	1.5–5.1
Institution-based	10–33
Cancer	7.4–34
Diabetes	1.6–9.1
Obesity	29.5–50.5
Dental	
Caries	24–56
Gingivitis	60–90
Seizure disorder	8.8–32

common types of mental health disorders reported in people with mental retardation in a community study by Ryan and Sundheim (1993) were anxiety disorders (30%), including posttraumatic stress disorder (19% to 72%). Psychotic disorders (2% to 5%) are found at slightly above the general population rate, and personality disorders (3%) are most often missed due to mental retardation being assumed to be the cause of personality style. Mood disorders are reported to affect 6% of people with mental retardation, but this is generally thought to be a low estimate due to underdiagnosis. Dementia is a particular problem and is more common among adults with Down syndrome. A summary of these prevalence data is found in Table 10.2.

The assessment of psychiatric illness must be made by careful notation of verbal and nonverbal self-reports by an individual as well as reports of that person's behavior by another individual who knows the person well. Attributing a set of behaviors, such as withdrawal, to one source of disorder, such as depression, is overly reductionistic. Pain, fear and anxiety, sensitivity to noise, shyness, disorganized thinking, psychotic perceptions (hallucinations), anger, or a misunderstood instruction are other possible causes of withdrawal behavior. When an individual with limited expressive language is assessed, hypotheses must be made about the most likely underlying cause of disturbance. This approach requires the treatment team to continue to examine the appropriateness of the hypotheses, given the responses they observe to their interventions and supports.

TABLE 10.2

**Prevalence of Common Mental Health Disorders in People
With Mental Retardation**

Disorder	%
Anxiety disorder	10–35
Posttraumatic stress disorder	22[a]
Psychosis	2–5
Depression	6–30
Personality disorder	~3
Substance abuse	2–20

[a] Range = 19% to 72%.

There has been a general tendency to attribute all changes in mood and behavior to the diagnosis of mental retardation. This phenomenon has been named *diagnostic overshadowing* (Reiss & Szyszko, 1983). Attributing all symptoms to mental retardation deprives the individual of access to appropriate treatment and of achieving maximal functioning. The same diagnostic error can be made from the other diagnostic side, leading to underrecognition of intellectual impairments among individuals with depression, psychosis, or anxiety disorders. Clinicians and teams who support individuals with mental retardation must remain attentive to the possibility of mistakes in *both* of these directions.

The diagnosis of mental retardation in and of itself does not guarantee the presence of psychiatric illness or disorder. In the *DSM–IV–TR* System, mental retardation is coded within the section on personality disorders. These disorders (Axis II) are considered to reflect traits of the individual. Often diagnoses on this axis do not require psychiatrist attention nor do they respond to psychotropic medications. Although earlier in our history, mental retardation was understood to represent a more stable trait of an individual and initially was thought to influence all aspects of a person's interaction with his or her environment, mental retardation is no longer considered a static condition. People with personality disorders improve with supports and treatment, which is also true of those with mental retardation. These are reasons that the coding of mental retardation under Axis II makes some sense. By convention of the *DSM* System, other medical conditions are coded under Axis III. Many disorders and diseases have known etiologies and specific treatments. Etiologic syndromes that cause mental retardation are coded under Axis III, in addition to identifying mental retardation under Axis II.

Seizures and epilepsy are more common among people with mental retardation

©American Association on Mental Retardation

compared to the general population. The prevalence of epilepsy is 0.6% in the general population but ranges from 8.8% to 32% among people with mental retardation. For individuals with both mental retardation and cerebral palsy, the prevalence of epilepsy is approximately 50%. Epilepsy is associated with autism, independent of the presence of mental retardation, and affects 11% to 35% of people with this diagnosis (Hauser & Hesdorffer, 1990). Several epileptic syndromes are strongly associated with mental retardation. For example, 70% to 90% of children with infantile spasms (West syndrome) or Lennox-Gastaut syndrome also have mental retardation.

A clinical challenge for any person with mental retardation and seizure disorder is whether to consider stopping anticonvulsant medication after being seizure free for more than 1 year. The risk of recurrence of seizures among individuals with mental retardation who have been seizure free for 4 to 5 years and who stop taking anticonvulsant medication is substantially higher (50%) compared to individuals without mental retardation who have been seizure free for the same time period and are off medication (25%). There are no reliable predictors, and the decision must be made in a thoughtful way for each individual. Seizure-related injuries represent a significant health risk for many people with mental retardation and epilepsy. For many individuals with epilepsy, the embarrassment of having a seizure in a public location is not worth the risk of stopping medication. Other injuries may be more time limited, such as damage to joints (dislocations), fractures (bones), and internal damage (including head injury) caused by hitting immoveable objects in the environment.

Substance abuse (2% to 20%) is increasingly recognized in people with mental retardation. Withdrawal from alcohol can contribute to seizures. When an individual is residing in a location where substance use is part of the social culture, his or her participation may be expected as part of normalizing his or her own behavior. In making a diagnosis of abuse or dependence, clinicians must look at the individual's drive to seek out the substance and his or her physiologic reaction to the absence of the substance. As more people with mental retardation are residing in the community, alcohol, marijuana, and cigarettes are the most frequently used legal and illegal substances of abuse. The long-term health risks and direct and indirect effects on their mental functioning (e.g., depression from alcohol; depression, apathy, and paranoia from marijuana; arousal and headaches from nicotine) must be taken into consideration by their health-care providers on a regular basis.

DIFFICULT BEHAVIORS

An important aspect of being human is to communicate within social groups. The purpose of most behavior is to care for oneself and to communicate with others.

©American Association on Mental Retardation

Any assessment of challenging, difficult, or dangerous behavior (formerly some-times referred to as maladaptive behavior) must include a comprehensive analysis of a person's life experiences, current situation, personality, and health condition.

ENVIRONMENTAL ASSESSMENT

Environmental assessment is a systematic method for collecting the information about a person's response to the many gross and subtle cues from the environments (physical and interpersonal) around him or her. Disorders that emanate from an individual's brain can influence his or her perception of changes around him or her, as discussed in the preceding section on health assessment. Misinterpreting altered behavior as a psychiatric disorder can make it more difficult to permit natural consequences of the behavioral pattern to evolve. It is important to avoid reinforcing or encouraging the altered behavior or inappropriate dependence. It is equally pointless to attempt to shape a person's behavioral responses purely by natural consequences when the person is suffering from progressive depression, for example. The importance of reevaluating the situation cannot be overly emphasized, including the response to different interventions and the meanings of the actions and in-actions of all participating team or family members.

For example, the most common cause of new onset of self-injury or aggressive behavior is pain. Diffuse sources, difficult to physically localize within the body, are more likely to increase overall irritability and to manifest as changes in behavior. For example, the innervation of the abdomen often makes it difficult to localize pain. Intestinal gas, ulcer of the stomach, reflux disorder, and menstrual cramps are all examples of sources of abdominal pain that may be difficult for an individual to pinpoint.

Head banging may be symptomatic of pain in the head from headache (sinus headache or migraine) or infection (ear infection, sinus infection). In a subset of in-dividuals, head banging may have developed as a means to increase endogenous opioid production (Sandman et al., 2000), analogous to the euphoric-like state ex-treme athletes achieve, such as long-distance runners. In other individuals, this may just be one manifestation of a ritualized or obsessive-compulsive action.

PSYCHIATRIC TREATMENT

Lack of order in normal brain function can be manifested in motor, sensory, psy-chological, and mixed-system problems. In clinical domains the term disorder is used to describe disruptions in normal function of tissues and organs for which we do not yet have a clear etiology. A person with a disorder may be well or sick (ill) at different points in time. Most psychiatric illnesses are chronic conditions result-ing from disruption of the neurophysiologic and neurobiologic functions of the brain. At present the causes are often not completely known but may be responses

©American Association on Mental Retardation

of the brain to insults elsewhere in the body, to the experience of external stress, or to prolonged imbalance of neurotransmitters. Thus different biological pathways may result in similar psychiatric symptoms.

Psychotherapy techniques, from counseling to insight-oriented and group therapies, may be very helpful in the treatment of anxiety and depressive disorders. Experiencing safe interactions with people who are trained to discuss issues such as trauma can truly alter people's perception of safety in the world around them. Brain-imaging techniques have shown that psychotherapy produces molecular changes in brain activity similar to those resulting from therapeutic medications. The time course to produce these changes is usually faster when using medications.

Pharmacology has advanced rapidly over the past 30 years, with new medications producing fewer toxic and unintended side effects. Readers are directed to *The International Consensus Handbook* (Reiss & Aman, 1998) and to a special issue of the *American Journal on Mental Retardation*, "Expert Consensus Guidelines on the Treatment of Psychiatric and Behavioral Problems in Mental Retardation" (Rush & Frances, 2000), for a comprehensive overview of psychotropic medications. Medications need to be examined periodically for their need and for possible drug–drug interactions. The fewest number of medications should be used as needed for specific symptoms. When starting any new medication, low dosages should be used and increases made slowly. This is done in order to look for possible side effects or unintended effects as well as for the body and brain to have time to adapt to the new medication. Some people have very strong responses to low oral doses of medicine, which may be due to protein-binding effects and interactions with other medications being taken or to individual variations in organ metabolism.

When administering medication, it is important to obtain informed consent from the prospective patient or treatment guardian. Important issues regarding consent have been detailed in a recent publication, *A Guide to Consent* (AAMR, 2001). Use of medications primarily for restraint is not recommended and is never indicated on a long-term basis.

HEALTH-RELATED SUPPORTS

Approximately 7.5 million individuals with mental retardation are living in the community in the United States (Office of the Surgeon General, 2002). Most of them live in the family home, even as adults, and are limited by low employment and difficulty in living independently. Many have associated health-care problems, such as obesity, hypertension, diabetes, seizures, mental health disorders, and orthopedic disorders. This has resulted in increased interest in the physical- and mental-health-care needs of people with mental retardation. Possible reasons for this include:

- More individuals with mental retardation are living in the community and seeking care from community health-care providers.

- Advances in health care have resulted in more and better treatments for chronic disorders, such as epilepsy or depression, that are often present in people with mental retardation.

- Families and self-advocates are more vocal about their needs for health-care supports.

- Advances in neonatology have enhanced survival of children with disabilities who often have complex health-care needs.

- Managed care organizations have encouraged the idea that individuals with disabilities should have a primary care clinician who can provide a "medical home" to coordinate health care, educational, and social services.

Many resources and supports are available to meet these needs. The role of the Internet has revolutionized the flow of information between providers and consumers. In the coming years, we will undoubtedly see a major change in how health-related supports are identified, assessed, and provided to consumers with mental retardation.

RESOURCES

Several textbooks describe health care for individuals with disabilities. Some are comprehensive texts in which the entire field is reviewed (Batshaw, 1997; Capute & Accardo, 1996; Jackson & Vessey, 1992; Nickel & Desch, 2000; Rubin & Crocker, 1989). Other texts are more focused on health-care concerns in specific disorders, such as Down syndrome (Pueschel, 1992). In addition, a number of monographs cover health-care topics that affect individuals with mental retardation. The AAMR publishes such monographs in an ongoing series called *Contemporary Issues in Health.*

Although there is no broad-based professional journal devoted to health-care concerns for people with mental retardation, articles on this topic can be found in a number of disability-related journals, such as the *American Journal on Mental Retardation, Mental Retardation,* the *Journal of Intellectual Disability Research,* and *Mental Retardation and Developmental Disabilities Research Reviews.* Medical journals such as *Developmental Medicine and Child Neurology, Pediatric Neurology,* and the *Journal of Child Neurology* as well as many psychiatric journals often contain information about health-care issues for people with developmental disabilities. Professional journals in the fields of nursing, physical and occupational therapy, as well as nutrition and speech therapy often contain articles about developmental disabilities. This information reflects the interest in the field and research on diagnosis and treatment of health disorders among individuals with mental retardation.

Consumers have much more opportunity to access this information because of the availability of new information technology. The Internet has provided a

©American Association on Mental Retardation

tremendous source of information through innumerable websites of varying quality. The National Library of Medicine at the National Institutes of Health maintains a computerized searchable database of information in the published literature. This database was previously restricted to professionals and researchers who paid a fee to obtain access. It was opened to the public and is now accessible via the Internet (www.4.ncbi.nlm.nih.gov/PubMed). Several agencies provide websites of reliable quality such as the American Association on Mental Retardation (www.aamr.org) and the Arc (www.thearc.org).

Consumers can search the Internet for information about a specific health-care problem or disorder and retrieve more information than may be known by their health-care provider. This is particularly true when the problem is highly specialized or unusual and the health-care provider is a generalist or primary-care provider. This has resulted in an equalization or reversal of the roles of professional and patient in sharing information. In the past, professionals had the information and decided how much to share with patients and in what form. Now patients and families can retrieve the information themselves and present it to the physician for discussion. Physicians now have the role of helping patient and families to evaluate the information derived from the Internet, some of which may be very questionable and unreliable. Physicians are no longer responsible for knowing everything and can work together with patients and families to use this information to decide upon the best treatment.

Interest in complementary and alternative treatments has also increased in recent years. The National Institutes of Health sponsors research on these treatments, and many websites discuss a wide variety of approaches. Traditional forms of healing, herbal treatments, and spiritually based therapies are widely used by many individuals. The intersection of spirituality and health for people with disabilities is the focus of a professional journal, the *Journal of Religion, Disability, and Health,* which publishes articles by pastors, theologians, parents, and individuals with disabilities. These activities reflect a broadening of the concept of health care to include a more holistic approach that considers health in the context of culture, religion, and lifestyle.

NEUROBIOLOGY RESEARCH

Advances in neuroscience and genetics have fueled tremendous interest among professionals and the public. The 1990s were proclaimed "The Decade of the Brain" by the National Institutes of Health, and during this time we witnessed advances in research on how the brain works in health and disease. Two areas of research are particularly noteworthy. Research has shown that much of early brain development before birth is controlled by a number of genes. *Organizer genes* direct and control cell proliferation, tissue type, body segmentation, and symmetry. *Regulator genes* control differentiation of specific structures and cell lineages. These genes have complex actions and interactions that result in formation of the infant brain (Sarnat & Menkes, 2000). Brain development occurs in stages and includes primary neurolation, prosencephalic development, neuronal proliferation, neuronal migration, synaptic organization, and myelination (Volpe, 2000). Specific genetic mutations have been identified in humans that result in abnormal development during each of these stages. Individuals with these genetic abnormalities have brain malformations that may result in mental retardation of varying degrees. Thus this research is expanding the scope of known biomedical etiologies of mental retardation. The availability of knowledge about the human genome will undoubtedly revolutionize our understanding of the genetic basis of mental retardation.

The second noteworthy area of research on brain development has focused on the importance of optimal care during the first few years of life. In contrast to the research on genetic control, this research has emphasized the effect of environmental influences on brain development. Brain development is the result of the interaction of genetic and environmental influences during early childhood (Zuckerman, Frank, & Augustyn, 1999). This research provides the basis for understanding the importance of early intervention services for infants and children at risk for developmental disabilities (Spiker & Hebbeler, 1999). These services are now mandated by federal law (Individuals With Disabilities Education Act Amendments of 1997 [IDEA], Pub. L. 105–17) and implemented in most states through a variety of programs. Indeed, failure to refer an infant at risk for developmental delay and inadequate early intervention services are risk factors for mental retardation.

New research into cellular metabolism has identified individual variation in mitochondrial genetic material. These findings support the clinical observations that individuals vary enormously in their response to the same medication, with differences in side effects experienced, rate of efficacy, dosages required, and drug-drug interactions. These empirical findings will continue to press the further development of research and integration of biology and clinical science.

HEALTH-CARE SUPPORTS

Individuals with special health-care needs have or are at risk for chronic physical, developmental, behavioral, or emotional conditions and require health-care-related supports of a type or amount beyond that generally required. One of these supports is a *medical home,* a place where these health-care needs may be met. The medical home concept was first developed for children and adolescents (American Academy of Pediatrics, 2001) but is also applicable for individuals across the lifespan. A medical home provides care that is accessible, family-centered, comprehensive, continuous, coordinated, compassionate, culturally competent, and for which the health-care provider assumes responsibility. The medical home provider interacts with

©American Association on Mental Retardation

specialists, mental-health-care providers, educational and vocational service providers, family support services, religious and spiritual advisers, and representatives of financial support agencies. The medical home provider accepts the person's health-care insurance, even if it is limited to Medicaid. The provider respects the individual's point of view and works together with family and significant others to ensure that the individual's choices are respected. Respect for cultural perspectives is also essential. Coordination of all health-care supports is a key role of the medical home provider. The concept of a medical home for individuals with special health-care needs is an ideal that is far from a reality for many individuals. Nonetheless, the concept incorporates the belief that every individual with special health-care needs, including everyone with mental retardation, should have a medical home that fulfills this ideal.

A key aspect of this model of health-care support is the role of *self-determination.* Self-determination is familiar in other areas of the life of a person with mental retardation, such as choice about where to live or work, but it is relatively new in the area of health care. Self-determination in health care requires a new way of looking at the relationship between individuals and health-care providers. In addition to requiring new training for providers, it requires the development of new skills for people with mental retardation. The basic tenets of self-determination include:

- *freedom:* the ability to plan, choose, and evaluate all desired supports;

- *authority:* the ability to control resources and to be a full partner in decision making;

- *support:* respect for diversity and strengths that allow an individual to live in the community with happiness and satisfaction;

- *responsibility:* acceptance by the individual of social and community roles.

In health care, freedom means the ability to choose health-care providers and other health-related supports. Authority means the ability to control funding and to participate in health-care decisions according to one's ability. Support means that providers respect the individual's aspirations and recognize his or her personal goals for a meaningful life. Responsibility means that when an individual assumes the right of self-determination in health care, the person also assumes the responsibility to follow agreed treatment plans and to promote a healthy lifestyle. Self-determination in health care requires that providers and individuals with mental retardation work together in new ways, but it also holds the promise of a better future for all. Additional recommendations for health-care supports for people with mental retardation are found in the report of the Surgeon General's Conference on Health Disparities and Mental Retardation (Office of the Surgeon General, 2002) and the report of the Healthy People 2010 project (Maternal and Child Health Bureau, 2002).

SUMMARY

For people with mental retardation, the effects of physical and mental health on functioning range from greatly facilitating to greatly inhibiting. Some individuals enjoy robust good health, with no significant activity limitations, that allows them to participate fully in chosen social roles, such as work, recreation, or leisure activities. On the other hand, some individuals have a variety of significant physical health conditions, such as epilepsy or cerebral palsy, that greatly impair body functioning in areas such as mobility and nutrition and severely restrict personal activities and social participation. Others are significantly affected by anxiety disorders or by challenging behaviors that may reflect mental or physical health problems. Most individuals with mental retardation function somewhere between these extremes. Contextual factors, such as the environments in which individuals live, learn, work, play, socialize, and interact with others, influence the degree to which these individuals are able to function and participate. Environmental factors may create actual or potential dangers or fail to provide appropriate protection and supports. Individuals with mental retardation may have difficulty recognizing health problems, negotiating the health-care system, communicating symptoms and feelings, and understanding treatment plans. Aggressive or self-injurious behaviors that originate in environmental factors may be misinterpreted as problems within the individual and treated inappropriately. Attention to these contextual factors is critical for understanding how people with mental retardation experience and overcome health limitations.

Health conditions can affect assessment of intelligence and adaptive behavior for people with mental retardation. Intellectual assessment may be influenced by impaired alertness that is caused by factors such as sleep disturbances and nutritional disturbances. Valid assessment of intelligence may be extremely difficult in an individual with major depression or a thought disorder. Medications (e.g., anticonvulsants and psychotropic drugs) may affect performance on intelligence tests, and chronic illnesses may cause tiredness and fatigue that influence test performance. Assessment of adaptive behavior can also be affected by drugs that influence gross- and fine-motor skills or by oral motor conditions that influence communication skills. What was termed maladaptive behavior in the past may now be understood as being the result of mental health disorders or of contextual environmental challenges.

Assessment of needed supports may also be affected by the presence of health conditions. Individuals with mental retardation may need health-related supports to promote functioning and participation to overcome limitations in mobility (e.g., wheelchair-accessible work settings) or safety (e.g., adaptations to prevent seizure-related injuries). Access to quality health care is a support that may be needed by some individuals to promote optimal functioning and participation.

©American Association on Mental Retardation

CHAPTER 11
PUBLIC RESPONSIBILITY IN THE PROVISION OF SUPPORTS

OVERVIEW

This chapter provides an overview of the responsibilities of public systems, particularly state mental retardation–developmental disabilities (MR-DD) agencies, in moving their service delivery systems to a supports-based approach. The 2002 definition of mental retardation, and its classification and supports planning components, provides a coherent framework for reconceptualizing the purposes and processes of public systems. This approach also provides a structure through which public systems can reconcile diffuse and often conflicting public policy. Making a meaningful commitment to a supports-based approach gives public systems the opportunity to develop clarity of mission that is more closely aligned with the expressed aspirations of people with mental retardation and their families and emerging public policy.

SHIFTING TO THE 2002 SYSTEM

A public service delivery system, in shifting to a supports-based approach, changes its focus and commitment away from programs to individuals. This paradigmatic shift defines the consumers of the service system as individuals with particular support needs and their families, rather than groups or numbers of individuals enrolled in particular services and programs. The role of public systems becomes one of facilitating society's responses to individual support needs. This is both a conceptual shift and a programmatic shift away from maintaining systems of care or services in which or into which individuals are placed, with the hope, often unrealized, that their needs will be addressed.

The view represented by the 2002 AAMR System emphasizes attitudes and practices that recognize the full citizenship of people with mental retardation while acknowledging that mental retardation constitutes a significant limitation and disadvantage to the individual. Supports, which enhance functioning, are a counterweight to this disadvantage.

The goal of a supports-based approach is to facilitate the inclusion of individuals in the full life of the community. Appropriate supports lessen functional limitations and allow individuals to participate and contribute to community life while also having their needs addressed in a more typical societal context.

A GROWING CONSENSUS ON SUPPORTS

Services, both generic and specialized, are a subset of the larger concept of supports as defined and explicated in chapter 9. Those specialized services traditionally provided directly by large state MR-DD service delivery systems, by regional or local governmental entities, or under contract with private provider agencies, are types of paid supports. Generic services (i.e., provided by nondisability-specific health and human services systems) are also types of paid supports. As the concept of supports and a supports-based approach has become more broadly promoted within the field, the term *supports* has begun to be used in many instances interchangeably and erroneously with *services*. This is both imprecise and a mischaracterization of supports. Supports are both a broader and a more overarching series of resources and interventions than are services. Perhaps more significantly, supports are a very different approach to addressing the needs and choices of people with intellectual and other disabilities.

The nature of systems of supports and the relative relationship between supports and services is illustrated in Figure 11.1. This can be compared to the description of the sources of support found in chapter 9. The person is at the center, surrounded by concentric rings. Moving from the person, these rings represent family and friends, informal supports, paid and nonpaid generic services, and specialized services. The services provided directly or under contract by state MR-DD agencies would typically be considered "specialized services." Growing exceptions to this would be family support services, which might hover between the "family and friends" ring and the "informal supports" ring.

The goal of typical service provision in a systems-centered approach had been to generate or use specialized services to the maximum extent. Graphically, these are the most distant from the person, as illustrated in Figure 11.1. They are also most distant from the person's social network and from the person in terms of choice and control over resources. The freedom and the flexibility of resources to address individual choices and needs by blending these rings is the essence of the supports approach.

A growing consensus is emerging in the field about the nature of supports. Hallmarks of this consensus reflect that *supports,* when the term is used to represent this shift in perspective,

- are community-based;

- are person-centered and individually planned, developed, and personalized;

©American Association on Mental Retardation

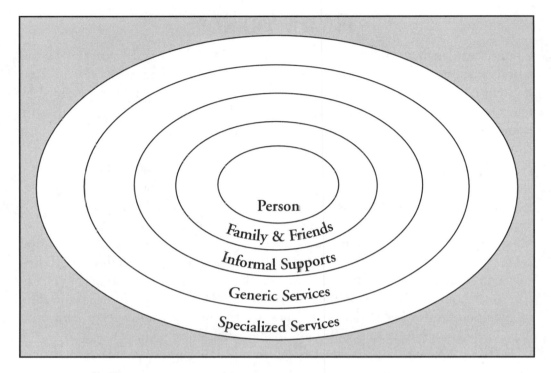

Figure 11.1. The nature of systems of supports.

- enhance individual functioning and participation;
- facilitate the exercise of self-determination; and
- are consumer directed.

There are two other significant hallmarks of a supports-based approach to service delivery. First, intensity of support needs is separable from the location where the supports will be delivered. The need for intensive or extensive supports does not dictate that they be delivered in a restrictive setting or a particular type of setting. Second, the intensity of an individual's support needs may vary across the areas in which he or she needs supports.

Matching these hallmarks with the present orientation of most state systems demonstrates notable gaps between the supports approach and present practice. Although many delivery systems have a stated philosophy of person-centered supports, the ways that resources are dedicated, and the types of options available to individuals and their families remain traditional system-centered services. To implement the 2002 AAMR *Definition, Classification, and Systems of Supports,* most public systems will need to further reconceptualize their purposes and dramatically change their practices.

POLICY TRENDS

Community membership, a term conceptualized by Bradley and Knoll (1990) and further elaborated by Bradley (1994), is a useful label for the present service paradigm as it seeks to evolve to a supports-based approach. Having been preceded by eras of segregation and deinstitutionalization, the era of community membership shares the hallmarks of the supports approach while also providing the context from which both the 1992 and 2002 definition arose.

Although a conceptual framework and not always an enunciated public policy, the idea of community membership has influenced and become embedded in other public policies. Many of these policies have been instrumental in moving state service systems to adopt more of a supports-based approach. These shifts are seen in family support services, the emphasis on natural environments in early intervention services (Part C of Individuals With Disabilities Education Act Amendments [IDEA] of 1997, Pub. L. 105–17), the decrease in reliance upon or elimination of congregate institutional settings, the increase in supported living and home ownership, employment and other forms of meaningful community contribution, and presence in the community of people with mental retardation.

Many public systems have evolved pockets of innovation, where some or all of these types of supports exist. Rarely is the provision of these types of supports systemwide or equally accessible to all eligible individuals. States, for the most part, have not embraced these innovations as their overarching policy framework, nor have they incorporated the conceptual framework for a supports approach as presented in the 1992 AAMR manual, *Mental Retardation: Definition, Classification, and Systems of Supports* (Luckasson et al.). Recent work by Denning et al. (2000) shows that about 6% of the states use the exact 1992 definition or have adapted it for their own use. (For a discussion of the diffusion of ideas, see chap. 2.)

Self-determination, both as a movement and an approach to supports provision, has become an important emerging public policy for people with mental retardation and other developmental disabilities. Model projects, first in New Hampshire and then in a number of other states, supported by the Robert Wood Johnson Foundation, provided a source of innovation in the states for demonstrating a consumer-driven supports approach. These grants to states or more local service entities serving individuals who had been in institutional and other traditional service settings have both raised consumer expectations as well as demonstrated the feasibility of consumer-directed support approaches and a retooling of service and support approaches.

Self-determination as an enunciated public policy is embedded in the Developmental Disabilities Assistance and Bill of Rights Act of 2000 (Pub. L. 106–402). The DD Act recognizes that a purpose of supports is to "promote self-determination" (§ 101(b)). Self-determination is also considered a principle, that "individuals with developmental disabilities, including those with the most severe developmental dis-

©American Association on Mental Retardation

abilities, are capable of self-determination" (§ 101(c)(1)). The U.S. Supreme Court decision in *Olmstead v. L. C.* (1999) upheld the rights of people with mental retardation to live in a community setting rather than in an institution. With its emphases on community support options, independent individual assessment, and consumer choice, *Olmstead* provides an additional policy voice for a supports-based approach.

Perhaps more significantly, because they involve the redirection of financial resources consistent with a supports-based approach philosophy, are the changes in some policies in the federal Center for Medicare and Medicaid Services (CMS), formerly the Health Care Financing Administration (HCFA). A series of directive letters from CMS to state Medicaid directors (HCFA, 2000, 2001) has clarified and shifted requirements to enable more supports that are requisite for community living. Through a series of grant offerings, CMS is providing incentives to states to use Medicaid money to move closer to a supports-based approach. Although some of these grant opportunities primarily apply to people with physical disabilities and frail older people, the larger grants in the Real Choice Systems Change program were created to assist states in moving their delivery systems, including those systems that serve people with mental retardation and their families, closer to a supports-based approach. These efforts, to ensure that federal policy is more coherent and enhances the implementation of the *Olmstead* decision, although small in comparison to the flow of Medicaid dollars into more traditional system-centered services, still represent the beginnings of a salient and tangible shift in federal policy toward a supports-based approach.

The supports-based approach is also inherent in federal policy through the Ticket to Work Incentives Improvement Act of 1999 (Pub. L. 106–170) recipients. The individual beneficiary, in need of employment services, controls the resources allocated for these purposes and picks his or her own provider, who allocates an individually tailored set of employment services. The structure of Ticket to Work and these Work Incentives reflects the hallmarks of a supports-based approach. Although it is a matter of debate how much individuals with mental retardation, in contrast to individuals with other disabilities, will directly benefit from this legislation, it nevertheless remains an important shift in federal policy toward a supports approach.

THE DEMAND FOR SUPPORTS OUTSTRIPS SUPPLY

Waiting lists for community services are a problem across the country. Eighteen states have had lawsuits brought by individuals and their families about their waiting list status and lack of access to services. The findings in Section 101 of the

DD Act (2000) (Pub. L. 106–402) recognizes that

> (11) many service delivery systems and communities are not prepared to meet the impending needs of the 479,862 adults with developmental disabilities who are living at home with parents who are 60 years or older and who serve as the primary caregivers of the adults. (§ 101(a)(11))

It is noteworthy that all these waiting lists are for community services. In most states the public demand for services and supports is outdistancing the supply of existing service and support options and the capacities and resources of the states. Most states and their specialized MR-DD service systems have done very limited planning to anticipate or address these demands or conducted any planning with individuals while they are waiting for services.

In a supports-based approach, continuous planning would be going on with individuals. An appropriately applied supports approach that provided adequate supports and services based on individual choices and needs might also serve to eliminate use of resources or services not wanted or valued by the individual and service packages that are bundled together as "one size fits all."

THE PURPOSES OF PUBLIC SYSTEMS

The goals and purposes of public service systems for people with mental retardation have shifted over time. From their initial founding in the 1860s, public systems for people with mental retardation have been state-operated and institutional, with an emphasis on custodial training and treatment, and misguided ideas of protecting individuals and society. As community-based services have become more the predominant mode of service delivery, public service systems have continued to implicitly or explicitly struggle with their role and purpose.

The essential task for public systems serving people with mental retardation is to become person-centered systems, balancing personal choices with safety and security (Gettings & Thaler, 2000). Moving to a supports-based approach is necessary to realizing these goals. As explicated in this manual and in the evolving thinking in the field, achieving a supports-based approach will require both evolution and transformations of public service systems if they are to become truly person-centered.

The framework of the 2002 AAMR System and each of its components, as in the 1992 System that preceded it, has implications for public systems. The implications of the three functions within the framework — diagnosis, classification, and supports planning as well as the demands and agenda they create for public systems — vary by function. Examining the three functions and assessing system capacity to address each of them can also serve as a tool in the process of reorganizing systems to a supports-based approach.

©American Association on Mental Retardation

DIAGNOSIS

State service systems typically do not have the responsibility for establishing the diagnosis of mental retardation for an individual. Rather, public systems use the decision, whether or not the individual is considered to have mental retardation, in their determinations of eligibility for services and benefits. The process of diagnosis typically precedes the determination(s) of eligibility for services and supports. In instances where there is no clarity about the diagnosis or insufficient documentation, public systems may seek additional evaluations and information to assist them in decision making for eligibility. There is great variation across public systems in how this additional information is developed, collected, and coordinated. Some systems perform some of these functions as part of the eligibility determination; other systems place the responsibility for additional information and data on the applicants and their families.

If public systems use these diagnostic decisions in their eligibility determinations, they have a responsibility to assure that the diagnosis was made in full adherence to professional practice (see chap. 6). As the nation becomes increasingly diverse, the application of Assumption 2 of the definition, "Valid assessment considers cultural and linguistic diversity as well as differences in communication, sensory, motor, and behavioral factors," has tremendous efficacy for the cultural competence and social legitimacy of public systems.

Some types of information obtained in the process of diagnosis may be useful in the process of planning supports. Under older, system-centered, nonsupports-based approaches, this might have included specific test scores or levels of functioning that may have been used to make placement or service decisions especially about the restrictiveness of the environment. Under the supports-based approach, however, only information that is specifically related to planning personal supports for the individual is used from the diagnostic process. Information that may become apparent during the diagnostic process, such as information about individual learning styles, the impact of physical limitations on participation in the diagnostic process, affective needs, and so forth, may be useful in designing personal supports.

CLASSIFICATION

In the 2002 System, classification is based, as it was in the 1992 System, primarily on intensity of support needs. Classification by degree of disability, functional level, IQ, or other statistical score is generally incompatible with the supports-based approach.

Large public systems that have made placement or financial allocation decisions based on functional level, as measured by level of mental retardation and/or based on test scores, will need to find other strategies for generating appropriate groupings and data on the individuals they serve. Previously, classification by levels of disability or impairment provided a short-hand way for systems to make decisions on placement or groupings. Functional levels created frameworks for the location and quantity of how much service might be received. Institutional care might have been advanced as appropriate for individuals at particular functional levels. Individuals with so-called milder impairments may have received fewer services. Perpetuating this approach was the underlying misassumption that the measurement of functional level was meaningful for these purposes. This viewpoint failed to take into account the varying strengths, gifts, and needs of individuals and the heterogeneity of groupings that were based on similar patterns of results on assessments.

Classifying individuals and groups of individuals on the basis of support needs provides the opportunity, as well as the challenge, for public systems of service to implement system planning and structure reimbursement patterns that are based on individual needs. Full embrace of a supports-based approach would require an intentional commitment to planning and this shift in planning modalities.

PLANNING SUPPORTS

Shifts inherent in a supports-based approach are most directly apparent in the function of planning supports. For individuals with mental retardation and their families, and for caregivers and other representatives of the delivery system, the function of planning supports makes real this shift in thinking. The supports-based approach moves systems, in collaboration with individuals, toward formulating personal outcomes for each individual. System goals shift from mere placement to enhancing and realizing personal outcomes. Personal appraisal and functional assessment measures are significant tools in this process. Mechanisms for seeking and honoring personal choices and aspirations, such as person-centered-planning techniques, are essential to the process of support planning.

The process of support planning, with its individual assessment component and the need to document support intensity needs, directly addresses the choices and aspirations of individuals with mental retardation and their families. The process of support planning also addresses requirements under the *Olmstead* (1999) decision for independent assessment, planning, and transition to community living. The support planning function of the framework if appropriately implemented enables states to address evolving public policy and consumer expectations.

IMPROVEMENTS IN FUNCTIONING

In the supports-based approach to service delivery, the supports available to individuals determine their functioning within the context of the interaction of their capabilities and the demands of their environment. Assumption 5 of the definition recognizes that "with appropriate personalized supports over a sustained period, the life functioning of the person with mental retardation generally will improve."

©American Association on Mental Retardation

Enhancement or improvements in individual functioning are a goal of the provision of supports and services. As public systems implement a supports-based approach, instances of improvement in individual functioning are a critical point. The importance of clinical judgment and ongoing communication with the individual, including personal appraisals, are essential to understanding the nature of improvement and its relationship to the continued provision of supports. Only through this highly personalized process can the system ascertain whether improvement is dependent on the continued provision of support or if the improvement represents developmental progress that may make possible the gradual fading of more intensive supports in favor of fewer or less intensive supports. Improvement in functioning may also shift the balance between paid supports and more natural supports.

RISKS OF PREMATURE REMOVAL OF SUPPORTS

People with mental retardation whose functioning improves risk premature removal of necessary supports. Inappropriate practices include:

- mistakenly removing as "no longer needed" the very systems of supports that are allowing the improvement;

- requiring individuals with mental retardation to repeatedly "re-prove" the disability, thereby discouraging applicants and cutting back on the number of recipients of services;

- inaccurately interpreting as improvement enhanced functioning in an undemanding or tolerant environment that does not generalize to more demanding environments.

Pressures upon public service systems to either decrease caseloads or serve more individuals with existing or limited financial resources can create pressure to remove supports from individuals who are "doing well." Similarly, reliance upon capitation approaches and rationing of resources may seek to arbitrarily limit supports. Responsible implementation of a supports-based approach requires the exercise of continuous vigilance in maintaining a focus on the individual.

SYSTEMIC CHANGES NECESSARY TO MOVE TO A SUPPORTS-BASED APPROACH

A supports-based approach will require traditional case management roles to shift. The role of coordinating supports and services through either case manager, supports broker, or personal agent will need to include these elements (Luckasson &

Spitalnik, 1994):

- empowering individuals rather than "remediating";
- developing a supports approach;
- facilitating person-centered forms of planning;
- viewing the individual and family as directors of their own supports.

Person-centered planning formats will result in individualized supports plans, in contrast to system-centered individual habilitation plans.

The supports-based approach makes it possible to separate the intensity of support needs from the location and type of setting where the supports will be delivered. Under this approach, support needs in one area of functioning do not determine the intensity of need in other areas; strengths and capacities may coexist with needs and limitations. More system-centered approaches assumed that intense support needs would need to be addressed in more restrictive settings and that having intensive support needs would require curtailing individual liberties in order to have these needs addressed. In contrast to this institutional model of interventions, the supports-based approach allows for consideration of place of delivery of supports as well as the nature and content of those supports and who will deliver them.

New types of support and service providers will be needed if public systems are to adopt a supports-based approach. Providers will need to vend specific supports desired by people with disabilities. Offering packaged programs in which the person is expected to fit will be less desirable to individuals who have control over the resources dedicated to their support needs. Although many individuals will have extensive support needs, including 24-hour supervision and assistance in all aspects of self-care and self-direction, the structure of how these types of supports are provided will shift.

Public systems will need to set different expectations as expressed in their contracting procedures. It will be important for systems to explore establishing funding patterns based on intensity of support needs rather than type of setting or severity of categorical disability. Entities that are exploring moving to capitated systems will need to develop rate structures based on intensity of support needs and the mix of supports through which individual needs are addressed.

Direct support professionals who understand supports and are trained in their roles as support providers and community connectors are essential in implementing a supports approach and assisting people with disabilities reach their desired outcomes. The growing crisis over the lack of direct support workers, the lack of professionalization of the role including low wages and unfavorable demographics for developing a future workforce, make these issues a potentially critical barrier in moving to a supports-based approach.

©American Association on Mental Retardation

SUMMARY

As public systems continue to move their service delivery systems to a supports-based approach, they will face a number of challenges, including the categorical organization of public systems, equity, education and training, assuring quality, and making innovation statewide practice.

THE CATEGORICAL ORGANIZATION OF PUBLIC SYSTEMS

There is a disjunction between individual clinical needs for supports and the ways that public policy may organize services. An individual who is diagnosed as having mental retardation may be eligible for MR-DD services. If that individual also has support needs for mental health services or services to support the aging process, his or her eligibility in the mental retardation system may preclude his or her access to services under a different organizational auspice.

EQUITY

Most public systems are plagued by the inequitable distribution of service resources. Some individuals receive costly comprehensive and often restrictive packages of services, whereas others, as evidenced by waiting lists, do not have access to services at all. A supports-based approach, in creating flexibility and reconfiguring how supports and services are provided, may make it possible to extend service resources to address the needs of a broader group of individuals.

Individuals of minority background tend to be underrepresented and underserved through public service delivery systems. The service models inherent in large public systems may not be responsive to diverse communities' views of disabilities, expectations about caregiving, and patterns of interaction with majority-dominated social institutions. By definition, a supports-based approach could be created to be responsive to individuals and families of diverse cultures and communities.

EDUCATION AND TRAINING ABOUT
SUPPORT APPROACHES

To enable large public systems to move to a supports-based approach, much education and training is needed. Workforce issues include the training of professionals as well as grappling with the training and other challenges in developing and maintaining an adequate supply of direct support professionals. Individuals with mental retardation and their families will need education and training to familiarize them with the supports-based approach and assist them in becoming effective participants in planning and directing their own supports.

ASSURING QUALITY

Monitoring and creating a climate for quality improvement is a critical task for systems moving toward a supports-based approach, as for any approach. Quality assurance in a supports-based model needs to mirror and measure the goals of the system: consumer choice and direction in the context of safety and security. Outcome-based models of quality enhancement are well-matched to the underlying assumptions of a supports-based approach. Participation of individuals and families in the development of any process of monitoring and quality enhancement is essential.

MAKING INNOVATION STATEWIDE PRACTICE

In every state there are kernels of innovation, demonstrating in a defined locality or for a specified number of individuals the efficacy of a supports-based approach. Within each state, and as a field, our challenge is to make a supports-based approach the norm, available to all who use services.

©American Association on Mental Retardation

PART 5

IMPLICATIONS

CHAPTER 12
IMPLICATIONS OF THE 2002 SYSTEM

> *Mental retardation* is a disability characterized by significant limitations both in intellectual functioning and in adaptive behavior as expressed in conceptual, social, and practical adaptive skills. This disability originates before age 18.

OVERVIEW

As discussed in chapter 2, the 1992 American Association on Mental Retardation (AAMR) System (Luckasson et al.) was a significant departure from previous diagnostic and classification systems in mental retardation, due primarily to its functional orientation and ecological perspective. The interactive role of capabilities (intelligence and adaptive behavior), environments, and supports was a major implication of the 1992 System. Compared to earlier systems, the 1992 System provided a better understanding of mental retardation and formed the foundation for the provision of needed and individualized supports to people with the disability (Luckasson & Spitalnik, 1994).

The 2002 AAMR System continues the functional and ecological perspective and incorporates changes in the understanding of the multidimensional aspects of the condition of mental retardation and its amelioration. Specifically, the 2002 System: (a) retains the term *mental retardation;* the essential features of the 1992 System, including its functional orientation and supports emphasis; and the three diagnostic criteria related to intellectual functioning, adaptive behavior, and age of onset; and (b) maintains a strong commitment to the belief that classification based on the intensities of needed supports should be the primary purpose of a classification system.

The 2002 System reflects the emerging consensus on the following seven aspects of the definition and classification of the condition of mental retardation:

1. Mental retardation is a disability characterized by significant limitations both in intellectual functioning and adaptive behavior as expressed in conceptual, social, and practical adaptive skills. The disability originates before age 18.

2. A disability is the expression of limitations in individual functioning within a social context and represents a substantial disadvantage to the individual. It is further conceptualized in the *International Classification of Functioning, Disability, and Health* (World Health Organization, 2001) as a significant problem in functioning related to problems in the capacity to perform ("impairment"), the ability to perform ("activity limitations"), and the opportunity to perform ("participation restrictions").

3. Adaptive behavior is the collection of conceptual, social, and practical skills that have been learned by people in order to function in their everyday lives. Its assessment should relate to an individual's typical performance during daily routines and changing circumstances, not to maximum performance.

4. Although far from perfect, intellectual ability is still best represented by IQ scores when obtained from appropriate assessment instruments. The criterion for diagnosis is approximately two standard deviations below the mean, considering the standard error of measurement for the specific assessment instruments used and the instruments' strengths and limitations.

5. Multiple classification systems may be used for a variety of purposes and based on a number of different factors to meet the varied needs of individuals and their families, researchers, clinicians, and practitioners. Aspects of an individual's mental retardation might be classified, for example, on the basis of the intensities of needed supports, etiology, levels of measured intelligence, or levels of assessed adaptive behavior.

6. The functions or reasons for applying a definition of mental retardation to a person are multiple and may include diagnosis, classification, and/or planning of supports. Within each function are multiple purposes. For example, the diagnosis function may be applied to determine eligibility for services, benefits, or legal protections. Likewise, there are different purposes for classification such as grouping for service reimbursement or funding, research, services, or communicating about selected characteristics. Supports planning for a given person should relate to the individual's strengths and needs in each of the five dimensions (see Figure 1.1) and focus on enhancing personal outcomes related to independence, relationships, contributions, school and community participation, and personal well-being.

7. Clinical judgment may play a key role in diagnosis, classification, and planning supports.

Reflective of these seven consensus statements, the 2002 System incorporates: (a) a standard deviation criterion to the intellectual and adaptive behavior components; (b) an added dimension that involves participation, interactions, and social

©American Association on Mental Retardation

roles; (c) recent factor-analytic work on adaptive behavior that identifies specific behavioral indicators for each of the three adaptive skill areas referenced in the definition — conceptual, social, and practical; (d) recent work in the conceptualization and measurement of supports and their intensity; (e) a systematic framework for assessment (see Table 1.1); and (f) an expanded discussion of the multidimensionality of mental retardation, clinical judgment, classification systems, etiology, physical health and mental health issues, and public responsibilities in the provision of supports.

The AAMR Terminology and Classification Committee is sensitive to the continued debate about "what is mental retardation?" and differing scientific paradigms used to explain and respond to it. For example, in a critique of the 1992 System, Switzky (in press) stated:

> The main problem with the 1992 manual is that it is strongly tilted toward the worldviews of stakeholders involved in the treatment, service provision, and social advocacy within the context of the community supports revolution and only minimally reflects the worldviews of researchers and scientists who may find the current [1992] AAMR definition too vague and ambiguous as well as arbitrary and misleading to be useful in carrying out the business of replicable research.

Reflecting these two very different paradigmatic approaches, Switzky and Greenspan (in press) in their final integrative chapter in the book *What Is Mental Retardation?* stated:

> We believe that our contributors' conceptions of mental retardation would cluster roughly into the Functionalist-Objectivist Paradigm, whose worldview is based on the presence of an objective reality and social stability, and into the Interpretative Paradigm, whose worldview is based on the presence of a subjective reality and social stability. This is the source of the paradigm clash that is now occurring in the field of mental retardation.

The nine implications of the 2002 System discussed in the following section of this chapter need to be considered in light of the current paradigm tension referenced by Switzky and Greenspan (in press) and the current discussion about terminology and the name *mental retardation.* There is no doubt that the field of mental retardation is in a state of flux regarding not just a fuller understanding of the construct of mental retardation, but also in the language and processes we use in naming, defining, and classifying. For example, we are, in early 2002, in the midst of discussions about the nature of intelligence; the relationship between intelligence and adaptive behavior; the implementation of the supports paradigm; and the relationships between people with mental retardation and those in other populations, including individuals with traumatic brain injury, those diagnosed with learning disabilities, those diagnosed with developmental disabilities, and those with cognitive disabili-

©American Association on Mental Retardation

ties; the best way to conceptualize disabling conditions; the impact of the consumer and reform movements; and the effects of terminology upon people's lives. Thus, in thinking about and discussing the "implications of the 2002 System," readers should realize that the field of mental retardation is in a state of transition and that knowledge and understanding is cumulative. The following nine implications are based on our current understanding of the condition of mental retardation and collective efforts to reflect current thinking in the field.

NINE IMPLICATIONS OF THE 2002 SYSTEM

In our opinion, there are nine major implications of the 2002 System for both the field of mental retardation generally and users of this manual specifically: (a) approach mental retardation from a multidimensional perspective; (b) employ an ecological approach to understand and investigate the impact on individual functioning of the person, the environment, and the individualized supports provided; (c) recognize differences in the relevance of assessment to the three functions of diagnosis, classification, and planning supports; (d) integrate further the supports paradigm into current education and habilitation practices; (e) modify research designs to reflect the current emphasis on inclusion, empowerment, and supports; (f) establish a needs-based approach to eligibility; (g) fund services on the basis of individualized support needs; (h) incorporate current thinking about mental retardation into legal procedures and the justice system; and (i) address the needs of the *forgotten generation,* defined as people with identified mental retardation at the higher IQ levels, those who currently reject or avoid the label but would be eligible for services or those who are not eligible for the label but experience significant problems due to cognitive limitations.

MULTIDIMENSIONAL APPROACH

In chapter 3 we discussed our current understanding of the five dimensions of a comprehensive model of mental retardation: Intellectual Abilities; Adaptive Behavior; Participation, Interactions, and Social Roles; Health; and Context (see Figure 1.1). As we continue to understand these dimensions better, at least four implications are apparent from a multidimensional approach to the condition of mental retardation: (a) an emerging appreciation of the parallel aspects of intelligence and adaptive behavior; (b) the importance of health and etiology in the process of diagnosis, classification, and the planning of individualized supports; (c) the need to analyze environments; and (d) the incorporation of an individual's desired outcomes into the provision of supports.

©American Association on Mental Retardation

Parallel Aspects of Intelligence and Adaptive Behavior

The current multidimensional approaches to — and understanding of — intelligence and adaptive behavior were discussed in chapters 4 and 5. In reference to intelligence, there is some empirical support (see, e.g., Greenspan & Granfield, 1992; McGrew et al., 1996; Schalock, 1999b) that intellectual functioning can be analyzed in terms of a tripartite model of intelligence that includes conceptual, social, and practical intelligence. Analogously, there is a growing consensus regarding a tripartite model of adaptive behavior whose major factors include personal independence (practical), responsibility (social), and cognitive or academic (conceptual). There is a close relationship between "tripartite" models of intelligence and adaptive behavior, especially in reference to (a) the conceptual similarity between practical intelligence and the adaptive behavior factor of independent living skills, (b) conceptual intelligence and cognitive and communication or academic skills, and (c) social intelligence and social competence. These close relationships have led some (e.g., Greenspan, 1999b; Schalock, 1999b) to suggest that the constructs of intelligence and adaptive behavior may be integrated through the broader, umbrella construct of personal competence.

Regardless of how this integration proceeds in the future, two major implications of the 2002 System are, first, to focus assessment on the multidimensional aspects of intelligence and adaptive behavior. In reference to intelligence, for example, profiles should be used that show relative strengths and limitations in the various subscale scores, such as those on the WISC–R and WAIS–III. The role of the evaluator is to interpret these scores and to discuss what the person's strengths and limitations suggest in terms of how that individual learns and processes information, and how the profiles can be used to maximize the person's learning and personal outcomes. The same is true for adaptive behavior profiles. The second implication of the "merging of intelligence and adaptive behavior" is that researchers need to identify and aggregate behavior indicators of each of the three adaptive behavior factors and different types of intelligence.

Sensitivity to Health and Etiology

Health is a fundamental aspect of living and includes several important personal capabilities, such as strength, alertness, and sensorimotor competence. Most individuals with mental retardation fall somewhere between a state of perfect physical health and severe physical problems. Health problems of people with mental retardation are not inherently different from those of individuals who do not have mental retardation, but, as discussed in chapter 10, the effects of these problems may be different because of environments, coping limitations, communication difficulties, and impediments in the health-care system.

The multifactorial approach to etiology discussed in chapter 8 expands the list of causal factors in mental retardation in two important directions: types of factors (biomedical, social, behavioral, and educational) and time of factors (whether these factors affect the parents of the person with mental retardation, the person with mental retardation, or both). From both a diagnostic and intervention perspective, these two directions have significant implications. First, with our increasing understanding of the causes of mental retardation, the specific conditions may, in time, replace the larger umbrella term *mental retardation;* second, current ideas about the intergenerational effects stress their origin in preventable and reversible influences of adverse environments and how understanding these effects should lead to enhanced individual functioning and family supports.

The Analysis of Environments

One of the major implications of the 2002 System is that the person's environment needs to be analyzed in reference to its characteristics and opportunities for personal growth, meaningful participation, and social interactions. This component of the multidimensional, ecological model of mental retardation requires one to consider (a) the specific settings in which the person receives educational services, lives, works, recreates, interacts, and socializes; (b) the extent to which the characteristics of these environments facilitate or restrict factors that influence a person's growth, development, and well-being; and (c) the optimum environments that provide opportunities and facilitate the person's independence, relationships, contributions, school and community participation, and personal well-being.

The Incorporation of Personal Outcomes Into the Supports Model

The provision of individualized supports should incorporate an individual's desired personal outcomes related to independence, relationships, contributions, school and community participation, and personal well-being (see Figure 9.1). The implication of this focus on personal outcomes — and the challenge to service providers and professionals alike — is to organize supports based on the desired outcomes for each person.

ECOLOGICAL APPROACH

The ecological perspective taken in the 2002 manual continues to focus on the dynamic interplay among the person, the environment, and supports. Our theoretical model has changed, however, from the 1992 manual (Luckasson et al., p. 10). In the 1992 "general structure of the definition of mental retardation" (shown here as Figure 12.1), the personal factors ("capabilities") of intelligence and adaptive skills were shown on the left side of the triangle to indicate that functioning in mental retardation was specifically related to limitations in intelligence and adaptive skills. This distinguished the functional limitation in mental retardation from other states of limited functioning related to other causes. Placing these personal as-

©American Association on Mental Retardation

pects on only one side of the triangle indicated that they are necessary but not sufficient for a full understanding of the concept of mental retardation. In the 1992 model, the right side of the triangle represented environmental factors that influenced functioning: home, work or school, and community. The equilateral nature of the triangle indicated that a description of these environments is also necessary for a full understanding of the concept of mental retardation. By placing these components (capabilities and environments) on two sides of a single structure (the triangle), the model indicated that the interaction between them was central to the concept of mental retardation. The 1992 model also noted that the needs for supports can reciprocally influence functioning.

The 2002 System's theoretical model (see Figure 1.1) continues this ecological approach to mental retardation. As shown in this figure, there is a clear focus in the 2002 System on the key elements in understanding the condition of mental retardation and individual functioning: the person, environments, and supports. However, the ecological model has been changed to reflect the current understanding of the multidimensionality of mental retardation and the mediational role that sup-

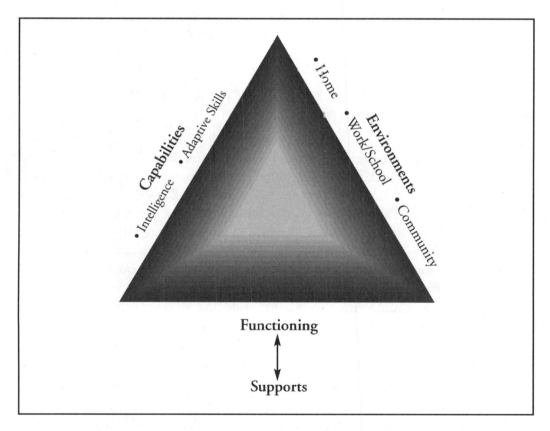

Figure 12.1. General structure of the 1992 AAMR definition of mental retardation.

ports play in individual functioning. As shown in Figure 1.1, each of the multidimensional influences on the individual's functioning (i.e., Intellectual Abilities; Adaptive Behavior; Participation, Interactions, and Social Roles; Health; and Context) is mediated through the supports available to the person. Figure 1.1 also indicates that the needs for supports can reciprocally influence functioning.

RELEVANCE OF ASSESSMENT

Table 1.1 in the 2002 manual provides a framework for assessment. In this framework, each of the three functions basic to the 2002 System (i.e., diagnosis, classification, and planning supports) has identified purposes, measures and tools, and important considerations for assessment. A major implication of the 2002 System is to realize that the reliable and valid assessments of supports, context, and health are also important to the three functions of diagnosis, classification, and planning supports. For example, the assessment of intelligence is appropriate for making a diagnosis of mental retardation and potentially classifying individuals; the assessment of adaptive behavior, for diagnosis, classification, and planning supports; the assessment of supports, for classification and planning supports; the assessment of context for all three functions; and the assessment of health for classification and planning supports.

SUPPORTS INTEGRATED INTO CURRENT EDUCATION AND HABILITATION PRACTICES

The supports model is being implemented within the context of the broader movement toward (a) person-centered planning that emphasizes personal growth and development, choices, decisions, and empowerment; (b) an ecological approach to disability that stresses the power of person-environment interactions and the reduction of functional activity limitations through person-centered support strategies; (c) a quality revolution that emphasizes quality of life, quality enhancement techniques, and quality outcomes; and (d) the provision of services and supports in natural environments, based on the principle of inclusion and opportunity development. As services and supports for people with mental retardation continue to move into the community and the important distinction between being *in* versus *of* the community becomes clearer, the use of "natural supports" also comes into play. In addition, there are at least seven implications resulting from the 2002 System's continued strong commitment to the supports paradigm:

- Understand all possible support functions. As described in chapter 9 (Figure 9.1, "Supports Model for People With Mental Retardation"), these support functions are teaching, befriending, financial planning, employee assistance, behavioral support, in-home living assistance, community access and use, and health assistance.

204   ©American Association on Mental Retardation

- Human service staff need to adopt a "facilitative support role," with the overriding goal of developing solutions within the person's natural environment in response to support needs. For this to occur, staff roles need to change to the following: (a) *planner role:* responsibility for analyzing the services that the person is seeking and assisting him or her in developing a plan to achieve the identified outcomes; (b) *community resource role:* responsibility for having knowledge of community resources in order to assist the person in accessing and obtaining needed devices and services; (c) *consultant role:* responsibility for entering into a consultant relationship with the person and provide recommendations based on knowledge and expertise; and (d) *technician role:* responsibility for staying versed in the latest assistive technology to identify appropriate strategies to ensure skill acquisition and maintenance.

- With appropriate supports over a sustained period, the life functioning of the person with mental retardation generally will improve.

- One needs to distinguish between training and treatment efforts that are designed primarily to improve the individual's inherent skills and those environmental and social accommodations that reduce the consequences of the person's condition.

- There is an emerging technology of supports stressing that (a) the technology should blend public and private sources of support in a coherent, manageable model; (b) ongoing supports should address assistance needs in all parts of a person's life; (c) models for providing ongoing supports should reflect realistic cost constraints; (d) supports should enhance opportunities for integration and participation; and (e) supports should be linked to measures of individual benefits and outcomes.

- Acceptance and inclusion of the spiritual life of the community is an important source of support that is frequently overlooked for individuals with mental retardation.

- Support levels are *not* substitutes for levels of deficiency. There are several ways in which the 2002 System's levels of support intensities differ from levels of mental retardation based on IQ scores. These differences include: (a) the intensities of needed supports are based upon a person's strengths and limitations across the five dimensions of the theoretical model (see Figure 1.1); by contrast, level of deficit based on IQ levels is limited to assessment only in Dimension I and is often simply dependent upon an IQ or IQ plus a global adaptive behavior score; (b) supports assessment involves many disciplines working as a team and analyzing a variety of assessment findings; (c) levels of needed supports are founded upon the strengths and limitations of an individual and his or her environment, not simply upon an individual's intellectual limitations; (d) levels of needed supports are viewed as potentially changing and thus requiring reassessment, not as static descriptions of intellectual traits; and (e) with an individual's supports profile at any given time, there is likely to be a varied array of needed supports and intensities, making a global summary label meaningless.

MODIFIED RESEARCH APPROACH AND DESIGNS

The concept of mental retardation and its definition have undergone numerous changes in terminology, IQ cutoff levels, and the diagnostic role of adaptive behavior over the past 5 decades (see chap. 2). Each change has reflected the field's continuing attempt to develop a clearer understanding of mental retardation and to implement a more precise and applicable terminology, classification, and habilitation-oriented system.

The research community is also undergoing change that is influenced significantly by the current emphasis on inclusion, empowerment, and supports. There is an emerging "pragmatic research paradigm" that emphasizes longitudinal studies and a more comprehensive framework for evaluating outcomes (Schalock, 2001). As these shifts merge with the 2002 System, one can expect significant changes in mental retardation research. Four of these changes are to:

- Employ greater precision in describing individuals with mental retardation, because a comprehensive description includes intelligence and adaptive skill levels, intensity of needed supports, and etiology.

- Employ participatory action research strategies that involve consumers in the design, implementation, and analysis of research projects and results.

- Employ methodological pluralism (quantitative and qualitative methods) to measure personal outcomes.

- Use multivariate research designs that allow researchers to determine the personal and environmental factors that lead to desired outcomes for people with mental retardation. These designs also place less emphasis on the person as the independent variable and more emphasis on environments and supports as independent variables and the person's independence, relationships, contributions, school and community participation, and personal well-being as dependent variables.

NEEDS-BASED ELIGIBILITY

Consistent with the theoretical framework of the 2002 System, eligibility determinations should move toward a decision-making process that is more functional in orientation. In some situations, a categorical decision based on a limited evaluation of whether the individual does or does not have mental retardation will suffice. For example, the history of the person is consistent over years and a diagnosis of mental retardation is no longer a question, the agency is not concerned with provision

206

©American Association on Mental Retardation

of supports, or the person will permit only a conclusory assessment. In most cases, however, eligibility determinations should more frequently be a result of a functional determination of how the person functions, on what factors the disability should be classified, what supports the person needs and wants, and what modifications and accommodations the person is eligible for. The old IQ-based classification system (mild, moderate, severe, profound) is particularly troublesome in eligibility because people's needs often do not correspond to their IQ levels; just because someone has an IQ at the higher end of mental retardation (mild) does not necessarily mean that his or her needs are "mild."

NEEDS-BASED FUNDING BASED ON INDIVIDUALIZED SUPPORTS

Similarly the 2002 System will have an important impact on the funding of services. For example, there will be a continuing shift toward individual supports as opposed to group services and individual- and family-controlled funding as opposed to buildings in which categorical services are concentrated and applied to people. Funding will also reflect more precisely an array of an individual's needed and desired supports rather than a categorical price structure based on IQ level (see chap. 11).

LEGAL ACCOMMODATIONS

Many of the legal procedures that might apply to people with mental retardation are based on centuries-old formulations of mental retardation or adapted from only tangentially related human vulnerabilities. For example, the idea of legal guardianship emerged in the 1300s in England to assure the king's access to the property of "idiots"; most criminal justice doctrines in mental disability emerged from the problems of mental illness; and victimization principles arose from issues surrounding children.

A move toward genuinely seeing the person with mental retardation and analyzing actual functioning should result in modern legal accommodations that reflect the complexity of mental retardation and begin to address the harsh injustices currently faced by defendants and victims with mental retardation, especially those who function at the higher levels of IQ. Use of the old system (mild, moderate, severe, profound) provokes especially grave injustices in this area, because "mild" mischaracterizes the challenges and misleads decision makers in the justice system. Because most individuals — even if identified in childhood based on IQs — lack supports as adults, many of the following circumstances have occurred: victimization and exploitation, maltreatment, acts of violence against them, unjust incarceration, lowered life satisfaction, lowered living standards, limited competence in

©American Association on Mental Retardation

parenting skills, child removal, family disintegration, placement of children in out-of-home care, criminal justice system failure, inadequate physical and mental well-being, school failure, illiteracy, dropping or being pushed out of school, homelessness, and joblessness (Tymchuk, Lakin, & Luckasson, 2001). Implementation of the 2002 System, with its emphasis on the interaction of supports and individual functioning, should reduce the mismatch within the legal system between individual needs and personalized supports.

THE FORGOTTEN GENERATION

In addressing the needs of the "forgotten generation," Tymchuk et al. (2001) called for specific strategies to meet the support needs of the substantial number of people with mild cognitive limitations that are not being addressed in American society (pp. 32–35). They urged (a) the development of models of living that genuinely address the lives of people; (b) the development of functional systems of assessment, classification, and direct service provision; and (c) coordination and integration of efforts. The 2002 manual is consistent with these themes, emphasizing that people with higher IQs (sometimes referred to as "mild") do not necessarily have "mild" needs for supports; that the rich multidimensional lives of people with mental retardation must be considered in planning supports; that mental retardation is a state of functioning and, therefore, assessment, classification, and supports planning must evaluate functioning; and that team input and coordination is critical at every stage.

SUMMARY

In summary, with the 1992 System, the concept of mental retardation was expanded significantly with the emphasis on a functional orientation, an ecological perspective, and the use of the supports paradigm for both classification and service-provision purposes. Based on the reactions to the 1992 System (see chap. 2), the Terminology and Classification Committee recognized that although we were attempting to respond to the paradigm shift in mental retardation, we needed to attend to ensuring adequate and appropriate services to users of the system. Although our primary challenge in 1992 was to reflect the paradigm shift, the challenge in the 2002 System has been to integrate the vast amount of commentary and research that has occurred since the 1992 System's publication and to operationalize more clearly the multidimensional construct of mental retardation and best-practice guidelines regarding diagnosis, classification, and planning supports for people with mental retardation.

As discussed throughout this chapter, there are at least nine major implications of the 2002 System. There are undoubtedly other implications that users of the

©American Association on Mental Retardation

2002 System will encounter. Each implication will, we hope, be evaluated and discussed over the next decade, which has been the case with the 1992 System. The challenges and opportunities reflected in these nine major implications will require multiple diffusion efforts. *Diffusion* is typically defined as "the process by which innovation is communicated through certain channels over time among the members of a social system" (Rogers, 1995, p. 5). Successfully addressing the four elements of the diffusion process — innovation; communication channels; time to involve knowledge transfer, persuasion, decision, implementation, and confirmation; and the system into which the information and change is to be infused — sets an important agenda for the next decade.

REFERENCES

Adams, G. L. (1999). *Comprehensive Test of Adaptive Behavior–Revised.* Seattle, WA: Educational Achievement Systems.

American Academy of Pediatrics. (2001). *Medical homes initiative for children with special needs.* Elk Grove Village, IL: Author.

American Association on Mental Retardation. (2001). *A guide to consent.* Washington, DC: Author.

American Educational Research Association, American Psychological Association, & National Council on Measurement in Education. (1999). *Standards for educational and psychological testing.* Washington, DC: American Educational Research Association.

American Psychiatric Association. (1952). *Diagnostic and statistical manual: Mental disorders.* Washington, DC: Author.

American Psychiatric Association. (1968). *Diagnostic and statistical manual: Mental disorders* (2nd ed.). Washington, DC: Author.

American Psychiatric Association. (1980). *Diagnostic and statistical manual: Mental disorders* (3rd ed.). Washington, DC: Author.

American Psychiatric Association. (1987). *Diagnostic and statistical manual: Mental disorders* (3rd ed., rev.). Washington, DC: Author.

American Psychiatric Association. (1994). *Diagnostic and statistical manual: Mental disorders* (4th ed.). Washington, DC: Author.

American Psychiatric Association. (2000). *Diagnostic and statistical manual of mental disorders* (4th ed., text rev.). Washington, DC: Author.

American Psychological Association. (1992, December). Ethical principles of psychologists and code of conduct. *American Psychologist, 47,* 1597–1611.

American Psychological Association. (1999). *Standards for educational and psychological testing.* Washington, DC: Author.

Aronowitz, R. A. (1998). *Making sense of illness: Science, society, and disease.* Cambridge: Cambridge University Press.

Arvey, R. D., Bouchard, T. J., Carroll, J. B., Cattell, R. B. et. al. (1994, December 13). Mainstream science on intelligence. *Wall Street Journal,* p. B1.

Bateman, B. D., & Linden, M. A. (1998). *Better IEPs* (3rd ed.). Longmont, CA: Sopris West.

Batshaw, M. L. (Ed.). (1997). *Children with disabilities* (4th ed.). Baltimore: Paul H. Brookes.

Bayley, N. (1993). *Bayley Scales of Infant Development* (2nd ed.). New York: Psychological Corp.

Beebe, D. W., Pfiffner, L. J., & McBurnett, K. (2000). Evaluation of the validity of the Wechsler Intelligence Scale for Children–Third Edition: Comprehension and picture arrangement subtests as measures of social intelligence. *Psychological Assessment, 12,* 97–101.

Beirne-Smith, M., Ittenback, R. F., & Patton, J. R. (1998). *Mental retardation* (5th ed.). Upper Saddle River, NJ: Merrill/Prentice Hall.

Benton, A. L. (1964). Psychological evaluation and differential diagnosis. In H. A. Stevens & R. Heber (Eds.), *Mental retardation* (pp. 16–56). Chicago: University of Chicago Press.

Biasini, F. J., Grupe, L., Huffman, L., & Bray, N. W. (1999). Mental retardation: A symptom and a syndrome. In S. Netherton, D. Holmes, & C. E. Walker (Eds.), *Comprehensive textbook of child and adolescent disorders* (pp. 6–23). New York: Oxford University Press.

Bracken, B., & McCallum, R. (1998). *Universal Nonverbal Intelligence Test.* Itasca, IL: Riverside.

Bronfenbrenner, U. (1979). *The ecology of human development: Experiments by nature and design.* Cambridge, MA: Harvard University Press.

Brown, M. C., Hanley, A. T., Nemeth, C., Epple, W., Bird, W., & Bontempo, A. (1986). *The Developmental Disabilities Profile: The design, development, and testing of the core instrument.* Albany: New York State Office of Mental Retardation and Developmental Disabilities.

Bruininks, R. H., Hill, B. K., Weatherman, R. F., & Woodcock, R. W. (1986). *ICAP: Inventory for Client and Agency Planning.* Chicago: Riverside.

Bruininks, R., McGrew, K., & Maruyama, G. (1998). Structure of adaptive behavior in samples with and without mental retardation. *American Journal on Mental Retardation, 98,* 265–272.

Bruininks, R. H., Morreau, L. E., Gilman, C. J., & Anderson, J. L. (1991). *Adaptive living skills curriculum.* Itasca, IL: Riverside.

©American Association on Mental Retardation

Bruininks, R. H., Woodcock, R.W., Weatherman, R. F., & Hill, B. K. (1996). *Scales of Independent Behavior–Revised.* Itasca, IL: Riverside.

Buntinx, W. H. E. (in press). Mental retardation: The relation between the AAMR definition and the WHO *International Classification of Functioning, Disability, and Health.* In H. Switzky & S. Greenspan, *What is mental retardation?* Washington, DC: American Association on Mental Retardation.

Butterworth, J., Hagner, D., Kiernan, W. E., & Schalock, R. L. (1996). Natural supports in the workplace: Defining an agenda for research and practice. *Journal of the Association for Persons With Severe Handicaps, 3,* 103–113.

Butterworth, J., Steere, D. E., & Whitney-Thomas, J. (1997). Using person-centered planning to address personal quality of life. In R. L. Schalock (Ed.), *Quality of life. Vol. 2: Application to persons with disabilities* (pp. 5–24). Washington, DC: American Association on Mental Retardation.

Campbell, E. M., & Heal, L. W. (1995). Prediction of cost, rates, and staffing by provider and client characteristics. *American Journal on Mental Retardation, 100,* 17–35.

Capute, A. J., & Accardo, P. J. (Eds.). (1996). *Developmental disabilities in infancy and childhood* (2nd ed.). Baltimore: Paul H. Brookes.

Carr, E. G., Horner, R. H., & Turnbull, A. P. (1999). *Positive behavior support for people with developmental disabilities: A research synthesis.* Washington, DC: American Association on Mental Retardation.

Carroll, J. B. (1993). *Human cognitive abilities: A survey of factor-analytic studies.* New York: Cambridge University Press.

Carroll, J. B. (1997a). Psychometrics, intelligence, and public perception. *Intelligence, 24,* 25–52.

Carroll, J. B. (1997b). The three-stratum theory of cognitive abilities. In D. P. Flanagan, J. L. Genshaft, & P. L. Harrison (Eds.), *Contemporary intellectual assessment: Theories, tests, and issues* (pp. 122–130). New York: Guilford Press.

Cattell, R. B. (1963). Theory of fluid and crystallized intelligence: A critical experiment. *Journal of Educational Psychology, 54,* 1–22.

Chen, J. Q., & Gardner, H. (1997). Alternative assessment from a multiple intelligences theoretical perspective. In D. P. Flanagan, J. L. Genshaft, & P. Harrison (Eds.), *Contemporary intellectual assessment: Theories, tests, and issues* (pp. 105–121). New York: Guilford Press.

Cohen, J. (2001). World Health Assembly adopts revised classification system. *APA Monitor, 32*(7), 21–26.

Coulter, D. L. (1991). The failure of prevention. *Mental Retardation, 29*(6), iii–iv.

Coulter, D. L. (1992). An ecology of prevention for the future. *Mental Retardation, 30,* 363–369.

Coulter, D. L. (1996). Prevention as a form of support. *Mental Retardation, 34,* 108–116.

Craig, E. M., & Tassé, M. J. (1999). Cultural and demographic comparisons of adaptive behavior. In R. L. Schalock (Ed.), *Adaptive behavior and its measurement: Implications for the field of mental retardation* (pp. 109–140). Washington, DC: American Association on Mental Retardation.

Curry, C. J., Stevenson, R. E., Aughton, D., Byrne, J., Carey, J. C., Cassidy, S., Cunniff, C., Graham, J. M., Jr., Jones, M. C., Kaback, M. M., Moeschler, J., Schaefer, G. B., Schwartz, S., Tarleton, J., & Opitz, J. (1997). Evaluation of mental retardation: Recommendations of a consensus conference. *American Journal of Medical Genetics, 72,* 468–477.

Das, J. P., Naglieri, J. A., & Kirby, J. R. (1994). *Assessment of cognitive processes: The PASS theory of intelligence.* Boston: Allyn & Bacon.

Davidson, J. E., & Downing, C. L. (2000). Contemporary models of intelligence. In R. J. Sternberg (Ed.), *Handbook of intelligence* (pp. 34–49). Cambridge: Cambridge University Press.

Denning, C. B., Chamberlain, J. A., & Polloway, E. A. (2000). An evaluation of state guidelines for mental retardation: Focus on definition and classification practices. *Education and Training in Mental Retardation and Developmental Disabilities, 35,* 226–232.

Developmental Disabilities Assistance and Bill of Rights Act Amendments, Pub. L. No. 103–230, 108 Stat. 284 (1994).

Developmental Disabilities Assistance and Bill of Rights Act of 2000, Pub. L. No. 106–402, 114 Stat. 1678 (2000).

Developmental Disabilities Services and Facilities Construction Amendments of 1970, Pub. L. No. 91–517, 84 Stat. 1316 (1970).

Developmentally Disabled Assistance and Bill of Rights Act, Pub. L. No. 94–103, 89 Stat. 486 (1975).

Doll, E. A. (1941). The essentials of an inclusive concept of mental deficiency. *American Journal of Mental Deficiency, 46,* 214–219.

©American Association on Mental Retardation

Doll, E. A. (1947). Is mental deficiency curable? *American Journal of Mental Deficiency, 51,* 420–428.

Dosen, A., & Day, K. (Eds.). (2001). *Treating mental illness and behavior disorders in children and adults with mental retardation.* Washington, DC: American Psychiatric Press.

Durand, V. M., & Crimmins, D. B. (1988). Identifying variables maintaining self-injurious behavior. *Journal of Autism and Developmental Disorders, 18,* 99–117.

Dykens, E., Hodapp, R., & Finucane, B. (2000). *Genetics and mental retardation syndromes: A new look at behavior and interventions.* Baltimore: Paul H. Brookes.

Education for All Handicapped Children's Act Amendments of 1986, Pub. L. No. 99–457, 20 U.S.C. § 1400 et seq., 97 Stat. 1357.

Evans, I. M. (1991). Testing and diagnosis: A review and evaluation. In L. H. Meyer, C. A. Peck, & L. Brown (Eds.), *Critical issues in the lives of people with severe disabilities* (pp. 25–44). Baltimore: Paul H. Brookes.

Evans, L. D., & Bradley-Johnson, S. (1988). A review of recently developed measures of adaptive behavior. *Psychology in the Schools, 25,* 276–287.

Felce, D. (2000). Engagement in activity as an indicator of quality of life. In K. D. Keith & R. L. Schalock (Eds.), *Cross-cultural perspectives on quality of life* (pp. 173–190). Washington, DC: American Association on Mental Retardation.

Ficker-Terrill, C. (in press). The future. In D. Croser, P. Baker, & R. Schalock (Eds.), *Embarking on a new century.* Washington, DC: American Association on Mental Retardation.

Field, M. A., & Sanchez, V. A. (1999). *Equal treatment for people with mental retardation: Having and raising children.* Cambridge, MA: Harvard University Press.

Furlong, M. J., & LeDrew, L. (1985). IQ = 68 = mildly retarded? Factors influencing multidisciplinary team recommendations on children with FS IQs between 63 and 75. *Psychology in the Schools, 22,* 5–9.

Gardner, H. (1983). *Frames of mind.* New York: Basic Books.

Gardner, H. (1993). *Multiple intelligences: The theory in practice.* New York: Basic Books.

Gardner, H. (1998). Are there additional intelligences? The case for naturalist, spiritual, and existential intelligences. In J. Kane (Ed.), *Education, information, and transformation* (pp. 111–132). Englewood Cliffs, NJ: Prentice Hall.

Gettings, R., & Thaler, N. R. (2000). A state perspective: Balancing individual choice and control with personal health and safety. *Wingspread conference proceedings* (pp. 43–61). Silver Spring, MD: National Center on Outcomes Resources.

Giangreco, M. F. (2001). Interactions among program, placement, and services in educational planning for students with disabilities. *Mental Retardation, 39,* 341–350.

Glutting, J., Adams, W., & Shelsow, D. (2000). *Wide Range Intelligence Test: Manual.* Wilmington, DE: Wide Range.

Gottfredson, L. S. (1997). Mainstream science on intelligence: An editorial with 52 signatories, history, and bibliography. *Intelligence, 24*(1), 13–23.

Gould, S. J. (1981). *The mismeasure of man.* New York: Norton.

Greenspan, S. (1981). Defining childhood social competence: A proposed working model. In B. K. Keogh (Ed.), Advances in special education (Vol. 3, pp. 1–39). Greenwich, CT: JAI Press.

Greenspan, S. (1996). There is more to intelligence than IQ. In D. S. Connery (Ed.), *Convicting the innocent: The story of a murder, a false confession, and the struggle to free a "wrong man"* (pp. 136–151). Cambridge, MA: Brookline Books.

Greenspan, S. (1997). Dead manual walking? Why the 1992 AAMR definition needs redoing. *Education and Training in Mental Retardation and Developmental Disabilities, 32,* 179–190.

Greenspan, S. (1999a). A contextualist perspective on adaptive behavior. In R. L. Schalock (Ed.), *Adaptive behavior and its measurement: Implications for the field of mental retardation* (pp. 61–80). Washington, DC: American Association on Mental Retardation.

Greenspan, S. (1999b). What is meant by mental retardation? *International Review of Psychiatry, 11,* 6–18.

Greenspan, S. (in press). Perceived risk status as a key to defining mental retardation: Social and everyday vulnerability in the natural prototype. In H. Switzky & S. Greenspan (Eds.), *What is mental retardation?* Washington, DC: American Association on Mental Retardation.

Greenspan, S., & Driscoll, J. (1997). The role of intelligence in a broad model of personal competence. In D. P. Flanagan, G. Genshaft, & P. L. Harrison (Eds.), *Contemporary intellectual assessment: Theories, tests, and issues* (pp. 131–150). New York: Guilford Press.

©American Association on Mental Retardation

Greenspan, S., & Granfield, M. (1992). Reconsidering the construct of mental retardation: Implications of a model of social competence. *American Journal on Mental Retardation, 96,* 442–453.

Greenspan, S., Loughlin, G., & Black, R. S. (2001). Credulity and gullibility in people with developmental disorders: A framework for future research. In L. M. Glidden (Ed.), *International review of research in mental retardation* (Vol. 24, pp. 101–133). New York: Academic Press.

Greenspan, S., & Love, P. E. (1997). Social intelligence and developmental disorder: Mental retardation, learning disabilities, and autism. In W. E. MacLean, Jr. (Ed.), *Ellis' handbook of mental deficiency, psychological theory, and research* (pp. 311–342). Mahwah, NJ: Lawrence Erlbaum.

Greenspan, S., Switzky, H. N., & Granfield, J. M. (1996). Everyday intelligence and adaptive behavior: A theoretical framework. In J. W. Jacobson & J. A. Mulick (Eds.), *Manual of diagnosis and professional practice in mental retardation* (pp. 127–135). Boston: Addison-Wesley.

Gresham, F. M., & Elliott, S. N. (1987). The relationship between adaptive behavior and social skills: Issues in definition and assessment. *Journal of Special Education, 21,* 167–181.

Grossman, H. J. (Ed.). (1973). *A manual on terminology and classification in mental retardation* (rev. ed.). Washington, DC: American Association on Mental Deficiency.

Grossman, H. J. (Ed.). (1983). *Classification in mental retardation* (rev. ed.). Washington, DC: American Association on Mental Deficiency.

Haerer, A. F. (1992). *DeJong's the neurologic examination* (5th ed.). Philadelphia: Lippincott.

Hamill, D., Pearson, N., & Wiederholt, J. (1997). *Comprehensive Test of Nonverbal Intelligence.* Austin, TX: Pro-Ed.

Harrison, P. L. (1987). Research with adaptive behavior scales. *Journal of Special Education, 21,* 37–68.

Harrison, P. L., & Oakland, T. (2000). *ABAS: Adaptive Behavior Assessment System.* San Antonio, TX: Psychological Corp.

Harrison, P. L., & Robinson, B. (1995). Best practices in the assessment of adaptive behavior. In A. Thomas & J. Grimes (Eds.), *Best practices in school psychology—III* (pp. 753–762). Washington, DC: National Association of School Psychologists.

Hawkins, G. D., & Cooper, D. H. (1990). Adaptive behavior measures in mental retardation research: Subject description in *AJMD/AJMR* articles (1979–1987). *American Journal on Mental Retardation, 94,* 654–660.

Health Care Financing Administration. (2000). *State Medicaid director letters: Olmstead updates 1, 2, 3.* Washington, DC: U.S. Department of Health and Human Services.

Health Care Financing Administration. (2001). *State Medicaid director letters: Olmstead updates 4, 5.* Washington, DC: U.S. Department of Health and Human Services.

Heber, R. (1959). A manual on terminology and classification in mental retardation. *American Journal of Mental Deficiency, 64* (Monograph Suppl.).

Heber, R. (Ed.). (1961). *A manual on terminology and classification in mental retardation* (rev. ed.). Washington, DC: American Association on Mental Deficiency.

Hennike, J. M., Myers, A. M., Realon, R. E., & Thompson, T. J. (1999). *NC–SNAP: North Carolina Support Needs Assessment Profile: Examiner's guide.* Butner, NC: Murdoch Center Foundation.

Hernstein, R. J., & Murray, C. (1994). *The bell curve: Intelligence and class structure in American life.* New York: Free Press.

Hill, B. (1999). *Adaptive and maladaptive behavior scales.* ICAP User's Group Home Page. Available: http://www.isd.net.bhill/compare.htm

Hodapp, R. M. (1995). Definitions in mental retardation: Effects on research, practice, and perceptions. *School Psychology Quarterly, 10,* 24–28.

Hodapp, R. M., Burack, J. A., & Zigler, E. (1990). *Issues in the developmental approach to mental retardation.* Cambridge: Cambridge University Press.

Horn, J. L., & Cattell, R. B. (1966). Refinement and test of the theory of fluid and crystallized general intelligences. *Journal of Educational Psychology, 57,* 253–270.

Horner, R. H. (2000). Positive behavior supports. In M. L. Wehmeyer & J. R. Patton (Eds.), *Mental retardation in the 21st century* (pp. 181–196). Austin, TX: Pro-Ed.

Horwitz, S. M., Kerker, B. D., Owens, P. L., & Zigler, E. (2000). *The health status and needs of individuals with mental retardation.* Washington, DC: Special Olympics.

Imrie, R. (1997). Rethinking the relationship between disability, rehabilitation, and society. *Disability and Rehabilitation, 19*(7), 263–271.

Individuals With Disabilities Education Act Amendments of 1997, Pub. L. No. 105–17, 111 Stat. 37 (1997).

Institute of Medicine. (1991). *Disability in America: Toward a national agenda for prevention.* Washington, DC: National Academy Press.

©American Association on Mental Retardation

Jackson, P. L., & Vessey, J. A. (1992). *Primary care of the child with a chronic condition.* St. Louis: Mosby-Yearbook.

Jacobson, J. W., & Mulick, J. A. (1996). Psychometrics. In J. W. Jacobson & J. A. Mulick (Eds.), *Manual of diagnosis and professional practice in mental retardation* (pp. 75–84). Washington, DC: American Psychological Association.

Jones, K. L. (1997). *Smith's recognizable patterns of human malformation* (5th ed.). Philadelphia: Saunders.

Jones, M. L., Risley, T. R., & Favell, J. E. (1983). Ecological patterns. In J. L. Matson & S. E. Breuning (Eds.), *Assessing the mentally retarded* (pp. 311–334). New York: Grune & Stratton.

Kamphaus, R. W. (1987a). Conceptual and psychometric issues in the assessment of adaptive behavior. *Journal of Special Education, 21,* 27–35.

Kamphaus, R. W. (1987b). Critiques of school psychological materials. *Journal of School Psychology, 25,* 97–100.

Kaufman, A. (1994). *Intelligent testing with the WISC–III.* New York: Wiley.

Kaufman, A., & Kaufman, N. (1983). *Kaufman Assessment Battery for Children.* Circle Pines, MN: American Guidance Service.

Kaufman, A. S., & Doppelt, J. E. (1976). Analysis of WISC-R standardization data in terms of the stratification variables. *Child Development, 47,* 165–171.

Kihlstrom, J. F., & Cantor, N. (2000). Social intelligence. In R. J. Sternberg (Ed.), *Handbook of intelligence* (pp. 359–379). Cambridge: Cambridge University Press.

Kraijer, D. W. (1993). *Use of the International Classification of Impairments, Disabilities, and Handicaps (ICIDH) in the field of mental retardation.* Strasbourg, France: Council of Europe Press.

Lambert, N., Nihira, K., & Leland, H. (1993). *AAMR Adaptive Behavior Scale–School and Community.* Austin, TX: Pro-Ed.

Landesman-Dwyer, S. (1981). Living in the community. *American Journal of Mental Deficiency, 86,* 223–234.

Landesman-Ramey, S., Dossett, E., & Echols, K. (1996). The social ecology of mental retardation. In J. W. Jacobson & J. A. Mulick, *Manual of diagnosis and professional practice in mental retardation* (pp. 55–65). Washington DC: American Psychological Association.

Larson, S. A., Lakin, K. C., Anderson, L., Kwak, N., Lee, J. H., & Anderson, D. (2001). Prevalence of mental retardation and developmental disabilities: Estimates from the 1994/1995 National Health Interview Survey Disability supplements. *American Journal on Mental Retardation, 106,* 231–252.

Lipsitz, J., Dworkin, R., & Erlenmeyer-Kimling, L. (1993). Wechsler Comprehension and Picture Arrangement subtests and social adjustments. *Psychological Assessment, 5,* 430–437.

Lubin, R., Jacobson, J. W., & Kiely, M. (1982). Projected impact of the functional definition of developmental disabilities: The categorically disabled population and service eligibility. *American Journal of Mental Deficiency, 87,* 73–79.

Luckasson, R., Coulter, D. L., Polloway, E. A., Reiss, S., Schalock, R. L., Snell, M. E., Spitalnik, D. M., & Stark, J. A. (1992). *Mental retardation: Definition, classification, and systems of supports* (9th ed.). Washington, DC: American Association on Mental Retardation.

Luckasson, R., & Reeve, A. (2001). Naming, defining, and classifying in mental retardation. *Mental Retardation, 39,* 47–52.

Luckasson, R., Schalock, R. L., Snell, M. E., & Spitalnik, D. (1996). The 1992 AAMR definition and preschool children: A response from the Committee on Terminology and Classification. *Mental Retardation, 34,* 247–253.

Luckasson, R., & Spitalnik, D. (1994). The 1992 definition of mental retardation. In V. J. Bradley, J. W. Ashbaugh, & B. C. Blaney (Eds.), *Creating individual supports for people with developmental disabilities* (pp. 81–95). Baltimore: Paul H. Brookes.

MacMillan, D. L., Gresham, F. M., Bocian, K. M., & Lambros, K. M. (1998). Current plight of borderline students: Where do they belong? *Education and Training in Mental Retardation and Developmental Disabilities, 33,* 83–94.

MacMillan, D. L., Gresham, F. M., & Siperstein, G. N. (1993). Conceptual and psychometric concerns about the 1992 AAMR definition of mental retardation. *American Journal on Mental Retardation, 98,* 325–335.

MacMillan, D. L., Gresham, F. M., & Siperstein, G. N. (1995). Heightened concerns over the 1992 AAMR definition: Advocacy versus precision. *American Journal on Mental Retardation, 100,* 87–97.

MacMillan, D. L., Gresham, F. M., Siperstein, G. N., & Bocian, K. M. (1996). The labyrinth of IDEA: School decisions on referred students with subaverage general intelligence. *American Journal on Mental Retardation, 101,* 161–174.

©American Association on Mental Retardation

MacMillan, D. L., Siperstein, G. N., & Gresham, F. M. (1996). A challenge to the viability of mild mental retardation as a diagnostic category. *Exceptional Children, 62,* 356–371.

MacMillan, D. L., Siperstein, G. N., & Leffert, J. S. (in press). Children with mild mental retardation: A challenge for classification practices. In H. Switzky & S. Greenspan (Eds.), *What is mental retardation?* Washington, DC: American Association on Mental Retardation.

Maternal and Child Health Bureau. (2002). *Healthy people 2010.* Washington, DC: Author.

McGrew, K. S., & Bruininks, R. H. (1990). Defining adaptive behavior and maladaptive behavior within a model of personal competence. *School Psychology Review, 19,* 53–73.

McGrew, K. S., Bruininks, R. H., & Johnson, D. R. (1996). Confirmatory factor analytic investigation of Greenspan's model of personal competence. *American Journal on Mental Retardation, 100,* 535–545.

McLaren, J., & Bryson, S. E. (1987). Review of recent epidemiological studies of mental retardation: Prevalence, associated disorders, and etiology. *American Journal on Mental Retardation, 92,* 243–254.

Medicode. (1998). *International classification of diseases, ninth revision, clinical modification* (6th ed.). Salt Lake City: Medicode Publications.

Mercer, J. R. (1973). *Labeling the mentally retarded.* Berkeley: University of California Press.

Mercer, J. R. (1992). The impact of changing paradigms of disability on mental retardation in the year 2000. In L. Rowitz (Ed.), *Mental retardation in the year 2000* (pp. 15–38). New York: Springer-Verlag.

Meyers, C. E., Nihira, K., & Zetlin, A. (1979). The measurement of adaptive behavior. In N. R. Ellis (Ed.), *Handbook of mental deficiency: Psychological theory and research* (2nd ed., pp. 431–481). Hillsdale, NJ: Lawrence Erlbaum.

Naglieri, J. A., & Das, J. P. (1997). *Cognitive Assessment System: Interpretive handbook.* Itasca, IL: Riverside.

Naglieri, J. A., & Rojahn, J. (2001). Intellectual classification of Black and White children in special education programs using the WISC–III and the Cognitive Assessment System. *American Journal on Mental Retardation, 106*(4), 359–367.

Neisser, U., Boodo, G., Bouchard, T. J., & Boykin, A. W. (1996). Intelligence: Knowns and unknowns. *American Psychologist, 51*(2), 77–101.

Nickel, R. E., & Desch, L. W. (Eds.). (2000). *Physician's guide to caring for children with disabilities and chronic conditions.* Baltimore: Paul H. Brookes.

Nihira, K. (1999). Adaptive behavior: A historical overview. In R. L. Schalock (Ed.), *Adaptive behavior and its measurement: Implications for the field of mental retardation* (pp. 7–14). Washington, DC: American Association on Mental Retardation.

Nihira, K., Leland, H., & Lambert, N. (1993). *AAMR Adaptive Behavior Scale–Residential and Community Version* (2nd ed.). Austin, TX: Pro-Ed.

Nunnally, J. (1967). *Psychometric theory.* New York: McGraw Hill.

O'Brien, J. (1987). A guide to personal futures planning. In G. T. Bellamy & B. Wilcox (Eds.), *A comprehensive guide to the activities catalog: An alternative curriculum for youth and adults with severe disabilities* (pp. 123–145). Baltimore: Paul H. Brookes.

Office of the Surgeon General. (2002). *Closing the gap: A national blueprint to improve the health of persons with mental retardation.* Washington, DC: Author.

Olmstead v. L. C. 527 U.S. 581 (1999).

Paine, R. S., & Oppe, T. E. (1966). *Neurological examination of children.* Philadelphia: Lippincott.

Polloway, E. (1997). Developmental principles of the Luckasson et al. (1992) AAMR definition of mental retardation. *Education and Training in Mental Retardation and Developmental Disabilities, 32,* 174–178.

Polloway, E. A., Smith, J. D., Chamberlain, J., Denning, C. B., & Smith, T. E. C. (1999). Levels of deficits or supports in the classification of mental retardation: Implementation practices. *Education and Training in Mental Retardation and Developmental Disabilities, 34,* 200–206.

Pope, A. M. (1992). Preventing secondary conditions. *Mental Retardation, 30,* 347–354.

Pueschel, S. (1992). *Biomedical concerns in persons with Down syndrome.* Baltimore: Paul H. Brookes.

Rapley, M. (2000). The social construction of quality of life: The interpersonal production of well-being revisited. In K. D. Keith & R. L. Schalock (Eds.), *Crosscultural perspectives on quality of life* (pp. 155–172). Washington, DC: American Association on Mental Retardation.

©American Association on Mental Retardation

Reardon, M., & Hitzing, W. (1994). *Implementation of H.B. 569: The results thus far and the recommendations for the Planning Council.* Columbus: Ohio Developmental Disabilities Alliance.

Rehabilitation, Comprehensive Services, and Developmental Disabilities Amendments of 1978, Pub. L. No. 95–602, 92 Stat. 2955 (1978).

Reiss, S. (1994). Issues in defining mental retardation. *American Journal on Mental Retardation, 99,* 1–7.

Reiss, S., & Aman, M. G. (Eds.). (1998). *The international consensus handbook: Psychotropic medications and developmental disabilities.* Columbus: Ohio State University, Nisonger Center.

Reiss, S., & Szyszko, J. (1983). Diagnostic overshadowing and professional experience with mentally retarded persons. *American Journal of Mental Deficiency, 87,* 396–402.

Reschly, D. J. (1982). Assessing mild mental retardation. The influence of adaptive behavior, sociocultural status and prospects for nonbiased assessment. In C. R. Reynolds & T. B. Gutkin (Eds.), *The handbook of school psychology* (pp. 140–156). New York: Wiley Science.

Reschly, D. J. (1987). Learning characteristics of mildly handicapped students: Implications for classification, placement, and programming. In W. C. Wang, M. C. Reynolds, & H. J. Walberg (Eds.), *The handbook of special education: Research and practice* (pp. 35–58). Oxford, England: Pergamon Press.

Reschly, D. J. (1990). Best practices in adaptive behavior. In A. Thomas & J. Grimes (Eds.), *Best practices in school psychology* (pp. 29–42). Washington, DC: National Association of School Psychology.

Risley, T. R., & Cataldo, M. E. (1973). *Planned activity check: Materials for training observers.* Lawrence: University of Kansas, Center for Applied Behavior Analysis.

Rogers, E. M. (1995). *Diffusion of innovations* (4th ed.). New York: Free Press.

Roid, G. H., & Miller, L. J. (1997). *Leiter International Performance Scale–Revised.* Wood Dale, IL: Stoelting.

Romer, D., & Heller, T. (1983). Social adaptation of mentally retarded adults in community settings. A social-ecological approach. *Applied Research in Mental Retardation, 4,* 303–314.

Rowitz, L. (1986). Multiprofessional perspectives on prevention. *Mental Retardation, 24,* 1–3.

Rubin, I. L., & Crocker, A. C. (Eds.). (1989). *Developmental disabilities: Delivery of medical care for children and adults.* Philadelphia: Lea & Febiger.

Rush, A. J., & Frances, A. (2000). Expert consensus guidelines on the treatment of psychiatric and behavioral problems in mental retardation [Special issue]. *American Journal on Mental Retardation, 105,* 159–228.

Sackett, G. P., & Landesman-Dwyer, S. (1977). Toward an ethology of mental retardation. In P. Mittler (Ed.), *Research to practice in mental retardation. Vol. 2: Education and training* (pp. 27–37). Baltimore: University Park Press.

Salvia, J., & Ysseldyke, J. E. (1991). *Assessment* (5th ed.). Boston: Houghton Mifflin.

Sandman, C. A., Hetrick, W., Taylor, D. V., Marion, S. D., Touchette, P., Barron, J. L., Martinessi, V., Steinberg, R. M., & Crinella, F. M. (2000). Long-term effects of naltrexone on self-injurious behavior. *American Journal on Mental Retardation, 105,* 103–117.

Sarnat, H. B., & Menkes, J. M. (2000). Neuroembryology, genetic programming and malformations of the nervous system. In J. H. Menkes & H. B. Sarnat (Eds.), *Child neurology* (6th ed., pp. 277–400). Philadelphia: Lippincott, Williams, & Wilkins.

Sattler, J. M. (1988). *Assessment of children's intelligence and special abilities* (3rd ed.). San Diego: Author.

Schalock, R. L. (1995). Assessment of natural supports in community rehabilitation services. In O. C. Karan & S. Greenspan (Eds.), *Community rehabilitation services for people with disabilities* (pp. 209–230). Boston: Butterworth-Heinemann.

Schalock, R. L. (Ed.). (1997). *Quality of life. Vol. 2: Application to persons with disabilities.* Washington, DC: American Association on Mental Retardation.

Schalock. R. L. (1999a). The concept of adaptive behavior. In R. L. Schalock (Ed.), *Adaptive behavior and its measurement: Implications for the field of mental retardation* (pp. 1–5). Washington, DC: American Association on Mental Retardation.

Schalock, R. L. (1999b). The merging of adaptive behavior and intelligence: Implications for the field of mental retardation. In R. L. Schalock (Ed.), *Adaptive behavior and its measurement: Implications for the field of mental retardation* (pp. 209–222). Washington, DC: American Association on Mental Retardation.

Schalock, R. L. (2001). *Outcome-based evaluation* (2nd ed.). New York: Kluwer Academic/Plenum.

©American Association on Mental Retardation

Schalock, R. L., & Jensen, C. M. (1986). Assessing the goodness-of-fit between persons and their environments. *Journal of the Association for Persons With Severe Handicaps, 11,* 103–109.

Schalock, R. L., Stark, J. A., Snell, M. E., Coulter, D. L., Polloway, E. A., Luckasson, R., Reiss, S., & Spitalnik, D. M. (1994). The changing conception of mental retardation: Implications for the field. *Mental Retardation, 32,* 181–193.

Scharnhorst, U., & Buchel, F. P. (1990). Cognitive and metacognitive components of learning: Search for the locus of retarded performance. *European Journal of Psychology of Education, 5,* 207–230.

Scheerenberger, R. (1983). *A history of mental retardation.* Baltimore: Paul H. Brookes.

Schorr, L. B. (1997). *Common purpose: Strengthening families and neighborhoods to rebuild America.* New York: Anchor Books, Doubleday.

Scott, K. G. (1988). Theoretical epidemiology: Environment and lifestyle. In J. F. Kavanagh (Ed.), *Understanding mental retardation* (pp. 23–33). Baltimore: Paul H. Brookes.

Seltzer, G. B. (1983). Systems of classification. In J. L. Matson & J. A. Mulick (Eds.), *Handbook of mental retardation* (pp. 143–156). Elmsford, NY: Pergamon Press.

Slosson, R. L. (1983). *Slosson Intelligence Test (SIT) and Oral Reading Test (SORT) for children and adults.* East Aurora, NY: Slosson Educational Publications.

Smith, J. D. (1994). The revised AAMR definition of mental retardation: The MRDD position. *Education and Training in Mental Retardation and Developmental Disabilities, 20,* 179–183.

Smith, J. D. (1997). Mental retardation as an educational construct: Time for a new shared view? *Education and Training in Mental Retardation and Developmental Disabilities, 20,* 179–183.

Smith, J. D., & Polloway, E. A. (1979). The dimension of adaptive behavior in mental retardation research: An analysis of recent practices. *American Journal of Mental Deficiency, 84,* 203–206.

Snell, M. E., & Voorhees, M. D. (in press). Mental retardation: Does the label bring support or stigma? In H. Switzky & S. Greenspan (Eds.), *What is mental retardation?* Washington, DC: American Association on Mental Retardation.

Social Security Administration (2001). *Understanding Social Security Income (SSI).* Available: http://www.ssa.gov/notices/supplemental-security-income/text-understanding-ssi.htm

Sparrow, S. S., Balla, D. A., & Cicchetti, D. V. (1984). *Vineland Adaptive Behavior Scales.* Circle Pines, MN: American Guidance Service.

Spearman, C. (1927). *The abilities of man: Their nature and measurements.* New York: Macmillan.

Spiker, D., & Hebbeler, K. (1999). Early intervention services. In M. L. Levine, W. B. Carey, & A. C. Crocker (Eds.), *Developmental-behavioral pediatrics* (3rd ed., pp. 793–802). Philadelphia: Saunders.

Spitalnik, D. M., & White-Scott, S. (2001). Access to health services: Improving the availability and quality of health services for people with mild cognitive limitations. In A. J. Tymchuk, K. C. Lakin, & R. Luckasson (Eds.), *The forgotten generation: Individuals with mild cognitive limitations in American society* (pp. 203–220). Baltimore: Paul H. Brookes.

Spreat, S. (1999). Psychometric standards for adaptive behavior assessment. In R. L. Schalock (Ed.), *Adaptive behavior and its measurement: Implications for the field of mental retardation* (pp. 103–117). Washington, DC: American Association on Mental Retardation.

Spreat, S., Roszkowski, M., & Isett, R. (1983). Adaptive behavior. In S. Breuning, J. Matson, & R. Barrett (Eds.), *Advances in mental retardation and developmental disabilities* (Vol. 1). Greenwich, CT: JAI Press.

Stanley, J. (1971). Reliability. In R. L. Thorndike (Ed.), *Educational measurement* (2nd ed., pp. 50–72). Washington, DC: American Council on Education.

Sternberg, R. J. (1988). *The triarchic mind: A new theory of human intelligence.* New York: Penguin.

Stevens, H. A. (1964). Overview of mental retardation. In H. A. Stevens & R. Heber (Eds.), *Mental retardation* (pp. 3–15). Chicago: University of Chicago Press.

Switzky, H. (in press). A cognitive-motivational perspective on mental retardation. In H. Switzky & S. Greenspan (Eds.), *What is mental retardation?* Washington, DC: American Association on Mental Retardation.

Switzky, H., & Greenspan, S. (in press). Summary and conclusions: Can so many diverse ideas be integrated? Multiparadigmatic models of understanding mental retardation. In H. Switzky & S. Greenspan (Eds.), *What is mental retardation?* Washington, DC: American Association on Mental Retardation.

©American Association on Mental Retardation

Tassé, M. J., & Craig, E. M. (1999). Critical issues in the cross-cultural assessment of adaptive behavior. In R. L. Schalock (Ed.), *Adaptive behavior and its measurement: Implications for the field of mental retardation* (pp. 161–184). Washington, DC: American Association on Mental Retardation.

Temkin, O. (1965). The history of classification in the medical sciences. In M. M. Katz, J. O. Cole, & W. E. Barton (Eds.) *The role and methodology of classification in psychiatry and psychopathology* (pp. 11–19). Chevy Chase, MD: Public Health Service.

Thompson, J. R., Hughes, C., Schalock, R. L., Silverman, W., Tassé, M. J., Bryant, B., Craig, E. M., & Campbell, E. M. (in press). The emerging supports paradigm: A suggested approach to assessment, planning, and evaluation. *Mental Retardation.*

Thompson, J. R., McGrew, K. S., & Bruininks, R. H. (1999). Adaptive and maladaptive behavior: Functional and structural characteristics. In R. L. Schalock (Ed.), *Adaptive behavior and its measurement: Implications for the field of mental retardation* (pp. 15–42). Washington, DC: American Association on Mental Retardation.

Thorndike, R., Hagen, E., & Sattler, J. (1986). *Technical manual for Stanford-Binet Intelligence Scale* (4th ed.). Chicago: Riverside.

Thurstone, L. L. (1938). Primary mental abilities. *Psychometric Monographs,* No. 1.

Ticket to Work Incentives Improvement Act of 1999, Pub. L. No. 106–170, 113 Stat. 1860 (1999).

Tredgold, A. F. (1908). *Mental deficiency.* London: Baillere, Tindall, & Fox.

Tredgold, A. F. (1937). *A textbook of mental deficiency.* Baltimore: Wood.

Trent, J. W., Jr. (1994). *Inventing the feeble mind: A history of mental retardation in the United States.* Berkeley: University of California Press.

Turnbull, A. P., & Turnbull, H. R. III (2000). Fostering family-professional partnerships. In M. E. Snell & F. Brown (Eds.), *Instruction of students with severe disabilities* (5th ed., pp. 31–66). Upper Saddle River, NJ: Merrill/Prentice Hall.

Turnbull, H. R. III, & Brunk, S. L. (1990). Quality of life and public philosophy. In R. L. Schalock (Ed.), *Quality of life: Perspectives and issues* (pp. 193–210). Washington, DC: American Association on Mental Retardation.

Turnbull, H. R. III, & Turnbull, A. P. (2000). Family support: Retrospective and prospective. In M. L. Wehmeyer & J. R. Patton (Eds.), *Mental retardation in the 21st century* (pp. 3–17). Austin, TX: Pro-Ed.

Tymchuk, A. J., Lakin, K. C., & Luckasson, R. (2001). *The forgotten generation: The status and challenges of adults with mild cognitive limitations.* Baltimore: Paul H. Brookes.

Voelker, S. L., Shore, D. L., Brown-More, D., Hill, L. C., Miller, L. T., & Perry, J. (1990). Validity of self-report of adaptive behavior skills by adults with mental retardation. *Mental Retardation, 28,* 305–309.

Volpe, J. J. (2000). Normal and abnormal human brain development. *Mental Retardation and Developmental Disabilities Research Reviews, 6,* 1–5.

Vygotsky, L. S. (1986). *Thought and language.* Cambridge, MA: MIT Press.

Wechsler, D. (1944). *The measurement of adult intelligence.* Baltimore: Williams & Wilkins.

Wechsler, D. (1991). *Wechsler Intelligence Scale for Children–Third Edition.* San Antonio, TX: Psychological Corp., Harcourt Brace.

Wechsler, D. (1997). *Wechsler Adult Intelligence Scale–Third Edition.* San Antonio, TX: Psychological Corp., Harcourt Brace.

Widaman, K. F., Borthwick-Duffy, S. A., & Little, T. D. (1991). The structure and development of adaptive behaviors. In N. W. Bray (Ed.), *International review of research in mental retardation* (Vol. 17, pp. 1–54). San Diego: Academic Press.

Widaman, K. F., & McGrew, K. S. (1996). The structure of adaptive behavior. In J. W. Jacobson & J. A. Mulick (Eds.), *Manual of diagnosis and professional practice in mental retardation* (pp. 97–110). Washington, DC: American Psychological Association.

Widaman, K. F., Stacy, A. W., & Borthwick-Duffy, S. A. (1993). Construct validity of dimensions of adaptive behavior: A multitrait-multimethod evaluation. *American Journal on Mental Retardation, 98,* 219–234.

Wilbur, H. B. (1877). *The classifications of idiocy.* Proceedings of the Association of Medical Officers of American Institutions for Idiotic and Feeble-minded Persons (pp. 29–35). Philadelphia: J.B. Lippincott.

World Health Organization. (1948). *Manual of the international statistical classification of diseases, injuries, and causes of death* (6th rev.). Geneva: Author.

World Health Organization. (1969). *Manual of the international statistical classification of diseases, injuries, and causes of death* (8th rev.). Geneva: Author.

World Health Organization. (1977). *Manual of the international statistical classification of diseases, injuries, and causes of death* (9th ed. rev.). Geneva: Author.

©American Association on Mental Retardation

World Health Organization. (1980). *International classification of impairments, disabilities, and handicaps. A manual of classification relating to the consequences of disease (ICIDH)*. Geneva: Author.

World Health Organization. (1993). *International statistical classification of diseases and related health problems* (10th ed.). Geneva: Author.

World Health Organization. (2000a). *International classification of functioning and disability (ICIDH–2). Full version*. (Beta-2). Geneva: Author.

World Health Organization. (2000b, December). *International classification of functioning, disability and health: Prefinal draft (ICIDH–2)*. Geneva: Author.

World Health Organization. (2001). *International classification of functioning, disability, and health (ICF)*. Geneva: Author.

Zigler, E., & Trickett, P. K. (1978). IQ, social competence, and evaluation of early childhood early intervention programs. *American Psychologist, 33,* 789–798.

Zuckerman, B. S., Frank, D. A., & Augustyn, M. (1999). Infancy and toddler years. In M. D. Levine, W. B. Carey, & A. C. Crocker (Eds.), *Developmental-behavioral pediatrics* (3rd ed., pp. 24–37). Philadelphia: Saunders.

SUBJECT INDEX

Adaptive Behavior,
And a diagnosis of mental
retardation, 74–75
And its components, 76
And the definition of mental
retardation, 24–25
Acquisition vs. performance,
73–74
Assumptions about adaptive
behavior, 74–75
Correspondence between three
dimensions of adaptive
behavior and factors on
existing measures, 77
Definition, 76
Domains, 82
Examples of conceptual, social,
and practical adaptive skills, 42
Measures of, 87–90
Operational definition, 14
Relation of 1992 to 2002 skill
areas, 81
vs. problem behavior, 79
Adaptive Behavior Assessment,
Cutoff scores, 78–79
Equal weights with assessed
intelligence, 80
Guidelines for test selection,
83–84
Performance requirements, 78
Purposes of, 82
Selection of AB measures, 82–84
Selection of raters or third party
informants, 84–85
Special considerations, 81–87
Assessment,
Framework, 12

Considerations for, 12
Assumptions (of definition of MR),
8–9

Behavioral phenotypes of selected
genetic disorders, 136–139

Classifying, 6–7
Classification,
Measures and tools, 12
Purposes, 12, 100
See also Classification systems
Classification systems, 99–115
By intensity of needed supports,
100–101
Comparison of ICF and AAMR
Systems, 109–113
Developmental Disabilities Act,
115–118
Diagnostic and Statistical
Manual of Mental Disorders
(DSM–IV), 112–115
International Classification of
Diseases; ICD (9 & 10),
101–104
International Classification of
Functioning, Disability, and
Health (ICF), 105–108
Medicaid (ICF-MR & Waivers),
119–120
Social Security, 118–119
State MR Program and funding
classifications, 120–121
Clinical judgment,
Definition, 95
Guidelines, 85–87, 95–96
Situations requiring, 94

©American Association on Mental Retardation

©American Association on Mental Retardation

AUTHOR INDEX

©American Association on Mental Retardation

©American Association on Mental Retardation

©American Association on Mental Retardation

THE Reputation of the Triumphant Beast